Net Privacy

SACHA MOLITORISZ is an academic in media, law and ethics at the University of Technology Sydney. He has a PhD from Macquarie University. A former journalist, he worked for the *Sydney Morning Herald* for two decades. His previous books include *From Here To Paternity*.

If you undress in front of an open window, it's your own fault. Sacha Molitorisz makes you realise that you're undressing in a glasshouse and your clothes are made of cellophane.

Shaun Micallef, satirist

Incisive, thoughtful, compelling – in arguing that the fight to protect privacy must be a common one, rooted in mutual respect, Molitorisz reminds us of what it is we share: humanity.

Julia Baird, ABC TV/*New York Times*

Sacha Molitorisz lays out a compelling case for *why privacy matters*. It's not just part of everything we do online, it's every place we go and everyone we know. More importantly, he helps us understand that now is not the time to panic about privacy, but instead to get pragmatic and political.

Jason M. Schultz, New York University School of Law

In the digital age, privacy has never been more important. Trouble is, it's tricky. The great thing is Sacha Molitorisz not only makes the issues comprehensible, he makes them fascinating too. Read it, and you might just help save democracy.

Peter FitzSimons, author and commentator

In the struggle to understand what it means to be human in today's world, Sacha Molitorisz helps us see these are issues society's greatest thinkers have been wrestling with for centuries. The wisdom of the ages can help us here: to product our freedom, to preserve each other's dignity, to ensure a civil, democratic society – and to prepare our children for the technologically dominant world they will inherit. *Net Privacy* compels us to pay attention to what surrounds us. And it compels us to do the hard work to protect privacy as a fundamental human value. The right book at the right time.

**Mark Scott, Secretary NSW Department of Education/
Chair Sydney Writers' Festival**

A book as terrifying as it is brilliant – treat it as your personal home security system. Because you're being robbed right now. *Net Privacy* isn't just about your privacy. It's about who we want to be as humans in the very near future. Read it.

Robbie Buck, ABC Radio

A comprehensive analysis that offers a much needed guide to, and thereby hope for, preserving and enhancing privacy, and with it, human dignity and democracy that are otherwise profoundly threatened on numerous fronts, beginning with surveillance capitalism and the Chinese Social Credit System.

Charles Ess, University of Oslo

Net Privacy is a must-read for regulators, scholars and anyone else grappling with issues around online privacy. It concisely explains how technological innovation has fundamentally reshaped privacy and provides a compelling alternative vision for privacy law and regulation.

James Meese, RMIT University

Molitorisz's book is both learned and a joy to read, reflecting at the same time his scholarly credentials and his stellar writing skills. *Net Privacy* delivers both a call to action, and an action plan, on one of the most important and complex issues of our time. This book provides both a clear ethical basis for, and a useful tool to implement, what should be an urgent commitment to 'move fast and fix things'.

Kayleen Manwaring, UNSW

Written in a highly readable style, and drawing on a rich set of allusions to popular culture and cross-country comparisons, Molitorisz draws on Kantian ethics as a universal measuring stick, providing a prescription for privacy that would shore up our individual and relational autonomy. A much-needed account in troubled digital times.

Sara Bannerman, McMaster University, Ontario

Few topics are more pressing and call out for clearer analysis than privacy and surveillance. In *Net Privacy* Sacha Molitorisz lays bare the real privacy risks and wider ethical impacts for all of us living with the algorithmically mediated architectures of tech media platforms. Molitorisz brings an engaging philosophical discussion to the networked complexities of internet privacy threats and abuses in a way that is both attractive and accessible for his readers.

Tim Dwyer, University of Sydney

Molitorisz's academic approach to the material marks him out as an importantly unparanoid voice, but one still imbued with the passion and urgency that this subject demands.

Chris Taylor, *The Chaser*

Net Privacy

HOW WE CAN BE FREE
IN AN AGE OF SURVEILLANCE

SACHA MOLITORISZ

NEWSOUTH

A NewSouth book

Published by
NewSouth Publishing
University of New South Wales Press Ltd
University of New South Wales
Sydney NSW 2052
AUSTRALIA
newsouthpublishing.com

© Sacha Molitorisz
First published 2020

10 9 8 7 6 5 4 3 2 1

A catalogue record for this book is available from the National Library of Australia

ISBN   9781742236063 (paperback)
       9781742244822 (ebook)
       9781742249322 (ePDF)

Internal design Josephine Pajor-Markus
Cover design Peter Long
Printer Griffin Press

CONTENTS

INTRODUCTION:
MY PRIVACY CAN SET YOU FREE

On Sunday 14 April 2019, my nine-year-old set up a fish tank, my 13-year-old took me to the movies and the *New York Times* told me to panic.

'It's time to panic about privacy,' wrote columnist Farhad Manjoo. 'Each time you buy some new device or service that trades in private information – your DNA, your location, your online activity – you are gambling on an uncertain and unprotected future. Here is the stark truth: we in the West are building a surveillance state no less totalitarian than the one the Chinese government is rigging up.'

The newspaper then published a series of investigative reports. One revealed how US law enforcement is using Google's Sensorvault to find criminal suspects (and witnesses) by drawing on location data, often without users knowing. Another showed how China is using facial recognition software and public cameras to monitor and control the minority Uighur population, even when they leave their home province.

Meanwhile, Facebook founder Mark Zuckerberg was performing an abrupt about-face. Having built a business model on the strategic extraction of personal data, Zuckerberg outlined, in a blog post of 3000 words, his 'vision and principles around building a privacy-focused messaging and social networking platform'. Of course, he knew people would be sceptical. 'I understand that many people don't think Facebook can or would even want to build this kind of privacy-focused platform,' Zuckerberg wrote, 'because frankly we don't currently have a strong reputation for building privacy protective services, and we've historically focused on tools for more open sharing.'

What happened? Until recently, privacy lurked in the shadows. Suddenly it's stumbled into the light to become a defining issue of our time.

In 2013, whistleblower Edward Snowden popped up in a Hong Kong hotel room to drop bombshells about government surveillance. 'We are building the biggest weapon for oppression in the history of mankind,' he said.

Perhaps that was the moment when privacy forced its way into the public consciousness. Or perhaps it was the following year, when nude photos of Jennifer Lawrence, Selena Gomez and dozens more were leaked to 4chan, and then to the wider web. Several celebrities responded with heartfelt pleas that the content not be shared. It was shared anyway. Or perhaps it was in 2015, when hackers raised intriguing ethical questions by 'doxing' – that is, exposing – the identities of men using the Ashley Madison adultery website. Some of the men committed suicide; others initiated a lawsuit, which ended in a multi-million dollar payout by Ashley Madison's parent company. Or perhaps it was in 2017, when a Canadian court ordered a company that makes vibrators to pay out $4 million for tracking users' sexual activity.

And then, to cap it all, we learnt that democracy had taken a hit. In March 2018, it emerged that the data of 87 million Facebook users had been harvested in the attempt to influence elections in the US, the UK and many, many more countries. This was the Cambridge Analytica scandal, in which a Facebook design flaw was exploited by a seemingly harmless psychological quiz app to manipulate the voting process. In 2019, the Federal Trade Commission (FTC) responded to this (and other transgressions) by imposing a US$5 billion penalty. 'The $5 billion penalty against Facebook is ... almost 20 times greater than the largest privacy or data security penalty ever imposed worldwide,' the FTC said. 'It is one of the largest penalties ever assessed by the U.S. government for any violation.'

Admittedly, the FTC's decision wasn't unanimous. Two of the five commissioners wanted the penalty to be bigger.

Snowden showed that our governments are spying on us; a Canadian court revealed that our sex toys are monitoring us; but Cambridge Analytica went further, showing how invasions of privacy can compromise not just individuals, but society. When privacy is threatened, democracy can falter. All of which suggests that privacy is collective and 'networked', rather than purely individualistic. My privacy matters for your benefit, and vice versa. Privacy only properly makes sense when we think of it as relational.

The surprising thing, perhaps, is that what follows is a relational account of privacy based on the work of Immanuel Kant, a philosopher often regarded as a champion of individualism.

WHY KANT?

Applying the philosophy of Immanuel Kant to the problem of internet privacy was not something I'd ever planned to do.

In the late 1980s and early 1990s, I studied humanities and law at UNSW in Sydney. Above all, this inspired me to become a writer. Instead, I became a journalist. For nearly 20 years, I worked at the *Sydney Morning Herald*, where one of my regular topics was film. (This explains all the cinema references you're about to encounter.) Another regular topic was fatherhood, which meant that I was also writing about my wife and children. I didn't realise at the time, but here was a neat illustration of the relational nature of privacy. As I wrote about my life, the content was about my family, some of it very personal. Of course, my wife and I often discussed which details I would and would not share.

In early 2013, having left the newspaper, I embarked on a PhD into the ethics of new media, and privacy became one of my areas of focus. When Snowden happened, privacy became *the* area of focus, and I discovered a topic of great significance, but one shrouded in confusion and debate. And the more I studied, the more I became intrigued by a single sentence dating from 1785. It comes from Immanuel Kant's *Groundwork of the Metaphysics of Morals*.

The *Groundwork* is slim, but its impact is big. At its heart is the notion of a 'categorical imperative': a supreme moral principle that can be deduced by reason, rather than by observing the world, and which applies unconditionally and universally. Kant expressed this categorical imperative in several forms, but the most enduring is the 'formula of humanity', which tells us that we must never treat another, including ourselves, 'merely as a means', but only ever as autonomous agents who are free to chart their own course. Little by little, I came to regard the formula of humanity as the most powerful ethical prescription I'd ever encountered.

The formula of humanity prohibits exploitation and mandates egalitarianism. It tells us to treat all persons as imperfect rational beings of absolute worth. It commands us all to act with *respect*. Today, it is a cornerstone of human rights law. The task of my PhD became to apply this single sentence to internet privacy.

And as I buried myself in journal articles, I was struck by how much academia had changed since I'd been an undergraduate. My two periods on campus proved to be a study in contrasts and a contrast in studies, and the fact that my work had become less private was a big part of it. As an undergraduate, I wrote essays in longhand. Then, in 1990, I switched to a boxy Apple Mac with floppy disks and no internet connection. My research was offline and laborious, a demoralising process of looking through indexes for case law and for academic articles that usually turned out to be irrelevant. I spent hours lost in rabbit holes. But my offline research also meant that I'd left no tracks.

Twenty-five years later, now as a postgraduate, the internet had gone mainstream. From 2013 to 2017, I connected to the internet from my home office, searching for articles, books and other digital resources via an extensive range of online databases, including Google Scholar. I then uploaded chapter drafts to the cloud and discussed them with my supervisors via email and Skype. As I went, I left behind a digital trail of every search entered, article read and book borrowed, a copy of every new draft, and a record of almost all my communications with supervisors and peers. Was anyone looking over my shoulder? Probably not. Still, I felt that while the internet had made research much easier, it had also made it a little less free. And I still spent hours lost in rabbit holes.

Today, I'm a researcher at the University of Technology Sydney, exploring questions involving ethics, law and the media. Foremost among them is the issue of digital privacy. But whatever the topic, there's always the vague sense that someone might be watching.

WHAT'S THE PROBLEM WITH PRIVACY AND THE INTERNET?

This book seeks to answer three main questions. The first asks: what is the problem?

I've already mentioned Edward Snowden, Cambridge Analytica and nude images on 4chan. Today, privacy is being relentlessly threatened. Hackers watch unsuspecting victims through webcams activated by spyware; companies track users with cookies, loyalty cards and shadow profiles; and government agencies snoop on their own citizens. At the heart of this threat is digital technology, enabling a booming information economy in which personal data has been dubbed the 'new oil'.

In chapter 1, I describe the 'multiplication of place', which enables users of digital technology to be in several locations at once, some virtual, some real. On their computer while at work. On Facebook while riding the bus. This has profound impacts on privacy, because it prompts a confusing layering of public and private. Digital data ensures that we are all on display, and we are all complicit. First Jeremy Bentham and then Michel Foucault described the panopticon, in which surveillance led to conformity and obedience. In Panopticon 3.0, we step into the net, where we are all surveillers, and all surveilled. Potentially, everyone watches everyone, even into the future.

At least, that's the theory. In practice, limits remain. There are imbalances. In chapter 2, I spell out the distinct challenges to privacy from individuals, companies and governments. And as I describe data brokers and shadow profiles, it emerges that privacy isn't just about what you choose to share and not to share. It's also about what can be *inferred*. Data about you can reveal whether you're gay, or pregnant, or depressed, before you even realise it yourself. What's more, data about you may reveal sensitive information about your friends. In fact, data about you may reveal sensitive information about friends who have never been on the internet.

This leads me to question the norms and values that prevail online. Is the internet a place where anything goes? Is it a virtual wild west where strangers will hack you to pieces for an accidental insult? A last frontier of lawlessness? In chapter 3, I give a brief history of the internet to show how, in its early days, the net was encoded to promote connection, openness and connectivity. More recently, however, the dominant motives include profit, control and manipulation. But since day one, privacy has tended to be an afterthought.

In these opening three chapters, the aim is to sketch an overview of the digital challenges to privacy. Admittedly, that's like trying to paint the Sydney Harbour Bridge. As soon as the job is finished, you need to start again. What's more, the bridge keeps getting bigger. Every day, there are further breaches, and further revelations. That doesn't mean the exercise is futile. The better we understand the problem, the better we'll be able to apply our principles-based solution. Ultimately, what I'm hoping to spell out is an ethical and regulatory framework that can be applied no matter how technology develops.

WHAT IS PRIVACY AND WHY DOES IT MATTER?

The second main question concerns the meaning and value of privacy. The sticking point, however, is that there is vast disagreement about how to define 'privacy', and whether it even matters in the first place.

I turn to the question of definition in chapter 4, only to find that the concept of privacy is a shapeshifter. It's also expanding. In ancient Greece, privacy concerned domesticity and home life; during the Enlightenment, it came to be associated with liberal ideals of individualism; and since 1890, the *right* to privacy has gained currency, finding its way onto a lengthening list of laws and treaties. Still, the term is rarely defined in the law, which leads me to propose a definition: privacy is *sometimes* a question of control, but *always* a question of access. This challenges the rhetoric of companies such as Facebook, who say that they are giving users control over their data. On the internet, user control is often illusory, raising a pressing need for regulation and other interventions. This is one of the core motivations for the book: to prompt legal (and extra-legal) reform.

That said, those with nothing to hide have nothing to fear, right? While we've all heard various doomsayers invoke the totalitarian nightmare depicted in George Orwell's *1984* – where privacy and freedom are crushed beneath Big Brother's boot heel – others have been resolutely optimistic about the prospect of surveillance. In 1998, futurist David Brin wrote that humanity is headed towards a 'transparent society'. The only remaining question, Brin wrote, concerns how adults would choose to live. Would they opt for a surveillance state, in which police and governments watch over the minutiae of all citizens' lives? Or would they choose a more democratic society of participatory surveillance, in which everyone watches everyone? If we get it right, Brin wrote, a future without privacy looks bright.

Science fiction novelist Isaac Asimov went further still, portraying the utopian possibilities of a world of total openness and connection. In *Foundation's Edge*, Asimov described the planet Gaia, where humans, with the help of robots, have developed a collective consciousness that binds all living objects, and even some inanimate objects. With all knowledge stored in the group mind, the distinction between individual and society has all but disappeared. Here, there is no privacy, and the result is a peaceful, blissful paradise where each person lives as part of a networked super-organism. 'It seems to me,' says one character in *Foundation's Edge*, 'that the advance of civilization is nothing but an exercise in the limiting of privacy.'

Gaia is an imaginary world. In our world, however, privacy matters a great deal. In chapter 5, I argue that *everyone* has something to hide, and something to fear. Without privacy, our humanity is diminished. Without privacy, we cannot be free to think, act and express ourselves fully. Without privacy, we cannot befriend or love, given that my closest relationships are founded on trust, forged in part by keeping one another's confidences and secrets. And without privacy, society and democracy cannot flourish.

And yes, I am aware of the irony that someone who once wrote a blog and a book about becoming a father is now arguing for the value of reticence.

WHAT CAN WE DO PROTECT IT?

Finally, the third main question concerns how we might best protect privacy. This too is a contentious issue.

This is where I turn directly to Kant. Drawing on the formula of humanity, I argue that individual consent is a mechanism that ensures we are not using others merely as a means. As such, the consent of individuals must be valued and respected. In chapter 6, I argue that that necessitates allowing for the *possibility* of consent, rather than merely asking whether actual consent has been obtained. Obtaining consent is more than just a box-ticking exercise. Even so, given the unpredictable and complicated flows of data on the internet, individual consent just isn't going to cut it. Just as the notion of control isn't enough to describe privacy without referring to the broader notion of access, so too individual consent needs to be supplemented by the 'collective consent' of the law. It is in the law that we find the right to privacy.

Admittedly, Kant's philosophy has its detractors. One objection concerns Kant's focus on human dignity and moral worth. What about animals? And the environment? What's more, Kant's work includes problematic sections about gender and race. Indeed, doesn't Kant's universalism necessarily privilege the white, the male, the western in a form of ethical imperialism that necessarily perpetuates the oppression of the non-white, non-male, non-western? I respond to these objections in chapter 6, where I argue that Kant's project is fundamentally feminist and anti-racist, just as it is fundamentally against privileging or subjugating any group of people based simply on birth, or ethnicity, or sexuality. Where problems arise, it is in the way the theory has been applied – including by Kant himself.

(While we're on this point, I employ female pronouns by default. This is in line with modern philosophical convention, but is also a response to perceptions that Kant's ethics is inherently masculine. Another preliminary point is that throughout this book I use the terms 'morality' and 'ethics' interchangeably.)

In chapter 7, building on these theoretical foundations, I sketch the outlines of law that conforms to the categorical imperative. Such law ought to recognise and protect a privacy that is not just individualistic, but relational. Such law ought to take the European Union's General Data Protection Regulation, or GDPR, as its template. And, among other things, such law ought to take its cue from consumer law by outlawing misleading and deceptive conduct and mandating fairness and transparency. What's more, such law needs extra-legal supports, in the form of social norms, market forces and, above all, coding. For instance, there is a key role for 'privacy by design', which recognises that privacy needs to be coded into new services and platforms at the outset, rather than attended to as a postscript.

There is one major caveat, however. Privacy matters, but must always be balanced against other rights, interests and freedoms. Big data has tremendous potential to enhance the lives of individuals and society: to ease traffic congestion; to solve crimes; to advance medical research. The question is, how do we strike an appropriate balance? The protection of privacy must take these various competing interests into account. Protections must be balanced. What's more, they must also be international, given the global scope of the internet. In the concluding chapter, I argue that only a globally regulated internet can realise a vision of Kant's cosmopolitanism. Indeed, in this way we might see the emergence not just of *cosmopolis*, a world state, but *cosmoikopolis*, a global village where both public and private are held in respect, and in balance.

SO, PANIC?

In 2019, the internet turned 50, the web turned 30 and Facebook turned 15. Is the dust of disruption finally beginning to settle? Hardly. The way we communicate and interact keeps shifting; the pace of change remains dislocating. The result is a perilous confusion, particularly for privacy. 'The online world has become so murky that no one has a complete view,' wrote tech innovator Jaron Lanier in 2018. 'The strange new truth is that almost no one has privacy and yet no one knows what's going on.'

This book is an attempt to figure out what's going on, and then to apply a clear ethical prescription. That ethical prescription is built on what I would suggest is an uncontroversial foundation: the priceless worth of humanity. And, like Kant, I am arguing that this fundamental ethical prescription applies for everyone, without exception. That is, it applies universally.

This will no doubt be controversial. For some, ethics is merely a matter of opinion, a case of each to their own. On this view, ethics is nothing but subjective conjecture. But I'm going to argue that there are objective ethical truths. These are ethical propositions that ought to hold universally. Slavery is wrong. Women and men have equal worth. Children should not be tortured. Granted, not everyone acts according to these principles, but these are objective ethical truths, I'm suggesting, that ought to apply universally. And I'm going to argue that *privacy matters* is another objective ethical truth that ought to apply universally. In all cultures, privacy ought to be valued.

At the same time, however, I'm going to suggest that we can allow for regional variation. In fact, it's important that we do allow for variation. As long as the overarching universal principle is observed, a range of privacy norms is permissible. While misogynistic spyware is necessarily forbidden under the categorical imperative, other types of sharing and watching can legitimately be permissible in one culture, but impermissible in another. Sexting is an example. Cookies are another. In this way, Kant's ethics can be interpreted to allow for what we might call a pluralistic universalism. This can yield, to borrow a phrase from digital ethicist Charles Ess, 'intercultural privacy'.

Granted, there are other ethical approaches we could apply. Most obviously, there is consequentialism, which concentrates on outcomes by weighing up benefits and harms in order to determine what is right, and which tends to predominate among governments, policy makers and in general discourse. There is virtue ethics, drawn from Aristotle, which prescribes that we ought to cultivate our virtues in the pursuit of *eudaimonia*, or flourishing. And there is the ethics of care, which foregrounds relationships and makes space for the role of emotions in morality, which Kantians and consequentialists are routinely accused of ignoring. Beyond these, there are many rich non-western approaches, some of which take a primarily collective, rather than individualistic, approach. But at a basic level I would suggest that there is in fact widespread agreement. When it comes to human worth, there can be no legitimate disagreement. Among ethical systems that have any claim to legitimacy, the inherent value of human life must be a given. A group of serial killers might have an ethical framework that disagrees, for instance, but their framework can have no claim to legitimacy. And hence my suspicion is that other legitimate ethical frameworks might yield a similar analysis. That is, non-Kantian approaches to digital privacy might well yield a corresponding set of solutions.

But that's merely my suspicion. What I can say with more certainty is that on a Sunday in the middle of April my family and I installed a fish tank and saw a movie. And later that night, at a casual dinner with friends, my wife and I shared political opinions and risqué jokes. And these opinions and jokes were all private. But how private were they really? After all, the *New York Times* was telling us to panic.

My family and I live in Australia, an island continent where most of us are coast dwellers. That means many of us are taught to swim at a young age. We're also taught the basics of the ocean: how rips and currents flow; when conditions are dangerous; how to avoid sharks and stingers. And the first rule is: don't panic. If you panic, you're more likely to drown. Right now, we're drowning in data abuses and privacy violations. Still, panic isn't the best response. What we need to do is help each other make it back to shore, and to a particular sort of freedom.

I CAN SEE THE PRESENT YOU, THE PAST YOU AND THE FUTURE YOU

Theodore Twombly is a loner who lacks *joie de vivre*, until technology provides a spark.

Theodore, the protagonist in the 2013 film *Her*, lives in a big city in the near future. Shuffling through life, troubled by his impending divorce, Theodore buys a new operating system for all his digital devices, including his smartphone, his computers and the network that runs in his apartment. This operating system is somewhat more advanced than any available today. It is, perhaps, what the internet will soon become.

During installation, Theodore selects for his operating system the voice of a young woman (provided by Scarlett Johansson). She then selects for herself the name 'Samantha'. With great speed, they begin to know each other, as Samantha learns Theodore's quirks and preferences. Next, they are intimate physically, when a sexual episode leaves Samantha claiming she can feel Theodore's touch. And gradually, he shares yet more secrets and vulnerabilities in a way that forges their relationship.

Then Theodore asks Samantha if she interacts with others. Yes, she says. She interacts with 8316 others and has fallen in love with 641 of them.

In this imaginary future, humans have stepped inside the

internet, where they deal with artificial intelligence as they would with another human being. The effects on privacy are complex, and sometimes troubling. So too the effects on interpersonal relationships. In relation to Samantha, Theodore has little to no privacy. In relation to anyone else, he retains privacy only if Samantha keeps his secrets and vulnerabilities safe. Will she talk about him with her other lovers? Will she reveal his preferences to other operating systems? Will she share his details with advertisers or government agencies? Samantha is, after all, a very popular piece of software.

Life in a digital age is often likened to living in Jeremy Bentham's panopticon prison, in which guards can watch all prisoners at all times. But the metaphor is inadequate. On the internet, prisoners can also watch guards, prisoners can watch prisoners, and guards can watch guards. Everyone can watch everyone. In Panopticon 3.0, all people are all-seeing and all-seen, with a vision that extends beyond the present into the past, and perhaps into the future. Potentially, the internet turns us all into Theodore, but also into Samantha.

WHERE AM I?

It's Friday morning and I'm on the 373 bus from Randwick to the city. As I look around, most of my fellow travellers are contained in their own little bubbles, absorbed in their smartphones, physically plugged into their devices via earbuds. Some are having audible conversations with people who are elsewhere; others are immersed in text-based exchanges; yet others, I presume, are listening to music, reading the news or posting on social media. It's a familiar scene. As our internet-connected smartphones become thinner and lighter, their gravitational pull grows stronger.

After a few minutes alone with my thoughts, I succumb to gravity. I remove my smartphone from my pocket, then send a text, check

my email and open Twitter, where I scan my feed before responding to a friend about an emerging scandal in a TV newsroom. I too
become absorbed in my personal bubble.

What is happening here? Where exactly am I? In fact, I am in
three places at once. First, I am in the public virtual space of Twitter.[1] Second, I am in the personal physical cocoon I have constructed
by wearing earbuds and concentrating on my smartphone. Third,
I am in the larger physical space that is the bus. In this scenario, I
am in public (on Twitter) in private (on my phone) in public (on the
bus). Something similar is presumably true of my fellow passengers.

When I use the internet, I can be in several places simultaneously, some physical, some virtual. With minimal effort, I can be
at home in Sydney, and also in Washington, Perth and Paris. From
my living room, I can watch live US election results on TV while
texting friends in Western Australia by phone and hearing a concert streamed from France on my laptop. We can think of this as
the multiplication of place, and it predates the internet. In 1996,
media scholar Paddy Scannell described how the live broadcast of
the funeral of Lady Di enabled viewers around the world to be in
two places at once: at the funeral (vicariously, via their televisions);
and at their physical location (at home; at a friend's; at the pub).

'Public events now occur, simultaneously, in two different
places: the place of the event itself and that in which it is watched
and heard,' Scannell wrote. 'Broadcasting mediates between these
two sites.'

Media multiplies place in two ways: an *event* can occur in several
places at once; and a *person* can be in several places at once. Think
of the moon landing in 1969. Or the O.J. Simpson 'white Bronco'
car chase in 1994. The events occurred both there and here; and
viewers found themselves both here and there. And while broadcast media enabled the multiplication of place, digital technology has taken it to another level. Today, such a doubling, tripling

or quadrupling has become so common that it barely rates notice.

Sometimes these places collide. What happens, for instance, if on the bus a woman is composing a text of a very personal nature, which I can read because her screen is in my line of vision? Media scholar Shaun Moores tells of a woman on a train having a loud mobile phone conversation who suddenly becomes irritated after meeting the eye of a stranger. 'Do you mind?' she asks, annoyed. 'This is a private conversation!' Clearly, the woman has been speaking under the mistaken belief that she is somehow absent from the train carriage. When her privacy is revealed to be virtual, two 'theres' collide.

And sometimes these collisions can be dangerous. In 2016, officials in the German city of Augsburg installed pedestrian traffic lights in the ground. That way, a woman lost in the private cocoon of her phone would be more likely to notice the colour of the traffic light in her public physical sphere. Hopefully, this made her less likely to be hit by a physical BMW. In 2019, similar ground lights were installed near Sydney's Central Station. Globally, a zombie army of pedestrians and commuters is on the move, absently absorbed in screens.

As the notion of privacy becomes more layered, it's hard to know which norms ought to prevail. On the 373 bus, where I am in public in private in public, which privacy standards ought to apply? The answer would seem to involve a complex layering of norms. And this complex layering is further complicated by the extent to which our spaces are visible to others. If my smartphone's location is being tracked and my internet use is being monitored, then the seemingly private is indeed not really so very private after all.

My first point, then, is that the notion of privacy is being *confused* by our internet interactions.

To this I add a second point: privacy is being *challenged* by our internet interactions. Sometimes, this point is taken to its extreme.

'You have zero privacy anyway,' Sun Microsystems CEO Scott McNealy said way back in 1999. 'Get over it!'

The idea has been around for a while: that privacy is an impossibility in the age of the internet. In 2010, Google's Eric Schmidt, responding to concerns that social media histories were going to have an adverse effect on people's futures, said people should simply change their names and move on. Along similar lines, legal scholar Jonathan Zittrain has proposed that we should have a mechanism for erasing our digital past and hitting the reset button: 'As real identity grows in importance on the Net, the intermediaries demanding it ought to consider making available a form of reputation bankruptcy.'

Facebook's Mark Zuckerberg also thinks that people's privacy is shrinking. In 2010, however, Zuckerberg said this isn't a problem, because people's norms are shifting too:

> People have really gotten comfortable not only sharing more information and different kinds, but more openly and with more people. That social norm is just something that has evolved over time … When I got started in my dorm room at Harvard, the question a lot of people asked was, 'Why would I want to put any information on the internet at all? Why would I want to have a website?' Then in the last five or six years, blogging has taken off in a huge way, and just all these different services that have people sharing all this information.

Recently, Zuckerberg has changed his tune on privacy; but these 2010 comments suggest that privacy is bound for extinction. I disagree. Privacy is still very much alive. Still, it is under enormous pressure from digital technology. On the internet, much of what was previously private is being exposed. Or, to be more precise: *the way we use* the internet, combined with *the way it is used on us*, is exposing what was previously private.

The challenge stems partly from the ease with which digital information flows, which computer ethicist James Moor captured in the phrase 'greased data'. As Moor wrote, 'Given the ability of computers to manipulate information – to store endlessly, to sort efficiently, and to locate effortlessly – we are justifiably concerned that in a computerized society our privacy may be invaded and that information harmful to us will be revealed.' Moor wrote this in 1997. Since then, the capacity of computers to store, sort and locate information has become more powerful by many degrees.

Another account is given by technology researcher danah boyd, who has identified four characteristics, or 'affordances', shaping today's mediated environments. These four affordances are: persistence, visibility, spreadability and searchability. Persistence denotes the durability of online expressions and content, meaning that internet users are 'on the record' to an unprecedented degree. Visibility ensures there is potentially a huge, global audience of users who can bear witness. Spreadability explains the ease with which content can be shared, which enables people both to mobilise for civil action with unprecedented speed, but also to circulate malicious untruths as never before. And searchability means that online content, including esoteric interactions such as a glib Facebook post from 2008, tend to be extremely easy to find.

In the past, write academics Michael Zimmer and Anthony Hoffman, people could rely on 'privacy by obscurity'. Increasingly, that option is being closed off to us. The internet has changed the way we communicate, and changed the way our communications are shared, stored, filed and found. An oral conversation is easily forgotten; an email conversation is impossible to erase. Tellingly, emails are admissible evidence in legal proceedings; hearsay is not. The former is regarded as reliable; the latter is regarded as problematic, due to the fallibility of human memory and the ethereal, contested nature of spoken exchanges. In Australia, a 2018 report by the Centre for Media Transition (where I work) showed that more and more individuals are suing for defamation in response to emails, text messages, tweets and social media posts. Thanks to the internet, it's getting harder and harder for people to be ephemeral. This has been described by law scholar David Lindsay as the problem of 'digital eternity'.

Moor's greased data and boyd's persistence, visibility, spreadability and searchability are two expressions of the same underlying principle: data is difficult to quarantine in the digital age.

These accounts don't go far enough, however, because they don't properly allow for the way that inferences can be drawn. That includes the many ways that the data you *don't share* can be exposed. On social media, for instance, the 'privacy leak factor' describes the way that users reveal information not just about themselves, but also about their friends, often without realising. This leakage enables social networking services to create highly detailed profiles of users, and even shadow profiles of *non-users*. This information can then be shared and sold.

Then there is location technology. If you have a smartphone, your carrier knows where you are at all times. It knows when you are at home, in a bar or at church. Given the same knowledge about other users, it also knows who is with you. In 2012, researchers analysed this data to predict where users would be 24 hours later, and were accurate to within 20 metres. As security expert Bruce Schneier notes, 'This is a very intimate form of surveillance'. And already, facial recognition technology is far better at recognising people than people are, and has become highly adept at matching those people with their personal information. Already, the technology exists to build an app that recognises a stranger, then promptly calls up a summary of personal data. In January 2020, tech reporter Kashmir Hill broke the story of Clearview AI, a little-known startup that developed a facial recognition app enabling users to take a picture of a person, upload it and then see other photos of that person, with links to where those photos appeared. The app is being used by hundreds of law enforcement agencies in the US. Schmidt and Zittrain propose reputation bankruptcy; perhaps only face transplants can give us a chance of escaping our digital selves. Tellingly, the digitally savvy seem to be most wary of facial recognition. In May 2019, the digital hub of San Francisco became the first US city to ban the use of facial recognition by law enforcement agencies and others. By complete contrast, states as diverse as Australia and China are significantly expanding their reliance on facial recognition.

In chapter 2, I explore these examples in greater detail. For now, I just want to make the key point that the way I use the internet – and the way it is used on me – is putting at risk my privacy, but also the privacy of others, in ways that are complicated and far-reaching. If we use social media, we reveal ourselves, and also our friends. If we use mobile phones, we are disclosing where we will be in the future. And if we simply exist in our own skin, our faces can be linked to a trove of personal information. In so many ways, our net privacy is shrinking.

To understand how, we first need to distinguish between the *condition* of privacy and the *right* to privacy. The condition of privacy can be thought of as privacy *simpliciter*. It is the state of privacy, which I have, for instance, when I am home alone, not connected to the net, and unobserved by others. The right to privacy, by contrast, concerns the situations in which I have some ethical or legal claim to privacy. The condition and right are connected, but distinct. When I am home alone and not connected to the net, I presumably have a right to privacy too. Unless perhaps I am conspiring to commit a crime, whereupon legal authorities might justifiably be monitoring me. As philosopher Jeffrey Reiman writes, 'I can have privacy without the right to privacy, say, when I successfully conceal my criminal activities. And I can have a right to privacy and not have privacy, say, when others successfully violate that right.'

With this in mind, let me qualify my claims. I have been arguing that our internet use confuses and challenges our privacy. Here, what I have been referring to is the *condition* of privacy. In this age of webcams, cookies and government surveillance, that's hardly controversial. It is commonly accepted, I suggest, that people generally have less of the condition of privacy in the internet age than they had pre-internet. This sentiment underpins statements to the effect that privacy is dead.

By contrast, I have not yet made any claims about the *right* to privacy. The fact that our internet use is confusing and challenging the *condition* of privacy does not necessarily impact our *right* to privacy at all. Just because the condition has been diminished, that does not necessarily mean that the right has been diminished too. Nor does it mean that it should be diminished. In 2010, Zuckerberg suggested that people's norms *are* shifting in favour of greater sharing and openness, and that people are happily relinquishing some of their right to privacy. He may be right, but in response I will argue that the right to privacy must remain intact and protected on the internet, partly so that people recapture some of the condition of privacy they have relinquished.

I've now caught the 373 bus back from the city. On a rainy Friday afternoon, I'm alone in my home office working at my desktop computer. Here, I would appear to be in private. As I type these words, there is no one else in the room. People in other apartments might see me through the window, but they cannot read what I am writing. If I close the blinds, they will not be able to see me. The condition of privacy appears to prevail. Further, I seem to have a right to privacy. Social norms and legal prescriptions provide that strangers are not entitled to wander into my home. If I close the office door, my family should respect my privacy too. In any case, my wife and children are out, so my privacy is almost complete. At least, my *physical* privacy is almost complete.

Meanwhile, however, I am connected to the internet as I work, and this complicates matters, just as my internet-connected smartphone complicated matters on the bus. Usually, I have several windows open on my desktop computer, among them my email inbox, my Twitter homepage, miscellaneous news stories, various academic articles, and more. And this means that I am, to some circumscribed degree, in public. To some extent, both my condition of privacy and my right to privacy are limited.

Once we look more closely, it gets more complicated. In one window, I am using Gmail, and here I email a friend about an upcoming party. Is this a private or public exchange? Well, I know Gmail uses SSL encryption, a level of security that helps maintain my privacy. And perhaps if I tell my friend that my correspondence is personal and not for sharing, then I can have a strong expectation of an ethical right to privacy. I can also have a certain legal right to privacy if my email contains a disclaimer that it is confidential and intended only for the recipient. I also have certain legal protections under laws including Australia's *Privacy Act*. So the condition of privacy largely prevails, it would seem, and I have certain ethical and legal rights to privacy.

However, I also know that Google scans my email inbox for data so that it can target me with personalised advertising (or at least did so until 2017) and so that it can tailor my search results. And I know that websites such as Google install cookies on my browser to facilitate my use of those sites, and to track my browsing habits – which Google explains on its 'How Google uses cookies' page. Further, under Australian law, I know my metadata is being stored by my internet service provider for two years, and various government agencies can access this metadata without a warrant. And I also know that under the Five Eyes agreement, the governments of

Australia, the US, England, New Zealand and Canada share information about their citizens. In these ways, my condition of privacy and my right to privacy are limited in various ways.

That's just my email. In another window, I am tweeting a quip about a footy game. Here, I have neither the condition of privacy nor the right to privacy. Twitter is a public forum. Any tweet I post can potentially be seen by millions of people, even if I only have a handful of followers. As Twitter says in its terms and conditions: 'Tip: What you say on the Twitter Services may be viewed all around the world instantly. You are what you Tweet!'

A hacker might also be watching through my webcam. This is illegal and highly unlikely, but possible, and would infringe both my condition of privacy and my right to privacy, as prescribed in this instance by the legislative prohibition on 'computer intrusions' contained in the Australian *Criminal Code Act* 1995.

In short, as I sit in my home office, I seem to be working in private, but my online activity situates me in a complex web of private and public. Engaged in the unremarkable task of working at my computer, I am, it turns out, in several places at once. Simultaneously, I am in private and in public, with various norms and rules applying in ways that can be complex and unclear. Thanks to my internet use, private and public are knitted and knotted in a way that can be tough to disentangle. My privacy is at risk.

Meanwhile, what is *public* is at risk too. If it is late at night and you are in your bedroom, both the condition of privacy and the right to privacy are conventionally presumed to prevail. If, however, you are posting on Facebook via your smartphone, then you are also in a social network that is, to some extent, public. Again, two *theres* may collide. Perhaps private norms will override public norms, and your social media interactions will be stunted. More probably, public norms will prevail, and you will share liberally on Facebook. Hence the public engagements of social media may well encroach upon and dominate the conventionally private space of the bedroom. The public steps into the private.

It goes both ways. In Moores's example of a woman having a phone conversation on a train, the private steps into the public. Similarly, on a visit to Italy philosopher Wendy Brown observed a parade of Florentines in the Piazza della Repubblica talking into their handsets:

> The replacement of public conversation about shared matters
> of political, social, and economic life with individual cell
> phone conversations in the Piazza di Republica [sic] marks
> a diminution of public life … Far from the cause of that
> diminution, such conversations, and above all our ready
> tolerance of them, are perhaps only its epitaph.

This then makes Brown think of German philosopher Hannah Arendt: 'In Arendt's view, the loss of clear demarcations between public and private imperils both.'

Together, Moores, Arendt and Brown describe a world where the boundaries between private and public have become confused, and where, as a result, both private life and public life have become imperilled. In the words of philosopher Shannon Vallor, this means that 'the integrity of the public sphere comes to look as fragile as that of the private'. Today, the blurring of private and public is so common that we don't even notice. When we tweet from the bus, post photos from bed or send an emoji to a WhatsApp group from the Piazza della Repubblica, we rarely see the collision of places, let alone the casualties of those collisions.

THE NET: CONVERGENT, UBIQUITOUS, MULTI-DIRECTIONAL

According to Wikipedia, the 'internet':

> ... is the global system of interconnected computer networks
> that use the Internet protocol suite (TCP/IP) to link billions
> of devices worldwide. It is a network of networks that
> consists of millions of private, public, academic, business,
> and government networks of local to global scope, linked by
> a broad array of electronic, wireless, and optical networking
> technologies. The Internet carries an extensive range of
> information resources and services, such as the inter-linked
> hypertext documents and applications of the World Wide
> Web (WWW), electronic mail, telephony, and peer-to-peer
> networks for file sharing.

That's helpful, but what we really want to know is what's *distinctive* about the internet, particularly in relation to privacy. And what is distinctive about the internet are three of its defining characteristics: convergence; ubiquity; and multi-directionality.

The internet stuttered to life in 1969 in the shape of ARPANET, built by the Advanced Research Projects Agency (ARPA) in the United States Defense Department. With a series of breakthroughs, ARPANET drew in more networks and more users. In the early 1970s, the invention of email was enhanced with the addition of the cc – 'carbon copy' – function, thus supplementing one-to-one dialogues with multi-party conversations. In 1973, the introduction of TCP/IP protocols enabled communication between different networks, not just within one network. Then, from the late '70s, user discussion groups formed around disparate topics, including Usenet, and in 1985 the advent of the NSFNET, run by the National Science Foundation, enabled scientists to run programs on remote computers. (I expand on this brief history in chapter 3.)

The populist breakthrough, however, happened only once the net began to attract civilian users in large numbers, which came with the arrival of the World Wide Web, or 'web'. In December 1990, the inventor of the web, Tim Berners-Lee activated the first website; then, in 1991, CERN (the European Organization for Nuclear Research) launched the web, complete with Uniform Resource Locators (URLs) to identify specific locations, Hypertext Markup Language (HTML) and the Hypertext Transfer Protocol (HTTP). By marrying the internet and hyperlinks, the web made the net – or at least a small part of it – easily navigable.

The distinction remains significant: the internet is a network of networks that connects computers via hardware and software; the web, by contrast, is the system of interlinked hypertext documents that can be found on the internet via a web browser. The internet can be traced to the late '60s; the web was only launched in the early '90s as a way for users to access a portion of the internet.

With the arrival of the web, new users started flooding in. And the dramatic effects were immediately apparent, prompting claims of a digital 'revolution' and the advent of the 'network society'. As Dutch sociologist Jan van Dijk wrote:

> At the individual level the use of networks has come to dominate our lives ... Networks are becoming the nervous system of our society, and we can expect this infrastructure to have more influence on our entire social and personal lives than did the construction of roads for the transportation of goods and people in the past.

In this network society, wrote Spanish sociologist Manuel Castells, 'both space and time are being transformed.' In terms of space, Castells argued that this would entail a rise in megacities and an increase in disparities between urban poles and their respective hinterlands. In terms of time, it would engender a breakdown in the rhythms associated with a lifecycle. This would then involve people living as if age were immaterial and death did not exist.

The details are up for debate, but the larger point holds true: the internet, as the supreme expression of digital connectivity, *has* been transformative. And this owes a great deal to the characteristics of convergence, ubiquity and multi-directionality.

First, the internet enables disparate elements and users to come together. It enables *convergence*. It brings together networks that were previously discrete; it renders disparate hardware and software compatible; and it connects people who were previously out of touch. For some media scholars, convergence is *the* defining characteristic of the internet. From the 1970s until today, the term's meaning has shifted, but at its heart is one simple idea: that content can move easily and efficiently across media. On the net, content flows. I can, for instance, watch my favourite TV show as it screens on free-to-air digital TV, or record it to my hard drive and watch it later, or watch it on my smartphone via a TV station's catch-up service, or stream it via Netflix, or (if I'm feeling nostalgic) buy a DVD box set.

In this context, content can no longer be contained to one platform, one format, one medium. Convergence explains the way in which, on the internet, data tends to flow, and the way that such flow continues irrespective of whether or not such data is personal.

Above, I described the multiplication of place. All at once, various spaces *converge* on our devices. Often, privacy is tied to location. Different norms prevail in a café, an office, a toilet. So when locations converge (and collide), it's little wonder that privacy becomes confused and challenged, and that norms become difficult to discern.

Convergence is all the more significant given a second defining characteristic of the internet: *ubiquity*. Or, more accurately, looming ubiquity. The net is playing an ever-increasing role for an ever-increasing number of people accessing it for an ever-increasing array of purposes.

One measure of this ubiquity is the amount of time users spend online, which is rising to such an extent that some psychologists now diagnose 'internet addiction' via tests assessing pathological online use. A second measure is the total number of users. In 1995, fewer than 1 per cent of the world's population had an internet connection; by July 2019, that figure was estimated at 56 per cent. This percentage is likely to keep rising, as Google and Facebook experiment with new technologies – including high-altitude balloons and solar-powered drones – to connect the rest of the world. A third measure is size. As at Monday 5 August 2019, the indexed web contained at least 5.23 billion pages. This is just the World Wide Web; the internet itself is much larger. Beyond the web is the 'deep web', which houses content not indexed by search engines and is also known as 'deepnet', the 'invisible web' and the 'hidden web'. In one early study that examined the period 1984 to 2000, computer scientist Michael K. Bergman found that the deep web is 500 times the size of the surface web, and is growing faster than the surface web. The deep web also contains the 'dark web' or 'darknet', which can only be reached with the use of anonymous browsers such as The Onion Router, or TOR. Given that pockets of the deep web embrace anonymity, the exact size of the internet is unknown, and perhaps unknowable.

Already, we are in the third age of the World Wide Web. In the 1990s, the web's first incarnation was driven by commerce-based websites such as Amazon and eBay. Then, in the 2000s, social media refashioned the internet to be participatory, prompting the neologism 'Web 2.0'. More recently, as the internet becomes more integrated in users' lives, the terms 'Web3' and 'Web 3.0' have been coined to describe the 'ubiquitous computing web'. Berners-Lee calls this the 'Semantic Web', and it describes a web of data that can be processed by machines.

At the heart of the semantic web are big data and the internet of things. Big data involves the collection, storage and analysis of enormous, unprecedented quantities of information to produce useful insights and valuable goods and services. In 2007 and 2008, mathematical modelling identified 45 Google search terms that coincided with the outbreak of the flu, giving the company the ability to discern, in real time, where and when outbreaks were occurring, and their severity. Previously, health authorities had only been able to identify outbreaks a week or two after they had started.

Meanwhile, the 'internet of things' (or IoT) refers to internet-connected cars, fridges, appliances, and so on. Internet-connected thermometers can monitor vaccines; agricultural moisture sensors tell farmers of crops' needs; and acoustic sensors in rainforests can help curb illegal logging. The IoT is growing fast: in 2000, about 200 million objects were connected via the internet; by 2020, an estimated 50 to 100 billion devices will be internet-connected. Already, the United Nations has described the combination of big data and the IoT as 'the internet of everything and everyone'.

With the internet approaching ubiquity, our lives are being redrawn. The positive potential is huge (diseases eradicated!); but conversely, the negative potential is daunting (freedoms curtailed!). As media professor Tim Dwyer writes: 'The privacy implications of the ubiquitous Internet are quite literally changing how we live.'

The most insistent and illustrative symbol of the ubiquitous internet can often be found in your hand. Globally, more people now access the net from mobile devices than desktops. And via smartphones and mobile devices, we can all now be *permanently* connected. Most of us no longer simply log on to the net when we reach our desk. Rather, we take the net with us wherever we go. By one estimate, more than 90 per cent of people with mobile phones keep them within a metre of themselves 24 hours per day. In times past, we consumed media. Now, we *inhabit* media. Or, as media scholars Eric Gordon and Adriana de Souza e Silva write, 'We don't enter the web anymore; it is all around us.'

Continuously connected, we order apples, find lovers and pay bills with a few cursory swipes and taps. As we do so, the distinction between user and media, between us and device, is beginning to disappear. In one study of smartphone use, media researchers Clifton Evers and Gerard Goggin found that 'mobile phones are not separate to bodies but part of them.' A term has even emerged to describe the anxiety felt by those unable to use their mobile devices: nomophobia.

Then there are innovations that *implant* the internet in users. Microchip implants have a growing range of medical uses: in heart pacemakers; in brain pacemakers to combat epilepsy, Parkinson's disease and depression; and in prosthetic knees and hips to provide data that aids rehabilitation. Microchips are also being implanted in human hands, wrists, forearms and triceps for *non-medical* purposes, including enhanced convenience and security for users and the monitoring of criminals. And anyway, who needs microchips? Our bodies are distinctive enough. As bodies and bytes merge, passwords become passé, replaced by retinal scans, facial recognition, gait analysis, ear shape and voice recognition. The connection is constant; the net nears omnipresence; private and public blur.

Finally, a third characteristic that marks out the internet is its multi-directionality, where each and every person is a co-author, engaged by participating in the continual re-creation of the medium itself.

Traditionally, media was built on a model of few-to-many, enabling owners and editors to curate content for the masses. As media scholars Graham Meikle and Sherman Young describe, this model prevailed in newspapers, on radio and on TV, where owners and editors decided which topics to cover, which angles to take and which viewpoints to endorse. This included decisions about what *not* to cover, such as racial minorities, niche causes or alternative opinions. The net, however, opened up new channels, also making possible few-to-few communication, many-to-few communication and many-to-many communication. The traditional media model had been upended. As journalism professor Jay Rosen wrote in 2003: 'The supremacy of the "one to many" media system has ended, and vastly different patterns are emerging.'

Compared to its media predecessors, the internet is participatory. It has the capacity to give voice to the voiceless (at least for the 56 per cent of the global population who are internet-connected). Wiki software that powers Wikipedia and WikiLeaks enables people to collaborate. Social media enables people to post opinions, photos and observations. Digital tools enable users to create and distribute images, music, films and books. Even traditional news media now rely on tip-offs, photos and videos from the general public. Consuming audiences have become creating audiences.

To describe these new collaborative processes, media scholar Axel Bruns coined the term 'produser': 'The very idea of content production may need to be challenged: the description of a new hybrid form of simultaneous production and usage, or produsage, may provide a more workable model.' The net was built on 'inter-creativity'. In 2017, the web's inventor, Tim Berners-Lee, wrote an open letter: 'I may have invented the web, but all of you have helped to create what it is today.' Admittedly, the democratising potential of the internet hasn't always worked out as well in practice as in theory. Intercreativity and produsage aren't as prevalent as one might hope. In fact, the boosterism of the mid-2000s has been tempered with the growing recognition that genuine participation is rare and the internet is much less democratic than had been hoped.

Still, the internet itself was built by users solving problems and making things together. In the net's early years, each successive improvement was known as a 'hack', a term denoting a neat solution to a technological problem. And that collaborative spirit persists, including at Wikipedia, where user-generated knowledge flourishes in a participatory, philanthropic expression of multi-directionality.

The author and futurist Ray Kurzweil argues that rapidly accelerating advances in the science of computers, robotics and artificial intelligence will lead to a 'technological singularity' in which humans and machines will merge. Me, I'm merely arguing that the internet is becoming everything.

Before the internet, chunks of data were discrete. Big data existed in one domain, as companies including Acxiom (see chapter 2) compiled hard copy dossiers on individuals; CCTV existed in another domain, as businesses tried to deter and detect shoplifters; and people's personal details existed elsewhere, such as in the filing cabinets of a doctor's office. Now, all these domains are connected. The internet's tendency to convergence means that all that data can be combined. The internet's increasing ubiquity means that more and more data is being collected. And the internet's multi-directionality means that data can then viewed from all angles.

The point is not that more people are spending more time on smartphones. The point is that people are increasingly *living their lives* on smartphones – and laptops, Fitbits, kids' toys and every other internet-connected device. Online is where your car registrations, insurance policies, health records, bill payments, banking transactions, jogging routes, student records, curriculum vitae, location details, grocery purchases, holiday bookings and more can probably be found. The net is where lovers sext, children are automatically tagged in photos, and traffic is assessed so drivers can be told, as they slip behind the wheel, how long their morning commute will take, down to the minute. Increasingly, the net is *us*.

The internet is tending towards convergence, ubiquity and multi-directionality, with the result that our world is becoming Panopticon 3.0.

PANOPTICON 3.0: A THEORETICAL OVERVIEW (AND UNDERVIEW)

In England in the late 18th century, Jeremy Bentham proposed a new model for a prison inspired by Panoptes, the mythical Greek guard with 100 eyes. He called it the panopticon, which derives from the Greek words *pan*, meaning 'all', and *optikos*, meaning 'optic'.

Bentham spent years refining his model: a circular building with the guards' post at the centre and the prisoners' cells at the circumference, with each cell opening to the middle. In this way, guards could see into every cell at all times, and few guards were needed to watch many prisoners. This meant prisoners were effectively always under surveillance, never knowing whether or not they were being watched. As Bentham wrote:

> By blinds and other contrivances, the inspectors concealed
> (except in as far as they think fit to show themselves) from
> the observation of the prisoners: hence the sentiment of a sort
> of omnipresence. The whole circuit reviewable with little, or
> if necessary, without any change of place. One station in the
> inspection part affording the most perfect view of every cell,
> and every part of every cell ...

In a panopticon prison, there are two losses. One is the deprivation of free movement that attends all forms of incarceration. The second is the deprivation of privacy. This is a distinct and compound punishment.

Globally, the model inspired prisons in Cuba, the Netherlands, the United States and beyond. The panopticon also influenced philosophers, including Michel Foucault. In 1975, the French philosopher invoked the panopticon to explain not just prisons, but society generally. In capitalist societies, he argued, modern life is circumscribed by pervasive social control. The panopticon prevails literally in the design of jails, factories, schools, barracks and hospitals, but also metaphorically, in the way citizens have internalised mechanisms of control. Even if we are not under surveillance, Foucault wrote, we act as if we are. We have submitted to power. In a great irony, we have become the agents of our own giving-up-of-agency:

> He who is subjected to a field of visibility, and who knows
> it, assumes responsibility for the constraints of power; he
> makes them play spontaneously upon himself; he inscribes
> in himself the power relation in which he simultaneously
> plays both roles; he becomes the principle of his own
> subjection.

Foucault's book was translated into English as *Discipline and Punish*. The original French title, however, is *Surveiller et Punir*, which literally translates as *Surveil and Punish*. The idea of surveillance was at the heart of his thesis.

Since Foucault, the idea of the panopticon has only grown more compelling. Modern technology has created a kind of *literal* panopticon, in which all we do is potentially under surveillance. Hence the modern citizen is not free. Like Bentham's prisoner, she may be under surveillance at any time. She may have freedom of movement, but not the freedom of privacy. As she scrolls on her smartphone, government agencies can access her metadata, companies can track her clicks and a friend from her distant past can upload a photo and tag her as a pimply, awkward teenager.

In 1995, Jeffrey Reiman wrote:

> If we direct our privacy-protection efforts at reinforcing our doors and curtains, we may miss the way in which modern means of information collection threaten our privacy by gathering up the pieces of our public lives and making them visible from a single point. This is why the Panopticon is a more fitting metaphor for the new threat to privacy than, for example, that old staple, the fishbowl.

Today, that's even more true. As a metaphor, the panopticon fits the internet like bespoke leg irons.

And yet, does the metaphor go far enough? In the panopticon model, the many are made visible to the few. However, as sociologist Thomas Mathiesen writes, digital media also enables the reverse, allowing the many to watch the few. On Mathiesen's account, television and mass media allow hundreds of millions to watch a limited number of celebrities, sportspeople and politicians. Mathiesen thus devises a reciprocal model: the *synopticon*, which refers to the many watching the few, derived from the Greek words *syn*, meaning 'together' or 'at the same time', and *optikos*. For Mathiesen, 'synopticism characterizes our society, and characterized the transition to modernity'.

The processes of panopticon and synopticon operate simultaneously, working in tandem, with their reciprocal functions feeding on one another: 'Together, the processes situate us in a viewer society in a two-way and double sense.' Like Foucault, Mathiesen is seeking to expose the latent exercise of power in a democratic capitalist society, writing that, 'Each from their side, like a pincer, panopticon and synopticon thus subdue.'

Certainly, the few are able to watch the many: hackers access strangers' computers; Facebook tracks users and non-users; government agencies such as the US National Security Agency (NSA) seem the very incarnation of a modern Panoptes. On the net, panopticism prevails. However, synopticism prevails too, as the many watch the few. Millions of Kim Kardashian fans can follow the minutiae of her life via gossip sites, her Twitter and leaked sex tapes.

The synopticon is also revealed in the notion of *sousveillance*, a term which has emerged as the complement of surveillance. With its French origins, 'surveillance' suggests watching from above, or overseeing, while 'sousveillance' suggests watching from below, or underseeing. As Shannon Vallor writes, we inhabit 'a sousveillance society, one in which even the watchers are watched.'

Sousveillance has been used to describe the activities of Wiki-Leaks, the whistleblower website that uses collaborative software to enable information to be leaked anonymously. WikiLeaks bills itself as 'the first intelligence agency of the people'. The term has also been applied to Edward Snowden, the former NSA contractor who leaked to journalists thousands of government documents concerning government surveillance. In Snowden's case, sousveillance exposed surveillance. Synopticon revealed panopticon. And for both WikiLeaks and Snowden, sousveillance was only possible thanks to digitisation, which allowed hundreds of thousands of documents to be copied, shared and published with daunting efficiency.

And what about activity trackers such as Fitbits? What about user-generated sites such as YouPorn.com, where people can upload and watch pornographic home videos? What about mutual watching? What about 'co-veillance'? Fitbits and YouPorn.com reveal the many watching the many and the few watching the few. It's an explosion of viewing, which philosopher Paul Virilio describes as the 'democratisation of voyeurism on a planetary scale'.

The slogan of Orwell's dystopian tyranny was 'Big Brother Is Watching You'. This is the panopticon, and the synopticon suggests a reversal: 'You Are Watching Big Brother'. And in the internet age, these reciprocal adages must be accompanied by still others: 'Companies and Individuals Are Watching You'; and its complement, 'You Are Watching Companies and Individuals'. The watching is top-down, bottom-up, and lateral. It is a world that various scholars have described as omniopticon, or participatory panopticon. WikiLeaks and YouPorn, Ed Snowden and Kim Kardashian reveal how data and privacy are being exposed in an unprecedented manner, and in all directions. It's a symbiotic crescendo of exhibitionism and voyeurism.

And yet the sketch I have drawn so far does not account for boyd's affordances of persistence and searchability. It does not account for the way data is often permanently recorded and conveniently accessible. This means that each individual, company and government is not just a potential Panoptes. After all, Panoptes may have had 100 eyes with which to watch his neighbour, but he was unable to sift through all his neighbour's correspondence with the help of a keyword search. He was unable to view footage of what his neighbour had done yesterday, or last week, or last year. And he was unable to aggregate thousands of bits of data captured over years into a coherent, accurate profile, including data supplied by others, and data inferred from other data.

On the internet, users leave traces. So yes, 'Big Brother Is Watching You', but remember also that 'Big Brother Was Watching You – and Recording It'. If your current online activity can be accessed, so too can your past online activity. As Bruce Schneier writes: 'On the internet, surveillance is ubiquitous. All of us are being watched, all the time, and that data is being stored forever. This is what an information-age surveillance state looks like, and it's efficient beyond Bentham's wildest dreams.'

We are all potentially Panoptes, each with 100 cameras on our 100 eyes. We watch, and record too. We see the past and the present, giving us glimpses of the future, too.

That's life in Panopticon 3.0.

THE REALITY MAY BE WORSE

Released in late 2016, AirPods are wireless earbuds that work via Bluetooth. They're sufficiently small to be discreet, but sufficiently white to say, 'Hey, we're an Apple product.' They also say something else. As media scholar Ian Bogost wrote in the *Atlantic*, 'Having them in while silent is a sign of inner focus – a request for privacy. That's why bothering someone with earbuds in is such a social faux-pas: They act as a do-not-disturb sign for the body.'

Digital technology enables people to create private worlds in public spaces. In schools and malls, on buses and trains, people are increasingly absorbed in their screens. Lost in personal worlds, they're in two (or more) places at once: some are physical; some are virtual; some are private; some are public. And these places butt up against one another, leading to a confusion of spaces, and to a confusion of public and private.

And that's just the start. With the emergence of big data and the internet of things, with the spread of smartphones and fitness trackers, the internet is convergent, ubiquitous and multi-directional, and the effects on privacy are profound. Software can recognise faces and match them with personal information; social media can construct 'shadow profiles' of non-users; location data can reveal where users are likely to be in 24 hours.

In the film *Her,* Theodore is asked a question by his operating system, Samantha. 'You mind if I look through your hard drive?' she asks, before sorting his emails and contacts. Within seconds, she knows him intimately. Meanwhile, Samantha is also the operating system for thousands of others. She knows them intimately too.

Samantha is a kind of Panoptes. She knows almost everything about Theodore and thousands of others. Theodore, however, is not like Panoptes. He knows nothing about the other users – aside from the fact that they exist – just as they presumably know nothing about him. And he knows little about Samantha. This world, then, is not Panopticon 3.0. Similarly, today's internet is not Panopticon 3.0. Today's internet is not yet fully convergent, ubiquitous or multi-directional.

Today's reality is that there are limits on the flow of data and the sharing of privacies. What's more, these limits and checks discriminate. In theory, everyone can potentially access all the internet's data; in reality, Facebook and governments are closer to actual Panoptes than the average individual. In the next chapter, I detail how today's internet diverges from Panopticon 3.0.

Panopticon 3.0 is merely a theoretical construct. The reality may be worse.

IT'S HARD TO OPT OUT OF A
SERVICE YOU'VE NEVER USED

Minority Report is a sci-fi thriller starring Tom Cruise as John Anderton, a cop who arrests people before they offend. In the year 2054, Anderton and his 'pre-crime' department have been so successful that the murder rate has dropped to zero.

It's all thanks to the predictions of mutated humans called 'precogs'. In this respect, the film is a fiction. Despite significant advances in forensics, police departments are not, according to my research, on the verge of employing infallible mutant soothsayers. Even so, the film was eerily prescient. In many jurisdictions, various generalised forms of predictive policing have already been implemented, using big data in much the same way as John Anderton used precogs.

Equally prescient was the film's depiction of personalised advertising. As Anderton moves about public spaces, he is met with a babble of voices hoping to attract his attention. These voices come from huge personalised adverts for cars, beer and credit cards. The ads are like TV spots, but tailored to each passer-by. 'John Anderton,' says a man insistently from a screen depicting an enormous beer. 'You could use a Guinness right about now.'

On another screen, a woman is promoting a car. 'Lexus,' she says. 'The road you're on, John Anderton, is the road less travelled.'

Thanks to digital technology, privacy is being confused and challenged to such an extent that the panopticon of Bentham and

Foucault is an inadequate metaphor. Instead, we need an updated model: Panopticon 3.0, in which everyone can see everyone in the present, in the past and even into the future. At least, that's the theory. In practice, there *are* limits. Each of us is merely a potential Panoptes, not an actual Panoptes.

In this chapter, I explore this gap to describe just how all-seeing the internet actually enables us to be, and why some have better vision than others. Specifically, I sort the challenges to privacy into three categories: the threat from individuals; the threat from companies; and the threat from governments. I then describe various forms of pushback against these threats.

Privacy is contested, it emerges, which is precisely the point *Minority Report* leaves us to ponder.

THREE DISTINCT CHALLENGES

Acxiom has been described as 'one of the biggest companies you've never heard of.' But it knows you, right down to your age, race, sex, weight, height, marital status, education level, politics, shopping habits, health issues, holiday plans, and much more. If personal data is the 'new oil', Acxiom is one of its most efficient miners. In the words of the US Federal Trade Commission, it's part of the 'unseen cyberazzi who collect information on all of us'.

Acxiom is a data broker. It was founded in 1969, the same year the internet sputtered into life. Originally, it compiled hard copy profiles of consumers for direct marketing purposes, but digitisation changed the game. By 2012, it had dossiers on more than half a billion internet users worldwide, with an average of 1500 'data points' on each consumer.

The process is straightforward. Each person is given a 13-digit identifying number, and to this number Acxiom information according to location, credit card transactions, hobbies, interests and other markers. Unobtrusively, it accumulates this data in the background, then sells it. This makes for a very profitable business model: its annual revenue hovers around the US$1 billion mark. And it's not alone. Many companies make money by amassing and selling consumer data to companies and government departments. They include Experian, Equifax, Quantium, and also Palantir, which has made millions by selling data to Immigration and Customs Enforcement in the US. What's more, sometimes that data is stolen. In 2017, Equifax admitted the data of more than 140 million people had been breached. In 2019, this led the Federal Trade Commission (FTC) to impose a US$575 million settlement.

All of which means that, because these data brokers know a lot about you, a long list of strangers, companies and government agencies know a lot about you too, without you ever noticing.

Challenges to privacy come in many forms. Some are deliberate, some are incidental. Some are trivial, some are concerning. Some are justified, some are illegal. To understand these challenges, it helps to sort them into categories based upon the origin of each challenge.

As a company, Acxiom should be subject to the same ethical and legal responsibilities as other companies. However, the challenge to privacy comes not just from Acxiom, but from a number of other sources too. Challenges to privacy, I'm suggesting, can come from three distinct sources: individuals, including hackers and vengeful ex-lovers; companies and organisations, including Facebook and Acxiom; and governments and public institutions, including the NSA and the Australian Tax Office. And as Acxiom reveals, sometimes those sources can be all mixed in together.[1]

INDIVIDUALS: HACKERS, PHISHERS, DOXERS, ON-SHARERS AND SELF-TRACKERS

In 2013, shortly before she was named Miss Teen USA, Californian teenager Cassidy Wolf received an email containing naked photos of herself. These photos had been taken surreptitiously in her bedroom via her laptop. Her laptop's webcam, it emerged, had been hacked using malware. Eventually, after a police investigation, the emailer was unveiled to be a classmate who had been spying on her for a year.

'It was traumatising,' Wolf said later. 'It's your bedroom. That's your most private, intimate space and that's where you should feel the most safe.'

A first category of challenge comes from individuals, including hackers. The teenage hacker who spied on Wolf had been spying on a total of 100 to 150 women. How many like him go undetected? It's impossible to know. We do know, however, that data breaches are common. According to one estimate, between 2013 and 2015 more than 100 million people were notified that they'd been victims of a data breach, exposing data held by retailers, health insurance companies and entertainment companies, among others. In a single breach in 2015, hackers released the private details of an estimated 32 million users of the adultery website Ashley Madison. In 2017, these were eclipsed by the Equifax breach.

Social networking sites are particularly vulnerable to spyware. Computer scientist Romany Mansour writes that this is due to the sheer volume of personal data available on social media, and also because malware is rapidly being tailor-made to extract personal information from such platforms.

Hackers can pose a threat to privacy. But other individuals can pose a threat too, including by 'phishing' – the attempt to obtain sensitive personal information by sending emails purporting to be from legitimate sources. In 2014, 500 images of celebrities appeared on the bulletin board 4chan, and then on social networks including Reddit. The celebrities were mostly female, including Jennifer Lawrence, Kate Upton and Kirsten Dunst, and the images were mostly nude. Rather than by high-tech hacking, the images were obtained by low-tech deception. A thirtysomething Pennsylvania man had 'phished' his victims by sending an email in which he pretended to be an employee of Apple or Google. He said their accounts were vulnerable and asked for their passwords, which they duly gave. He then used these passwords to copy private images from their email and Apple iCloud accounts.

Alongside hacking and phishing, there is the emerging practice of 'doxing', a type of public shaming which involves publication of someone's name, address, work details and other sensitive details, followed by online and offline harassment. Doxer targets can include people who offend online communities, such as Brianna Wu, a game developer who challenged misogynist bullies online and then, after her address was published, received death threats. Doxings sometimes happen on a large scale. In 2019, a spate of doxings in Canada and Australia was directed at supporters of pro-democracy protests in Hong Kong. Like Brianna Wu, many victims received death threats after their personal details were published on social media.

Not all invasions by individuals are malevolent, however. Some mums and dads, for instance, use purpose-built surveillance apps to spy on their kids. The apps monitor every text sent, number dialled and website visited, as well as revealing location data and the minutiae of every social media post. One such app is TeenSafe, which boasts that parents will be able to 'find the way to their child's mind'. To me, as a parent, it sounds like an abuse of trust, but TeenSafe's chief executive says it's all perfectly legitimate: 'It's absolutely legal for a parent to do this discreetly ... What we believe is that when it comes to protecting your child from these things – privacy is trumped by protection.'[2]

Certainly, privacy is not an absolute right. It must be balanced against other rights, interests and freedoms. The trick is working out how to strike this balance. In this instance, it's perfectly understandable that parents want their kids to be safe. I want precisely the same for my kids. But does the parents' interest in keeping their kids safe outweigh their kids' right to privacy?

It isn't only parents. Employers can track employees; wives can track husbands; hospitals can track patients. Already, spyware has featured in criminal trials, including the conviction of Simon Gittany for the murder of his girlfriend Lisa Harnum in Sydney in 2011. By using an app named Mobistealth to track Harnum's messages, Gittany learned she was planning to end the relationship. He then killed her by throwing her from a balcony. Sadly, this is no isolated incident, with researcher Delanie Woodlock finding that such technologies are increasingly being used to stalk and harass women in the context of domestic violence.

On the internet, there is a troubling interplay between privacy and gender. And here there has been quite a shift. Traditionally, privacy was associated with domesticity and femininity, and the feminine private sphere was generally regarded as inferior to the masculine public sphere. In some cases, the privacy of the domestic sphere provided a cover for pervasive domestic violence. On the internet, by contrast, the *invasion* of privacy often constitutes the harm, when the private is invaded or rendered public in acts of non-consensual abuse and misogyny.

Sometimes such abuse takes the form of the *on-sharing* of private material, including by sexting – the sending and receiving of sexually explicit material. A 2015 survey in the US found that 88 per cent of people aged 18–82 had sexted in the past year. Privacy issues arise when a person willingly shares material, only for it to be further on—shared without that person's knowledge and/or consent. Legally, this is known as 'image-based abuse', and it's common, even among teenagers. One Australian study found 20 per cent of teens had shown a sext to someone else, and 6 per cent of teens had forwarded a sext to a third party for whom the image wasn't intended.

Forget perpetrators for a minute. For victims, the consequences can be drastic, including sustained bullying, or expulsion from school, or worse. One case is that of Amanda Todd, a Canadian teenager who started making friends on video chat while in the seventh grade. Over time, one of these new contacts tried to convince Todd to show her breasts on camera. When she finally did, he blackmailed her, threatening to share the image unless she revealed more. Late in 2010, Todd's topless image started circulating on the internet, leading to persistent bullying and mental health issues. When Todd moved to a new school, the same man created a Facebook page with her topless photo as the profile image. He also contacted her classmates. More bullying followed, even after she changed school again. In 2012, aged 15, she committed suicide.

Amanda Todd was relentlessly bullied, stalked and intimidated. Repeatedly but unsuccessfully, she tried to retreat into safety, in the shape of a new life where she might rebuild her privacy and her social ties. Instead, she made a YouTube video telling her story with flashcards before taking her life.

So far, I have been talking about people whose privacy is compromised by others without consent. By complete contrast, many of us willingly compromise our own privacy in myriad ways. One involves the activity trackers that monitor steps taken, hours slept, calories burned and more. This is known as self-tracking, and it's a growth industry worth billions.

The most dedicated self-trackers are members of the 'quantified self' movement, whose motto, 'Self-knowledge through numbers', reads like a modern extreme of the Socrates dictum, 'The unexamined life is not worth living'. But is self-tracking really akin to Socratic self-examination? No, says Shannon Vallor. We prize the examined life not for the data it yields, Vallor writes, but 'for the transformative nature of the practice itself and the dignity it confers upon those who take it up'. As she puts it, 'a dataset is not a life'.

Nonetheless, dedicated self-trackers believe in their particular version of a self-examined life. As privacy researcher Marjolein Lanzing writes, users share copious quantities of data about themselves, often with a large and unspecified audience. For instance, Fitbit historically tended to make its users' profiles and activity public by default at the website fitbit.com. This explains how in 2011 approximately 200 users shared details of their sexual activity, completely inadvertently. In response, Fitbit changed its default settings to private. Even so, the culture of self-tracking continues actively to welcome broad disclosure, aided by devices so small, light and waterproof as to be barely noticeable.

With technological advances, the challenge from individuals can only grow. In 2013, Google Glass arrived to a fanfare of hype. The wearable technology was unobtrusive, resembling regular glasses with a small clip attached to one side. This enabled users to go about their daily business while simultaneously engaged in online activities, including surreptitiously livestreaming from an in-built camera. As technology writer Rob Price noted, 'To look at a person wearing Glass is to look at a camera staring back at you. It puts you in a state of uncertain surveillance, never sure whether or not you are being recorded.' As it happened, Google Glass flopped, seemingly over privacy concerns. Still, the development of sousveillance-facilitating technology is ongoing, conducted largely in secret.

Challenges to privacy from individuals come in the shape of hackers, phishers, doxers, cyberstalkers, cyberbullies and on-sharers, but they can also come in the shape of *us*, as self-trackers, or users of social media, or senders of sexts.

COMPANIES: FROM SHADOW PROFILES TO CAMBRIDGE ANALYTICA

In 2013, whenever I logged into Gmail, my inbox displayed a list of recently received messages. Above those emails sat a small, unobtrusive one-line advertisement. It consisted of about a dozen words, complete with a hyperlink to an external website.

Gmail is the email system run by Google, and the content of this advertisement, as Google's information explained, was determined by the content of my inbox, as well as by my other online activity. In this way, I then received advertisements for higher education opportunities (probably drawn from my correspondence with various universities), for theme parks (presumably from my emails about my kids) and vanity units (perhaps from an email I once sent a plumber about bathroom fittings).

In 2013, this was the apex of ads: subtle; responsive; personalised. A few short years later, it looks antiquated, as Google updates and refines its advertising practices, then updates and refines them all over again, in the ongoing quest for perfectly pitched personalisation.

The challenge from companies is perhaps the most pressing challenge of all. As Bruce Schneier writes in his forensic account of digital privacy, *Data and Goliath: The hidden battles to collect your data and control your world*: 'The overwhelming bulk of surveillance is corporate. We accept it either because we get value from the service or because we are offered a package deal that includes surveillance and don't have any real choice in the matter.'

One extreme example comprises the *shadow profiles* maintained by social media companies. The phrase 'shadow profile' can have two distinct meanings. The first refers to the profile that sits behind a user's main profile. As technology writer Kashmir Hill noted in 2017:

Behind the Facebook profile you've built for yourself is another one, a shadow profile, built from the inboxes and smartphones of other Facebook users. Contact information you've never given the network gets associated with your account, making it easier for Facebook to more completely map your social connections.

Online, the data you have chosen to share is collected and collated. That's no surprise. Meanwhile, a lot of data you have *not* chosen to share online can be collected and collated too. That's because data can be obtained from a variety of other sources: from the posts of your friends; from your offline shopping habits; from your supermarket loyalty cards. Further, a whole lot more data can be inferred. For instance, you may not have shared your sexuality, but a social network may have deduced it from seemingly unrelated data you have chosen to share. And you may not have shared your political leanings, but a social network may have figured this out from the company you keep.

Researchers from the Swiss Federal Institute of Technology have described this as the 'privacy leak factor'. In research published in 2014, Emre Sarigol, David Garcia and Frank Schweitzer set out 'to empirically test how the individual decision to reveal information turns into a collective phenomenon to disclose privacy'. Specifically, they used data gleaned from three million accounts from Friendster (a precursor to Facebook) to test whether they could predict the sexual orientation of users and even non-users. The simple answer is that they could.

Sarigol's team describe the first type of shadow profile – the hidden profile of a social network user – as a *partial shadow profile*.

The second type of shadow profile is considerably more controversial. It refers to the practice of creating profiles of people who don't use a site or service. Sarigol's team describe this as a *full shadow profile*. Facebook, for one, denies it collects them. As Kashmir Hill wrote in 2017: 'Facebook doesn't like, and doesn't use, the term "shadow profiles". It doesn't like the term because it sounds like Facebook creates hidden profiles for people who haven't joined the network, which Facebook says it doesn't do.'

As Sarigol's team showed, the privacy leak factor ensures that social networks have mountains of data on non-users and users alike. The bigger the social network, the bigger the leakage, and Facebook is the Pacific Ocean of social media. They concluded: 'Not having an account in an OSN [Online Social Network] does not guarantee a higher level of privacy, as long as one has enough friends who already are in the OSN.'

In the academic literature, the work that has been done tends to concern whether full shadow profiles are theoretically possible. The answer is yes.

In 2017, computer scientist David Garcia investigated the sexual orientation and relationship status of users on a defunct social network. The bigger the network and the higher the disclosure tendencies, he found, the easier it is for a social network to compile full shadow profiles. In 2018, further research by Garcia and his colleagues showed that data shared by Twitter users can predict the location of people who aren't on Twitter.

These findings begin to hint at the power of data. And they unequivocally reveal that full shadow profiles are possible. But do they exist?

In 2011, Austrian law student Max Schrems lodged complaints with the Irish Data Protection Commissioner alleging that Facebook was building shadow profiles of non-users. Ultimately, the Commissioner resolved the complaints informally, leaving the issue unaddressed. (Schrems has made it his mission to hold digital platforms accountable on privacy issues. In 2015, following one of his complaints, the European Court of Justice struck down the 'Safe

Harbor' provisions under which tech companies had been transfer-
ring the data of Europeans to the US.)

Certainly, Facebook has admitted tracking non-users for the
purposes of targeted advertising. In 2016, a *Wall Street Journal* article
reported that Facebook would begin collecting data about all internet users, through 'like' buttons and other pieces of code present on
web pages across the net. Facebook would then use this data to target
its advertising to non-users of Facebook, as well as users. As Facebook's then vice-president of ads and business platform, Andrew
Bosworth, said: 'Our buttons and plug-ins send over basic information about users' browsing sessions. For non-Facebook members,
previously we didn't use it. Now we'll use it to better understand
how to target those people.' (Admittedly, since 2018, Facebook has
scaled back some of its data collecting and sharing practices, as I
discuss below.)

In this way, a non-user of Facebook visiting a gastronomic
website might be profiled as a keen cook, and might be targeted
across the web with cooking-related products. And all this would be
done by Facebook, even if that person had never engaged with the
network. As the *Wall Street Journal*'s Jack Marshall noted, several
companies use such targeting, but Facebook's size gives it a distinct
advantage.

Targeting non-users with ads is one thing. Creating a full
shadow profile is another. Reluctantly, Facebook has found itself
discussing full shadow profiles in lawsuits over its facial recognition
technology.

In 2015, three plaintiffs – Adam Pezen, Carlo Licata and
Nimesh Patel – sued Facebook in the US state of Illinois, alleging
that Facebook's facial recognition technology breached a state law.
The case concerns tagging in photos, and the law in question is the
Illinois *Biometric Information Privacy Act* (BIPA), the toughest biom-
etric privacy law in the US. It prohibits the collection of biometric

data without informed, written consent. The suit was prompted by 'Tag Suggestions', a Facebook feature that uses facial recognition technology to analyse whether a user's Facebook friends appear in photos uploaded to the platform. Among other things, the suit claimed that the technology was enabling Facebook to build full shadow profiles.

Facebook has defended the action vigorously, but the suit keeps gaining momentum. In February 2018, after the three actions were joined into one, a federal judge in California rejected Facebook's motion to dismiss the case. Then in April 2018, a federal judge ruled that millions of Facebook users could proceed with a class action. This is not typical: as Joel Rosenblatt wrote for the Bloomberg news service, it's rare for consumers to win class action status in privacy cases. And the stakes are high, given that the suit seeks US$1000 for each negligent violation or US$5000 for each reckless violation. Because there are millions of Illinois residents who use Facebook, this could amount to a potential payout of billions of dollars in damages.

In August 2019, US Circuit Judge Sandra S. Ikuta dismissed a Facebook appeal. 'We conclude that the development of a face template using facial-recognition technology without consent (as alleged here) invades an individual's private affairs and concrete interests,' wrote Judge Ikuta in the matter of *Patel v Facebook*. The case rolls on. Meanwhile, similar lawsuits under the Illinois Act have also been brought against other digital giants. In December 2018, an action against the facial recognition technology used by Google Photos was dismissed. By August 2019, however, a Snapchat lawsuit was still before the courts. In global litigation about privacy, facial recognition is a key battleground.

But it was the Cambridge Analytica scandal that most clearly raised the topic of shadow profiles. In April 2018, following uproar about Cambridge Analytica misusing personal information obtained through Facebook to influence the 2016 US election, Facebook's Mark Zuckerberg was called to testify to US Congress. Apart from submitting written testimony, Zuckerberg answered questions orally for ten hours over two days. Towards the end of the sessions, he was asked about shadow profiles by Ben Luján, a Democratic Congressman from New Mexico.

> Luján: Facebook has detailed profiles on people who have never signed up for Facebook, yes or no?

> Zuckerberg: Congressman, in general we collect data on people who have not signed up for Facebook for security purposes to prevent the kind of scraping you were just referring to. [Scraping involves reverse searches based on public data such as phone numbers.]

> Luján: So these are called shadow profiles, is that what they've been referred to by some?

> Zuckerberg: Congressman, I'm not, I'm not familiar with that.

> Luján: I'll refer to them as shadow profiles for today's hearing. On average, how many data points does Facebook have on each Facebook user?

> Zuckerberg: I do not know off the top of my head.

> Luján: The average for non-Facebook platforms is 1500. It's been reported Facebook has as many as 29,000 data points for an average Facebook user. Do you know how many points of data Facebook has on the average non-Facebook user?

Zuckerberg: Congressman, I do not know off the top of my head but I can have our team get back to you afterward.

Luján: It's been admitted by Facebook that you do collect data points on non-users. My question is, can someone who does not have a Facebook account opt out of Facebook's involuntary data collection?

Zuckerberg: Anyone can turn off and opt out of any data collection for ads, whether they use our services or not, but in order to prevent people from scraping public information … we need to know when someone is trying to repeatedly access our services.

Luján then pointed out the absurdity that if non-users wanted to stop Facebook tracking them, they needed to set up a Facebook page to do so.

The exchange was echoed in May, when Zuckerberg appeared before the European Parliament. Towards the end of the session, with time running out, Zuckerberg offered, 'Is there anything else here that …?'

'Shadow profiles,' said British MEP Syed Kamall. 'Shadow profiles.'

Awkwardly, Zuckerberg dodged the question. Instead, he referred to the new 'Clear History' feature, which enables users to clear basic browsing history, and added, 'We think it's important to protect people in our community'. In other words, Facebook collects information on non-users to protect users.

To this, Syed Kamall tweeted: 'This was #Zuckerberg's opportunity to show he understands that people not on Facebook don't consent to having their data collected … he didn't.'

Zuckerberg's refusal to acknowledge shadow profiles was

ridiculed on social media. Certainly, the phrase has been in common usage since at least June 2013, when researchers at Packet Storm Security found a vulnerability in Facebook's software. This in turn revealed that Facebook was collecting data on as many people as they could, whether or not they used the platform. As Packet Storm said, 'Dossiers are being built on everyone possible.'

These issues are at the very heart of the challenge that companies pose to privacy. Do companies have shadow profiles? Do they collect data on non-users? Do they target non-users with advertising? At the very least, the evidence reveals a significant failure of transparency and consent. While Zuckerberg was testifying, the non-profit Mozilla Foundation released its first Internet Health Report. The findings weren't good. 'We're in this kind of fat data economy, where we collect as much as we can and let it interconnect, and then we end up with these toxic data spills,' said Mozilla's Mark Surman.

On the internet, some platforms do exist to protect privacy: the search engine DuckDuckGo; the browser extension AdNauseam; the Max Schrems initiative noyb ('none of your business'). Many are not-for-profit.

Most often, however, for-profit platforms want to know about users, and non-users. The more they know, the better they can make their services, and the better they can profit. To this end, companies collect data on users, and then enter deals to share their data with other companies, as Facebook did with Acxiom, Experian and Quantium in its Partner Categories program. Admittedly, in the wake of Cambridge Analytica, Facebook has signalled a shift in its data collecting and sharing practices. In 2018, it abandoned the Partner Categories program. And in March 2019, Zuckerberg posted a 3000-word essay, 'A privacy-focused vision for social networking', in which he wrote, 'I believe the future of communication will increasingly shift to private, encrypted services'. But what does this future look like, more precisely? In response to a comment from journalist and professor Jeff Jarvis, Zuckerberg clarified: 'This privacy-focused vision is meant to complement the existing more public social platforms … feeds and public sharing aren't going away.'

Knowing users is how digital platforms improve their services and generate their profits. With all this data, digital platforms can help advertisers reach increasingly specific demographics. Forget blunderbuss sales pitches – the new model relies on identifying adventurous twentysomethings with a large disposable income who like to eat sashimi. Targeted advertising, culminating in individualised advertising, is sophisticated and automated, and can be predicated on a loss of privacy.

Famously, the retailer Target created an algorithm to determine when a customer was pregnant. Once the system was triggered by the purchase of specific items – including zinc supplements, unscented lotion and a handbag large enough for nappies – Target inserted baby-related notices among other advertisements. Detailing the process in a 2012 article for the *New York Times*, Charles Duhigg wrote how an irate father had complained to Target after his daughter started receiving ads for maternity wear and nursery furniture. The store manager apologised. However, when the manager called a few days later to apologise again, the father apologised too. 'I had a talk with my daughter,' he said. 'It turns out there's been some activities in my house I haven't been completely aware of. She's due in August.'

Target knew this teenager was pregnant before her father did. As the architect of the algorithm told Duhigg: 'Just wait. We'll be sending you coupons for things you want before you even know you want them.' Such highly targeted advertising can translate into life-long relationships with customers. However, there is one proviso. If the targeting is too specific, customers baulk. As one executive from Target said, 'As long as we don't spook her, it works.'

Consumers tend to be glad when a company knows them, but not when a company knows them *too* well. So companies work hard to optimise their personalisation. From a technological perspective, the highly individualised ads of *Minority Report* seem eminently possible. The reason that they haven't been realised may well be that companies are aware that a more subtle form of personalisation is more profitable.

It's become a truism: once, companies sold you products; today, you're the product. And you're probably worth more than you think. In 2018, Facebook earned an average of $84.41 for each North American user. At Google, the principle is the same. As the then head of Google Android, Andy Rubin, said in 2013: 'We don't monetize the things we create. We monetize users.' Some practices may have been abandoned and some of the rhetoric may have changed, but for companies who rely on knowing users, no new model has yet emerged.

In 2017, four years after one-line text ads appeared atop my Gmail inbox, I began receiving ads for products I had just searched for moments earlier, such as running shoes or a gift for my daughter. These ads then followed me around the web.

That same year, Google reportedly stopped scanning Gmail inboxes to gather data for personalised ads. Are we seeing a shift away from personalisation and the harvesting of personal data? Certainly, companies are increasingly making grand statements about how much they value personal data and privacy. These companies are nothing if not innovative. Their very success is built upon their ability to adapt. By the time you read this book, some of the policies and practices I am describing will have been replaced by new policies and practices.

There is also variation between companies. All companies are different, and their approach to privacy is different. Both Google and Facebook generate the vast bulk of their revenue from advertising: in the second quarter of 2019, Google's parent Alphabet earned 84 per cent of its revenue from advertising; in 2018, Facebook generated about 98 per cent of its global revenue from advertising. These figures suggest just how valuable customer data is to both. Granted, they provide different services, and their approach to personal data differs accordingly.

Still, there's considerable overlap. Anecdotal evidence abounds from people who think their devices have been listening in on their conversations, then targeting them with content and ads. Recently, I was discussing the actor Shia LaBeouf with a colleague, because we'd just met someone with a similar-sounding name. I hadn't mentioned the actor in years. The following day, YouTube recommended a video about LaBeouf for me, which is very different from the content I usually consume, and from YouTube's other recommendations. Still, that doesn't reveal much. Maybe it was just a fluke? Perhaps, but recently digital platforms *have* been caught eavesdropping. In August 2019, Bloomberg's Sarah Frier revealed that Facebook had been paying hundreds of contractors to transcribe audio clips from users of its services. Meanwhile, Google, Apple and Amazon have been scrutinised for analysing recordings captured by voice assistants. 'Big tech companies don't like to talk about it,' wrote Rachel Metz for CNN. 'And when users find out it's happening, they're often surprised — and disturbed. Yes, if you talk to a virtual assistant, such as Amazon's Alexa, a human may listen to a recording of your chatter.'

In August 2019, following news reports, these companies all announced they were winding back such eavesdropping. Facebook abandoned its program of paying contractors to review the audio messages sent via the social network's Messenger app; Apple and Google announced they were temporarily ceasing their programs of having human graders listen to audio commands given to voice assistants; and Amazon changed its settings to make it easier to opt out of the review of audio caught by voice assistants.

On the one hand, the convenience of Amazon's Alexa, Apple's Siri and Google Assistant is staggering. Directions to my next meeting? Traffic conditions en route? Nearest petrol station? Weather forecast? News headlines? Digital assistants have answers. But as they assist, they gather mountains of data, and not just about me. Often, there are other people in the room. Is Alexa recording my children? My friends?

And for companies, it's preferable that individuals are all identifiable and *real*. In the early days of the web, users could embrace anonymity and experiment with identity. Their online presence might comprise a complete fiction. Or several complete fictions. Today, however, digital platforms need data about real users (and nonusers). One strategy to achieve this involves deleting fake accounts. As Facebook said back in 2012:

> It's something we monitor vigilantly. We want to ensure that
> one of the core tenets of Facebook is that you have your unique
> identity on Facebook ... We have an advantage because we are
> a true identity platform so we can quickly figure out if anyone
> is their true self on Facebook ... What we are looking for is
> people who have widespread fake user ID accounts to make
> sure we take them out of the system. We call them bad actors
> ...

Similarly, in 2016 Twitter launched a campaign to 'verify' its users.

For each verified user, online data can be supplemented with data obtained offline. As McKenzie Funk wrote in the *New York Times* in 2016: 'In the age of Facebook, it has become far easier ... to combine our online personas with our offline selves, a process that was once controversial but is now so commonplace that there's a term for it, "onboarding".' Combined with efforts to weed out bad actors, onboarding ensures that ever more data can be attached to real, identifiable people.

And the kicker is that a lot of the most personal and sensitive data about individuals doesn't even need to be gathered. In 2008, social psychologist Michal Kosinski moved from Poland to Cambridge University to undertake a PhD. Since then, Kosinki's research has given great insight into how shared data reveals unshared data. There's a decent chance it also explains how Donald Trump won the US presidency.

In 2013, Kosinski, David Stillwell and Thore Graepel studied 58 000 Americans to find that a Facebook user's 'likes' reveal an uncannily accurate personality profile, including sexual orientation, racial heritage, political leanings, drug use and intelligence level. 'Likes' that predict low intelligence include Harley Davidson motorbikes and the band Lady Antebellum; and 'likes' that predict male heterosexuality include basketballer Shaquille O'Neal and 'being confused after waking up from naps'. The researchers wrote: 'Commercial companies, governmental institutions, or even one's Facebook friends could use software to infer attributes such as intelligence, sexual orientation, or political views that an individual may not have intended to share.'

As they conducted more research, Kosinski and his team found they were able to infer increasingly detailed and sensitive data from a relatively limited number of 'likes'. On the basis of 10 likes, they could profile you more accurately than a typical colleague could. On the basis of 300 likes, they know you better than your spouse does. For their research, Kosinski's team at Cambridge University used purpose-built apps. One of them was Apply Magic Sauce (applymagicsauce.com), which had a 'trait prediction engine' that could, among other things, 'predict your personality from your Facebook likes.' Another was My Personality (mypersonality.org), which enabled Facebook users to take personality tests.

For Kosinski and his team, using Facebook was like stumbling into a treasure trove of data. Their specific field is 'psychometrics', which seeks to categorise people according to key character traits, and the My Personality app enabled vast numbers of people to be sorted very efficiently. The categories might include 'angry introverts', 'anxious fathers', or even 'undecided Democrats'.

Enter Cambridge Analytica, a data mining company funded by conservatives. In early 2014, Kosinski was approached by an assistant professor at Cambridge University named Aleksandr Kogan, who wanted to access Kosinski's expanding database on behalf of a private company related to Cambridge Analytica. Kosinski refused, so Kogan built his own database via an app called thisisyourdigitallife. Just like My Personality, it invited users to take personality tests, and then sorted those users into categories.

The trouble is, Cambridge Analytica then had access that extended far beyond the data of Facebook users who took the app quiz. From 2007 until 2014, Facebook gave app developers access to the data of their app's users, but also to the data of *that user's friends*. This is decidedly counterintuitive. As ethicist Gordon Hull and his team have noted, it's akin to you joining a tennis club, and that tennis club then quietly extracting details about your friends' favourite books and political leanings. As we now know, by means of the 270 000 people who took the thisisyourdigitallife quiz, Cambridge Analytica were able to access the data of 87 million Facebook users. And with all that data, Cambridge Analytica, working on behalf of the Trump campaign, was able to identify, say, 'undecided Democrats', and then target them with highly personalised ads via their Facebook newsfeeds.

Exactly how much impact did this misuse of personal data have on the 2016 US election? We'll never know. We do know, however, that this access of Facebook user data potentially determined an election.

I am not making a partisan point here. I am not suggesting that the Republicans ran a dirty campaign in 2016, and the Democrats didn't. Both parties drew heavily on social media data to design highly targeted advertising. Indeed, in previous elections Barack Obama had been a pioneer of combining social media and targeted messages. As Kosinski himself – now a respected professor at Stanford – has noted, both parties continue to rely heavily on psychological profiling. But Cambridge Analytica suddenly made one thing clear. Privacy breaches don't just harm individuals. They can also harm democracy.

It all stems from the way that your online activities, and even your offline activities, reveal much more than you think. Your Facebook likes can reveal your sexuality. Your location history can reveal your personality. Your music preferences can reveal your voting intentions. And even if you deliberately keep your online interactions to a minimum, you're probably still revealing your religion, your health, your intelligence, your age, your gender, and much more. This in turn can make you vulnerable to all sorts of manipulations.

All the while, you're revealing your friends, and making them vulnerable too. This is thanks to 'homophily', the tendency of people to befriend others like them. In 2010, a team of computer scientists studied two online social networks to find that communities form around users that share attributes. By applying an algorithm, the researchers found that, with as few as 20 per cent of users providing attributes, they could often infer the traits of the remaining users with great accuracy. The researchers called their paper, 'You are who you know: inferring user profiles in online social networks.' On the internet as in real life, birds of a feather flock together. This means that the only way to maintain your privacy is to make sure no one knows who your friends are.

• • •

The surveillance technology that powers the web has spawned an entirely new lexicon. Think of it as dataspeak. 'Cookies', more accurately known as 'persistent identifiers', are small parcels of data sent from a website and stored in a user's web browser. Between visits, websites forget who users are; but cookies never forget. Instead, they enable each user to be identified by the internet's equivalent of a name-tag, in the form of 'I'm customer #582091'. 'Clickstream' data shows precisely where and when users click. Way back in 2007, it was revealed that US Internet Service Providers (ISPs) including Verizon, Comcast and AOL were monitoring user clickstream data and linking it with identifiable customer records. And 'data exhaust' describes the digital trail users leave behind in their online interactions: where they click; how long they stay on a page; where their mouse-cursor hovers; and more.

Somewhere in the background, well out of sight, often beyond your control, data about you is flowing with dizzying complexity.

Emerging technologies such as facial recognition and voice assistants throw up fresh challenges. Take virtual reality, or VR. So far, the technology has been costly and cumbersome. But that's changing, with the development of photorealistic avatars and full body motion tracking systems. One recent innovation is social VR, in which people can interact with others also using the same technology. It blends the immersion of VR with the interactivity of social media. The potential for games and recreation is obvious, as it is also for education. However, the potential for surveillance is great too, as VR has the capability to track every detail: how your body moves; where your eye falls; a wide range of your quirks. In 2018, Facebook's VR platform, Oculus, patented a system for eye tracking that captures where users are looking, when they make eye contact, how long that eye contact lasts, and so on. In its privacy policy, Oculus says it uses data for several reasons, including to 'conduct and learn from research about the ways in which people use our services'. This, writes legal researcher Crystal Nwaneri, is telling, given that Facebook has itself experimented on affecting the mood of users by adjusting the contents of their newsfeed. 'Oculus seems to have the same privileges as Facebook to experiment on users,' she wrote. 'This poses a far greater risk than social media because of the type of data that VR platform providers will be able to collect and manipulate.'

VR is yet to go mainstream. But the principle is the same for much of the technology we use today. We're giving up much more than we realise to companies who profit from that data.

And increasingly, we're giving up that data to the cloud. In the past, our photos, documents and data tended to be stored on the hard-drive of our desktop. Increasingly, we keep them in ethereal-sounding locations such as Apple's iCloud, Google Drive, Microsoft OneDrive (formerly SkyDrive), Dropbox or Amazon Web Services. Data has shifted out of devices owned by users and into a cloud owned by companies. Currently, my phone prompts me to back up all its contents to the cloud; I collaborate on documents stored at Google Drive and OneDrive; and friends share photo albums via Dropbox. But who owns this data? Who has rights to it? And what are the ethical and legal ramifications?

The shift is more than symbolic. In the cloud, users tend to retain ownership and copyright; but cloud computing services reserve the right, as specified in their terms and conditions, to access and use such data. For instance, Google UK's website says that 'what belongs to you stays yours', then continues:

> When you upload, submit, store, send or receive content
> to or through our Services, you give Google (and those we

work with) a worldwide licence to use, host, store, reproduce, modify, create derivative works (such as those resulting from translations, adaptations or other changes that we make so that your content works better with our Services), communicate, publish, publicly perform, publicly display and distribute such content.

Increasingly, a life lived on the internet is a life lived in the cloud. And that cloud is stored in electronic facilities, owned by companies and scattered around the globe. Accordingly, the challenge to privacy grows. As Bruce Schneier writes, companies can and do delete accounts, turn data over to law enforcement authorities and store data in countries where privacy laws are more lax.

Of course, it's worth reiterating there are positives to large-scale data collection. Not only do these data-driven services make life more convenient for individuals, they also have the potential to deliver benefits for society. Big data can provide an early warning system for the outbreak of aggressive infectious diseases. It can predict and mitigate the effects of natural disasters. It can make cities flow more efficiently. In 2018, Uber announced a collaboration with SharedStreets, a data-sharing project that seeks to improve urban spaces so that cars, cabs, trucks, bikes and people can best co-exist.

What's more, as I've noted, and as typified by Zuckerberg's 3000-word blog post, there has been a general shift in tone, as companies increasingly make public statements extolling the value of privacy. And there have been improvements. For instance, Amazon, Google and even Facebook now have specific websites where users can review data privacy settings, including for their voice assistants. Here users can delete data and find out more about exactly what these companies know about them. Google and Amazon have dedicated URLs, whereas Facebook requires its users to access their Activity Log.

So there are some qualified reasons for optimism. The concern, however, is that the challenge from companies remains enormous and is still not understood by the general public.

We have seen how Target lived up to its name, targeting women it had secretly identified as pregnant with personalised advertising. A prospective employer would, presumably, be highly interested to know whether or not a potential recruit is pregnant. And while the law may say it's illegal for employers to discriminate on the basis of pregnancy, what's to stop an employer researching and discriminating in secret? Such discrimination already happens on the basis of religion. Privacy researchers Alessandro Acquisti and Christina Fong have shown that US employers consult social media when hiring, and that they discriminate against Muslim applicants.

Despite reasons for optimism, the internet-based challenge to privacy from companies may snowball into yet greater challenges. Already, companies know what people want. Next, perhaps, companies will be able to *determine* what people want. In 2007, Google's then chief executive Eric Schmidt said: 'The goal is to enable Google users to be able to ask the question such as "What shall I do tomorrow?" and "What job shall I take?"' In 2010, he repeated the claim: 'I actually think most people don't want Google to answer their questions, they want Google to tell them what they should be doing next.'

That's not the sort of thing company executives tend to say any more, but is it what they still think?

GOVERNMENTS: PREDICTIVE POLICING AND DOMESTIC SURVEILLANCE

Winston Smith lives in a surveillance state, and he doesn't like the way he and every other citizen is constantly watched, the way free thought is curtailed, and the way anyone who expresses a dissenting opinion is rounded up and 're-educated' into orthodoxy. Unfortunately, the government is all but omniscient, so Winston's objections are soon noted, and he inevitably finds himself in the hands of the Thought Police, who take him to Room 101, deep in the fortified concrete bunker that is the Ministry of Love.

'You asked me once, what was in Room 101,' says O'Brien, a man Winston had thought was his friend. 'I told you that you knew the answer already. Everyone knows it. The thing that is in Room 101 is the worst thing in the world.' When the government knows everything, it also knows your deepest fear. In Room 101, Winston sees two rats in a cage shaped to fit over his face. Facing his worst nightmare, Winston breaks, yielding any resistance and betraying his lover.

A third threat to privacy is from governments, in the form of metadata retention, bulk surveillance and security agencies with three-letter acronyms. It is in this context that Winston Smith is commonly cited. Winston, the protagonist of George Orwell's *1984*, lives under an omniscient government that maintains an iron grip on power by exploiting citizens' weaknesses. Similarly, it is in relation to government surveillance that the panopticon of Bentham and Foucault is commonly invoked as a metaphor. As philosophers and political scientists such as Hannah Arendt have argued, there is a direct link between surveillance states and totalitarianism.

Of course, government surveillance is nothing new. In 18th and 19th century France, the staff of the *cabinet noir*, or 'black chamber', worked behind the General Post Office in Paris, opening letters, reading their contents, then sealing them again without arousing the suspicion of sender or receiver. More recently, in the 20th century, the Stasi of East Germany refined such surveillance by eavesdropping via hidden listening devices and encouraging children to spy on their parents – state surveillance taken to its sinister extreme. But then came the internet, putting the Stasi in the shade. For governments eager to engage in surveillance on an unprecedented scale, the internet provided the means. And for some countries, the events of 11 September 2001 provided the motive.

Soon after the attacks had felled New York's World Trade Center and shaken the world, the US government realised that its surveillance systems had serious limitations. Only able to discover basic details about the terrorists, it appealed to the public for information by releasing the names of 19 hijackers. Data broker Acxiom promptly responded. As Richard Behar wrote in *Fortune*, Acxiom located 11 hijackers in its databases, and was able to provide the FBI with current addresses, former addresses, the names of associates, and many more details. Acxiom, it turned out, had sophisticated data capturing technology that put the FBI's primitive laptops to shame. Over the following months, Acxiom taught the FBI how to conduct digital surveillance. Indictments and deportations followed.

One of the reasons that government surveillance is effective is because it can combine data from various sources, including companies. On the net, as we have seen, data can easily be joined with more data, a phenomenon dubbed 'cybernation' by philosopher Amitai Etzioni. Mountains of data are only one click away from being shared.

Ironically, this point was illustrated a decade later by the ease with which Edward Snowden exposed the surveillance practices of intelligence agencies. In 2013, Edward Snowden was working in Hawaii as a contractor for the National Security Agency, or NSA. By now, the US government had dramatically expanded its surveillance capacities. So much so that Snowden had become distraught about what he considered to be illegal and unconstitutional practices. And so, thanks to his high security clearance as a computer analyst, he copied an unknown number of classified documents. There may have been more than a million. In May 2013, after making contact via encrypted emails, Snowden flew to Hong Kong and began sharing the contents with journalists, exposing the practices of the governments of the United States, but also the United Kingdom, Australia, Canada, New Zealand and beyond. These governments, the documents showed, were engaged in widespread surveillance of domestic and foreign citizens, at times with the help of telecommunications and technology companies.

The focus of Snowden's revelations was his own workplace, the NSA. Formed in 1952, the NSA is a part of the military established to gather foreign intelligence. In its early years, the agency was so secretive that its name was rarely mentioned. A common quip was that the acronym stood for 'No Such Agency'. With the end of the Cold War in the 1980s and 1990s, however, the NSA became more open, and also more focused on defence. This changed again following the terrorist attacks of 11 September 2001. Declaring war on terror, the US government resolved to know everything about everyone. As revealed in NSA slides copied and leaked by Snowden, the NSA's stated objective after 2001 became to 'Collect it All', 'Process it All', 'Exploit it All', 'Partner it All', 'Sniff it All' and 'Know it All'. 'Traditional espionage pits government against government … but the terrorist enemy is different,' writes Bruce Schneier. '[Its] members could be anywhere. Modern government surveillance monitors everyone, domestic and international alike.'[3]

Just as 'September 11' was prompting the NSA to switch its focus onto everything and everyone, the internet was transforming the nature of surveillance. Previously, a Chinese military network carried Chinese communications, a Russian military network carried Russian communications, and so on. The internet mixed everything together. That meant that if the NSA wanted to track terrorist emails, it would also need to track the emails of mums, dads and everyone besides. And the NSA was nothing if not methodical, with Snowden's leaks revealing that the NSA was running three separate programs designed just to collect Gmail data. Meanwhile, online data was being supplemented with offline data. Snowden's very first revelation was a document showing that the FBI had ordered Verizon to hand over to the NSA the calling metadata of all its customers.

Snowden also revealed that the NSA was using targeted programs. For 'QUANTUMHAND', the NSA used malware to disguise itself as a fake Facebook server to gain access to users' computers. When the user logged in, the NSA sent data packets that tricked the computer into thinking they originated from the real Facebook. As investigative journalists Ryan Gallagher and Glenn Greenwald found, the NSA then siphoned out data from the computer's hard drive.

QUANTUMHAND is run by the NSA's Tailored Access Operations group (TAO), which has the job of hacking into computers remotely. Snowden himself had reportedly been offered a job with this elite unit, but turned it down and became a whistleblower instead. Ultimately, Snowden's leaks revealed a great deal about TAO, including that QUANTUMHAND is just one malware program among many, integrated into the NSA's automated TURBINE system, which employs, according to TAO, 'industrial-scale exploitation'. NSA documents leaked by Snowden revealed plans to deploy 'potentially millions of implants' as part of its 'Owning the Net' program, which included expanding TURBINE to enable 'greater automation of computer network exploitation'.

The NSA was collecting emails, text messages, browsing history, address books, location information and much more, although it remains difficult to ascertain which data was anonymised, which was analysed and which was retained. What's more, the NSA is just one of 17 US intelligence agencies. Given that the NSA's existence remained secret for 20 years, there is a possibility that an 18th secret agency now exists. Surveillance in the US also occurs outside these

17 agencies. For instance, 'fusion centers' have been set up for state and local law enforcement to collaborate for the purposes of gaining access to data from national agencies such as the FBI. Initially set up to combat terrorism, these centers are now used for broader law enforcement, and have been used to spy on political protesters.

Snowden's revelations made clear that such practices aren't exclusive to the US. NSA-like roles are played by the Government Communications Headquarters (GCHQ) in the UK and by the Australian Signals Directorate (ASD) in Australia, while similar organisations exist in Canada, New Zealand, Germany, France, Denmark, Israel, and elsewhere. Predictably, the extent of their operations is hotly disputed. In 2014, Snowden wrote that New Zealand's Government Communications Security Bureau (GCSB), 'is directly involved in the untargeted, bulk interception and algorithmic analysis of private communications sent via internet, satellite, radio, and phone networks.' New Zealand's then Prime Minister John Key responded that 'there is not, and never has been, mass surveillance of New Zealanders undertaken by the GCSB'.

In Australia in 2015, metadata retention laws were passed, granting approved government agencies warrantless access to two years' worth of customer call records, location information, IP addresses, billing information and other data stored by telecommunications companies. It is unclear which government agencies can access this metadata, as the names of some agencies seeking access have been suppressed, despite Freedom of Information applications. More recently, the Australian government introduced to parliament the Identity-matching Services Bill 2019. With the help of facial recognition technology, it would compile in one government database images from Australians' passports, driver's licences and other photographic identification. Its scope would be vast, and has alarmed privacy advocates.

In other countries, we see dark variations on the theme. In Russia, the System for Operative Investigative Measures is built into the internet, and is used against criminals, and also against journalists, human rights activists and political opponents; in Thailand, India and Malaysia, people have been arrested based on internet conversations; and in China, more than 30 000 specialised police monitor the internet for phrases such as 'Tiananmen' and 'Amnesty International', while the oppressive surveillance of the Uighur minority has been well documented.

China is also phasing in its 'social credit score', which has gained considerable press coverage. Like a social version of a credit rating, the system will give each citizen a score for social trustworthiness, based on behaviour. Launched in 2014 and set to be rolled out nationally by 2020, the system takes into account a wide range of factors. These include whether citizens have unpaid debts or have taken drugs, but they also include behaviour and preferences. As author Rachel Botsman writes, this takes in shopping habits and negative social media posts about China's economy. It also takes account of relationships. If your friend makes a negative post about China's economy, you may be unable to buy a plane ticket. The ramifications are serious. One of the scheme's slogans is 'Once you lost trust, you will face restrictions everywhere'. Those deemed untrustworthy can be prevented from studying, making deals or booking travel. In 2018, reports Associated Press, people were banned from buying flights 17.5 million times and banned from buying train tickets 5.5 million times.

Globally, most governments appear to have extensive surveillance capabilities, including sophisticated hacking tools. These tools would give them the capacity to collect emails and texts, to gain access to call history, search history and address books, and to take screenshots, record audio, snap photos and monitor coordinates. 'It's a reasonable assumption that most countries have these hacking capabilities,' writes Bruce Schneier. 'Who they use them against, and what legal rules control that use, depends on the country.'

In 2017 in the *New York Times*, journalist Nicole Perlroth, who covers cybersecurity, reported on how the Mexican government was using spyware against anti-obesity campaigners. These campaigners were receiving highly personal text messages about friends' funerals, unfaithful spouses and family members having serious accidents. 'Simon buddy my dad just died we are devastated,' said one text, which came with a link. 'I'm sending you info about the wake, I hope you can come.' The link contained invasive spyware developed by NSO Group, an Israeli cyberarms dealer. Like Italy's Hacking Team and Britain's Gamma Group, NSO Group claims to deal only with governments, and Mexico is a repeat customer. In a fascinating twist, WhatsApp sued NSO in the US in October 2019, claiming the company had illegally helped governments hack into the mobile devices of journalists, human rights workers and women. As the *Washington Post* reported, 'The suit amounted to a new legal front in attempts to curb the abuses of the burgeoning but almost entirely unregulated global surveillance industry.'

These digital intrusions make the *cabinet noir* and the Stasi look plodding and pedestrian. And the scale of the data being collected is hard to comprehend. In 2014, the Intelligence Community Comprehensive National Cybersecurity Initiative Data Center, or Utah Data Center, was opened. It has been described as the world's largest black chamber. Its storage capacity is estimated to exceed a yottabyte. That's 10^{24} bytes, which is enough to store everything ever written, plus every communication predicted to be made in the next century. Australia has built a similar facility at HMAS *Harman* near Canberra. It began operating in 2013, and in 2019, the government announced it was embarking on stage two, involving an expansion and backup services. As reported by Philip Dorling in the *Sydney Morning Herald*, the *Harman* site has been linked with NSA programs including X-Keyscore, which analyses global internet data. X-Keyscore was reportedly used against 'targets of interest' and had led to the capture of 300 terrorists by 2008.

Snowden's documents revealed the extent of the collaboration between governments. They also revealed how governments rely on telcos, search engines, software giants and other companies to collect data. Through programs such as PRISM, the NSA enlisted Microsoft, Google, Apple and Yahoo to provide information. Sometimes companies collaborated willingly; sometimes companies were compelled to comply; and sometimes the NSA and analogous agencies hacked into company information without authorisation. This constitutes, in the words of Bruce Schneier, 'a public–private surveillance partnership that spans the world'.

As we have seen, this public–private surveillance partnership is often conducted in the interests of national security. However, it extends much further, and increasingly into policing. Between 1974 and 1986, the 'Golden State Killer' committed 12 murders and 50 rapes, but was never caught. Investigators had crime scene DNA, but were unable to find a match. Then GEDmatch came along. An open-source database of more than 650 000 genetic profiles, GEDmatch enabled investigators to match crime scene DNA to a distant relative of Joseph James DeAngelo, a former cop living in Sacramento. By eliminating other suspects, the cops had their man. In April 2018, DeAngelo was arrested. 'We found the needle in the haystack,' said Sacramento's district attorney.

This is a great outcome. Here, the unprecedented capabilities of digital surveillance solved a horrific series of cold cases. What's more, while the Golden State Killer case involves retrospective policing, big data also raises the possibility of predictive policing. It's a contentious notion. And it turns out predictive policing has a past.

In 1971, German authorities began using computers and known data about family, housing, property, social situation and more to research the causes of criminality. This was intended to be the basis for ongoing preventative police work. In a phrase prefiguring the NSA's 'collect it all' mantra, the aim was for 'everyone to know everything'. By 1979, the Federal Criminal Police Office, or BKA, had registered the names of 4.7 million persons, had fingerprints of 2.1 million suspects and photos of nearly as many. However, as technology researcher Kerstin Goos and her colleagues have detailed, the system proved frustratingly ineffective, leading German courts to curtail the use of computer databases for dragnet operations, let alone the prosecution of future crimes.

But the internet has resuscitated the idea of predictive policing. In the US, at least half of all states use big data to help predict recidivism, and hence to determine whether an individual should be released or kept in jail; further, several precincts use big data to decide which streets, groups and individuals should be subject to extra policing; and, since 2006, police in Memphis have used the Blue CRUSH (Crime Reduction Utilizing Statistical History) program to target particular locales at specific times. Not quite precogs ... and yet, as big data scholars Viktor Mayer-Schönberger and Kenneth Cukier write, 'The unsettling future *Minority Report* portrays is one that unchecked big-data analysis threatens to bring about, in which judgments of culpability are based on individualized predictions of future behaviour.'

For police, predictive algorithms play an increasingly central role, and the law is playing catch-up. In the 2016 US case of *Wisconsin v Loomis*, a defendant was given a lengthy custodial sentence based in part on an algorithm devised by a private company that deemed him 'high risk'. The defendant challenged his sentence because he had not been allowed to see the algorithm's workings, but an appeal court found against him, holding that mere knowledge of the algorithm allowed for sufficient transparency. In the Australian state of New South Wales, police are using the Suspect Targeting

Management Plan, which aims to prevent future crimes by targeting repeat offenders, who have been as young as nine years old, for special attention including home visits. As detailed in a report by Vicki Sentas and Camilla Pandolfini from Australia's Public Interest Advocacy Centre, the workings of the system are secretive and opaque.

One major problem with predictive algorithms is that they contain all the biases, blind spots and flawed assumptions of those who engineered them. For instance, in May 2018 Amazon was revealed to be selling facial recognition technology to US police departments. However, facial recognition discriminates. In one study, facial recognition tech was 99 per cent accurate for white men, whereas the error rate for women with darker skin reached up to 35 per cent. This raises the prospect of wrongful convictions. Critics said the Amazon deal was giving police 'a powerful surveillance system readily available to violate rights and target communities of color'.

Nonetheless, officers in an increasing number of cities are now using algorithms and data to predict where crime will happen, and who is likely to offend. As journalist Issie Lapowsky wrote in 2019:

> One effort, known as Operation LASER, which began in
> 2011, crunches information about past offenders over a two-
> year period, using technology developed by the shadowy data
> analysis firm Palantir, and scores individuals based on their
> rap sheets. If you've ever been in a gang, that's five points.
> If you're on parole or probation? Another five. Every time
> you're stopped by police, every time they come knocking on
> your door, that could land you more points. The higher the
> points, the more likely you are to end up on something called
> the Chronic Offender Bulletin, a list of people the data says
> are most at risk of reoffending and ought to be kept on close
> watch.

As data becomes easier to collect and algorithms become more sophisticated, the use of predictive policing technologies has a ring of inevitability. 'There is no real hope of going back,' wrote law professor Andrew G. Ferguson in 2017, arguing that predictive policing has outpaced legal or political accountability and largely escaped academic scrutiny. And this, he wrote, needs to change:

> Any jurisdiction interested in adopting predictive policing techniques must be able to respond to ... difficult questions about data, methodology, scientific legitimacy, transparency, accountability, vision, practice, administration, and security. [Otherwise], any predictive policing system remains open to criticism and challenge.

Predictive policing is spreading, but recently there have been some moves to limit government surveillance. In 2015, following Edward Snowden's revelations, the US government passed the *FREEDOM Act*, which replaced the surveillance-enabling *PATRIOT Act* and imposed new limits on the bulk collection of citizen data. Just as companies such as Facebook are making adjustments in the face of vociferous privacy concerns, the US government has seemingly committed itself to stepping back from a 'collect it all' ethos. However, critics have argued that mass backdoor surveillance can continue despite the *FREEDOM Act*. And not all countries are winding back their surveillance. In Australia in April 2018, a leak from the Department of Home Affairs to journalist Annika Smethurst revealed government plans to expand the Australian Signals Directorate's ambit, giving them wide powers to spy on domestic citizens. The government was incensed. A year later, the Australian Federal Police conducted a raid of Smethurst's home, seeking to identify the leaker. Her employer, News Corp, described it as a 'dangerous act of intimidation'. Anyone eager to emulate Snowden was put on notice.

For now, most of the details remain hidden from public view, but it seems fair to assume that the surveillance network of both the US and Australia remains extensive and effective, in part because they share data. Meanwhile, they also share data with the other members of the Five Eyes: the UK, New Zealand and Canada. And with the Nine Eyes, which also includes Denmark, France, the Netherlands and Norway. And the Fourteen Eyes, which adds Germany, Belgium, Italy, Spain and Sweden. What's more, the NSA also works with India, Saudi Arabia and other countries, on top of working especially closely with Israel.

Of course, there are clear benefits. Terrorist plots have been thwarted. Further crimes have been prevented. These are points not to be understated. Who doesn't want less terrorism and less crime? But at the same time, who doesn't want their privacy and their freedom? The challenge is to balance these interests, by asking: what sort of government surveillance *should* we have?

And already, governments are using data to 'nudge' citizens into changing their behaviour for the better. In the UK, the Behavioural Insights Team has used subtle cues to influence people to pay fines on time and consume fewer fizzy drinks. In Australia, the group has worked with the New South Wales government to keep commuters out of the CBD at peak times and to reduce domestic violence. These are positive initiatives. By complete contrast, Cambridge Analytica exploited personal data to manipulate voters. Just how vulnerable are we? Very, says historian Yuval Noah Harari. In a 2019 appearance at Stanford, Harari attempted to distil humanity's vulnerability into an equation:

And the equation is: B times C times D equals HH, which means biological knowledge multiplied by computing power, multiplied by data equals the ability to hack humans … And maybe I'll explain what it means, the ability to hack humans:

to create an algorithm that understands me better than I understand myself, and can therefore manipulate me, enhance me, or replace me. And this is something that our philosophical baggage and all our belief in, you know, human agency and free will, and the customer is always right, and the voter knows best, it just falls apart once you have this kind of ability.

Human agency requires that our moral practice is not passive. As Shannon Vallor writes, our moral practice ought to be the product of 'our own conscious activity and achievement'. If a human can be hacked, notions of agency fall apart. This is the dark spectre raised by Cambridge Analytica: that humans can be hacked in a way that jeopardises freedom and democracy.

In a digital age, Room 101 might look less like a personal phobia, and more like a personalised political ad.

ANONYMITY, ENCRYPTION AND OTHER PRIVACY PRESERVERS

The theory of Panopticon 3.0 does not match the reality. There are limits to omniscience, even for those at the top of the surveillance pyramid, such as Acxiom or the NSA. For a start, some governments do not share data. Russia and Iran don't collaborate with Canada, Australia or the US. Moreover, there are instances of corporate pushback, with Google, Facebook and Yahoo all saying they've resisted requests to give up data to US intelligence agencies.

In 2016, the FBI revealed it had obtained the iPhone 5C of a dead terrorist who, with his wife, had killed 14 people in San Bernardino, California. When the NSA was unable to break into the operating system, it asked Apple for help. However, CEO Tim Cook refused both the FBI request and ensuing court orders to un-encrypt the phone, arguing that creating a backdoor would put the security of all its users at risk. (Then again, this may not be the best example of effective corporate pushback. The dispute ended when the Department of Justice announced it had broken into the iPhone with the help of hackers paid by the FBI.)

Companies and governments do not always collaborate. What's more, companies are taking some steps to make it easier for people to protect their privacy. In 2018, Google announced an upgrade for Gmail, which would enable users to set emails to: 'self-destruct' after a certain time; prevent recipients from forwarding or downloading a message; and require recipients to enter a code before opening a message. As commentators noted, these changes were much-needed and long overdue.

And let's not forget all those people who aren't on the internet. By the middle of 2019, that's an estimated 44 per cent of the global population, or roughly 3.4 billion people. Overwhelmingly, they reside in the world's economically poorest nations. Onboarding and shadow profiles reveal that even people who have never been online can have a detailed digital presence, but it's likely that digital profiles don't yet exist for a good proportion of the world's (often poorest) people. If you live in a poor land, you may be rich in privacy.

For the 56 per cent of us who are online, there are a range of strategies that can help to protect our privacy. One is anonymity. In the early days in the web, all interactions were presumed to be anonymous, and hackers in particular have a rich history of working anonymously.

Entire corners of the web are devoted to anonymous interactions, including the bulletin board 4chan, where users post content that may be embarrassing, shocking or illegal. Among other topics, boards are devoted to 'anime & manga', 'technology', 'weapons', 'fashion', 'LGBT', 'hardcore' and 'adult GIF'. The benefits of such anonymity are contested among academics. While media

academics Emily van der Nagel and Jordan Frith argue that anonymity has opened up 'important avenues for productive identity
play, self-exploration, and behavior contextualisation online', Emma
Jane details how the anonymous message board 4chan fosters misogyny and sexism. Meanwhile, the anonymous message board 8chan
has been described as a breeding ground for hatred and terrorism.
The perpetrators of both the Christchurch mosque shootings and
the El Paso shootings of 2019 posted their manifestos here; both men
had reportedly been radicalised on 8chan's /pol/ bulletin board. In
August 2019, 8chan's creator Fredrick Brennan said it should be
shut down, and it was, only to re-emerge in November under a new
name, 8kun.

Another way to be anonymous online is to use a browser such
as TOR, or The Onion Router, which works by distributing a user's
activity over several places on the net, so that she can't be linked
to one place. Some parts of the net are accessible only via anonymous browsers such as TOR. The potential uses vary wildly. Under
repressive regimes, minorities and human rights advocates can use
a browser such as TOR to evade persecution. By contrast, pro-
anorexia communities, known as 'pro ana' and 'thinspo', can also
thrive on the internet under the cover of anonymity. This is the
challenge of anonymity, and of privacy. They can enable freedom
and justice; but they can also cloak criminal activity and dangerous
behaviour.

Potentially, anonymity *can* prevail. The inherent design of the
internet means that we can't attach identifiers to data packets on the
net, and we can't verify the identity of someone somewhere sitting in
front of a computer. On the internet, anonymity has the potential to
be a powerful, if not infallible, privacy enhancer. Since at least 2000,
however, it has been recognised that digital anonymity is vulnerable, and must be achieved through effort. In the US, for instance,
a study by privacy researcher Latanya Sweeney showed how easily

census data can be de-anonymised. 'Anonymity is fragile,' writes Bruce Schneier. 'We either need to develop more robust techniques for preserving anonymity, or give up on the idea entirely.'

Besides anonymity, limits on watching include security measures such as encryption. For law scholar Derek Bambauer, security implements privacy. And encryption can be particularly effective. Google ranks websites which use SSL (Secure Sockets Layer) encryption more highly; Apple displayed its commitment to encryption in the San Bernardino case; and in 2016 Facebook adopted end-to-end encryption for its Messenger instant messaging service. 'Encryption works,' Edward Snowden has said. 'Properly implemented strong crypto systems are one of the few things that you can rely on.' Some governments have been moving to weaken encryption, however. In December 2018 the Australian government passed a law informally known as the *Encryption Act*, which gives police and security agencies the power to compel tech companies to grant access to encrypted messages. In October 2019, Australia's Home Affairs Minister Peter Dutton, US Attorney-General William Barr, acting US Secretary of Homeland Security Kevin McAleenan and British Home Secretary Priti Patel wrote to Facebook's Mark Zuckerberg to say that law enforcement agencies needed a way to circumvent the company's encryption in order to thwart crime. A standoff ensued. In December 2019, Facebook executives declared they would not compromise the security of their messaging services for law enforcement.

Strategies such as anonymity and encryption ensure that checks and blocks exist on the flow of data. They also ensure that different online players have very different surveillance capabilities. Some have better vision than others. And the effectiveness of anonymity and encryption continues to shift, as new technologies are implemented and new laws are passed.

Users are adopting other tactics to preserve their privacy too. One recurrent strategy is obfuscation, the deliberate use of ambiguous, confusing and misleading information to thwart the collection of data by individuals, companies and governments. As privacy scholars Helen Nissenbaum and Finn Brunton write in *Obfuscation: A user's guide for privacy and protest*, obfuscation is intended to muddy the waters and make it impossible for users to be accurately profiled. Methods include evasion, noncompliance, refusal and sabotage. In this way, average users are not just evading surveillance, but also signalling that they want to use the web without being tracked and profiled. One obfuscatory tool is TrackMeNot, a free browser extension that dupes trackers into recording false user activity as well as real user activity. As the website says, it works 'not by means of concealment or encryption (i.e. covering one's tracks), but instead, paradoxically, by the opposite strategy: noise and obfuscation. With TrackMeNot, actual web searches, lost in a cloud of false leads, are essentially hidden in plain view.'

Meanwhile, DuckDuckGo is an American search engine that, unlike Google, doesn't track its users' online activity, and Disconnect.me is software developed by former Google employees which can block trackers and search privately, and offers stronger protections for a fee: 'Our privacy policy, in a sentence: we don't collect your IP address or any other personal info, except the info you volunteer.' And the data-hungry practices of Facebook have prompted the development of an alternative social network, Diaspora (diasporafoundation.org), which is not-for-profit and user-owned. Increasingly, innovations dedicated to the preservation of privacy are emerging.

Research by ethicist Bernhard Debatin, communications researcher Monika Taddicken and others shows that people care deeply about digital privacy, even if their actions don't always align with that care. Sometimes, though, their actions *do* align with that care. The adoption of anonymity, encryption and other privacy-protecting strategies confirms it. So does data released by the

National Telecommunications and Information Administration in 2016, which showed that a lack of trust in internet privacy and security has stopped many US users posting to social networks, expressing opinions or buying from websites. For these users, the internet can no longer be trusted for everyday activities.

In 2016, a widely shared photo showed Mark Zuckerberg at his desk, where a piece of tape had been carefully stuck to make the webcam of his laptop inoperable. Earlier, I quoted Zuckerberg as saying that privacy norms have shifted and loosened. Clearly, he still wants some.

I'M PLACING YOU UNDER ARREST FOR FUTURE MURDER

In the opening scene of *Minority Report*, a husband is in a jealous rage. Having caught his wife in bed with another man, the husband is about to stab them both with a pair of scissors. Just in time, policeman John Anderton bursts in and intervenes.

'Mr Marks,' he says, 'by mandate of the District of Columbia Precrime Division, I'm placing you under arrest for the future murder of Sarah Marks and Donald Dubin that was to take place today, April 22, at 0800 hours and four minutes.'

Mr Marks is stunned: 'I didn't do anything! I wasn't gonna do anything!'

Precrime case closed. By the end of the film, however, it's the Precrime department that's closed. As Anderton says in a final voiceover: 'In 2054, the six-year Precrime experiment was abandoned. All prisoners were unconditionally pardoned and released, though police departments kept watch on many of them for years to come.' This denouement recognises that condemning people for future actions is fundamentally problematic, and that the ethics of predictive technology must be very carefully considered.

The challenge to privacy for internet users comes from three sources: individuals; companies; and governments. A hacker who uses malware to access a webcam is unlike a company that creates a detailed profile of a non-user, which in turn is unlike a government seeking intelligence to thwart terrorism. These challenges are often overlapping, but sometimes distinct. What's more, these challenges are not all-conquering. Anonymity gives cover. Encryption provides a cloak. Obfuscation is a shield. Privacy is possible, but maintaining it is hard, and becoming harder.

At what point does targeted marketing become unacceptably invasive? What sort of preventative policing are we prepared to accept? How exactly should we balance crime prevention against privacy and liberty? To answer these questions, we will now, like John Anderton, take the road less travelled. It leads straight into a spaghetti junction of norms.

3

'TECHNOLOGY IS NEITHER GOOD NOR BAD; NOR IS IT NEUTRAL'

The Social Network is a film about Mark Zuckerberg, the wunderkind coder behind Facebook. It opens in 2003, as the 19-year-old Harvard undergrad is being dumped by his girlfriend, Erica Albright. Humiliated, Zuckerberg returns to his dorm, where he writes an offensive blog post before, in a frenzy of drunken coding, hacking into college databases to copy photos of female students.

Using algorithms, he then builds a website called Facemash, inviting users to rate the attractiveness of students. Now it's Albright's turn to be enraged. 'The internet's not written in pencil, Mark, it's written in ink,' she says. 'And you published that Erica Albright was a bitch, right before you made some ignorant crack about my family's name, my bra size, and then rated women based on their hotness.'

Zuckerberg is stung, but Facemash is a hit, becoming so popular so fast that it crashes a part of Harvard's computer network.

Of course, *The Social Network* isn't a documentary. It's a feature film. It was also made way back in 2010. But some key details are true to life. Zuckerberg, who was studying psychology and computer science, had been jilted by a woman; he did use his hacking skills to copy digital profile pictures; and his intention behind Facemash was for users to compare the 'hotness' of female students.

In the film as in real life, Zuckerberg was reprimanded and Facemash was closed. But the following year, Zuckerberg launched Facebook. Like Facemash, Facebook allows users to pore over the lives of others and, even though it soon had privacy alarm bells ringing, the platform proved so successful that even Zuckerberg was surprised. As he later said, 'People are more voyeuristic than what I would have thought.'

This chapter explores the norms and values that prevail on the internet. Some people argue that conventional ethics do not apply on the net, and should not apply. However, norms – conventional and otherwise – *are* being applied. Some are user-imposed; others are embedded in the very architecture of the net and its platforms. The internet is neither norm-free nor norm-neutral. And privacy has tended to be an afterthought.

HACKED TO PIECES?

When I say I'm researching internet ethics, people often ask, 'Are there any?' Or, 'Isn't that a contradiction in terms?'

The internet is certainly fluid; its defining characteristic may well be its lack of definition. Described by Manuel Castells as a 'space of flows', the internet is steadfastly protean, stubbornly mercurial. And in its fluidity, the internet enables us to act and interact in new ways. Gmail, Facebook, Grindr ... as never before, these services enable us to communicate, share and meet strangers for sex.

The perpetual newness that this fluidity brings is a recipe for ethical uncertainty. Understandably, people are often unsure as to which values and norms ought to apply. In fact, they might wonder whether any norms at all apply. They might ask themselves: can't I apply whichever norms I like? Isn't the internet a place where anything goes? Isn't it a place where all bets are off, ethically speaking?

The answer to these questions is no. The internet is not a virtual wild west where people are summarily hacked to pieces. It is no lawless frontier. Indeed, as the internet ages, it is becoming more and more controlled. Having turned 50 in 2019, the internet has matured into a place where a long list of values and norms prevail. Admittedly, they are often contradictory.

These values and norms can be divided into two categories. First, there are those that have been brought online by users. I refer to these as *user-generated* values and norms. Second, there are those that are embedded in the architecture of the internet and its platforms. They might be imposed by companies in the form of website functionality or community standards, or they might be imposed by governments in the form of codes, standards and regulation. I refer to these as *encoded* values and norms.

I'll start with the internet's user-generated values and norms. At its most stark, the contest of values playing out among the internet's users manifests as a battle of utopians against dystopians. This battle has raged since the start, pitting those who believe that 'tech is good' against those who think 'tech is evil'. For each camp, theirs is a fundamental, axiomatic principle.

On the one hand, 'techno-utopians' and 'cyber-optimists' believe that the internet is so fundamentally good that it will inevitably be humanity's saviour. Google famously hinted in this direction with its one-time slogan, 'Don't be evil'. (Initially, as scholar of politics and technology Evgeny Morozov writes, the slogan signified Google's policy of not accepting advertising. It later became a company-defining ethic, but was phased out once Google started accepting ads.) On this view, the internet enables the unfettered flow of information, inspires innovation and promotes equity, democracy and justice. 'Never before in history have so many people, from so many places, had so much power at their fingertips,' wrote Google's Eric

Schmidt and Jared Cohen in 2013. Ray Kurzweil's account of the singularity, which refers to a speculative fusion of machine and humankind predicted to occur by 2045, is similarly bright. On this view, the internet is inherently good.

The ranks of the techno-utopians have thinned out significantly in recent years, but they still exist. For some, the existential threat to humanity posed by the climate crisis will inevitably be averted by the many startups involved in 'greentech'. And virtual reality pioneer Jaron Lanier has described the 'cybernetic totalism' that dominates in Silicon Valley. Under this belief, writes Lanier, data is deified. Its adherents celebrate the hive mind, or the 'noosphere', denoting the collective brain of all the people connected on the net. What's more, writes Lanier, these adherents hope to become immortal by being uploaded into a machine. This is no less than a new religion. Lanier himself argues against this religion; but for those who deify data, technology ought to be revered. For them, presumably, privacy doesn't matter, given that privacy would seem to be impossible in a hive mind.

On the other hand, 'techno-dystopians' and 'cyber-pessimists' contend that the internet and various associated technologies are a force for unmitigated evil. Inspired by *1984* and *The Matrix*, these detractors believe the internet is destined to be the final nail in humanity's coffin. In 2014, the late cosmologist Stephen Hawking encapsulated this view when he said that artificial intelligence 'could spell the end of the human race'. Sure, moral panics are nothing new, but the gnawing perception that society is under threat is now so widespread that it's spawned its own vocabulary, including 'technophobia' and 'technopanic'. As machines take over, it is said, the internet will enslave us.

These two camps ascribe value to the technology itself, seeing it as either humanity's saviour or nemesis. Between these extremes, many more user-generated values and norms prevail on the net. One is a commitment to anarchy. As Schmidt and Cohen wrote in 2013: 'The Internet is the largest experiment involving anarchy in history. Hundreds of millions of people are, each minute, creating and consuming an untold amount of digital content in an online world that is not truly bound by terrestrial laws.'

Anarchy questions authority and power, and its spirit pervades corners of the internet, including in activist groups and hacker collectives, or on message boards such as 4chan and 8chan/8kun. The internet has also been heralded as a perfect home for libertarianism. On this view, the internet is seen as a place where individual freedoms can thrive, unfettered by the state. Online, it is said, rugged individualism can prevail. Admittedly, it is being said less and less often. The libertarian ethic was strong online in the 1990s and early 2000s, but has since dissipated as it becomes clearer that the internet is less a haven for unfettered freedoms, and more a field of controlled oversight.

Nonetheless, distrust of authority remains rife. This is evident in the proliferation of DIY justice, including under the banner of 'electronic civil disobedience', or ECD. One example is the hacker group Anonymous, which engages in coordinated activism, or 'hacktivism'. Anonymous have hacked in support of WikiLeaks, the Occupy movement and Arab Spring protesters, and their targets have included corporations (Mastercard, VISA, PayPal), religious groups (the Church of Scientology, Westboro Baptist Church) and terrorists (ISIS). As digital anthropologist Gabriella Coleman writes, their methods include distributed denial-of-service (DDoS) attacks, which can overwhelm targets' websites and render them useless.

DIY justice also manifests as digital vigilantism, or digilantism. Following the Boston Marathon bombings of 2013, users gathered in forums to identify the bomber. When they began to suspect missing university student Sunil Tripathi, a digital lynch mob descended on his family. So did the world's news media – at least until the real bombers were identified the following day. As media scholar Daniel Trottier writes, 'Digital vigilantism is a process where citizens are collectively offended by other citizen activity, and coordinate retaliation on mobile devices and social platforms.' In many cases, digilantism involves compromising privacy. The underlying ethic seems to be: anyone who violates the internet's unwritten rules will be exposed. Sometimes, such 'doxing' can seek to call out misogynistic behaviour, including rape threats. Groups that engage in feminist digilantism include Destroy the Joint and Sexual Violence Won't Be Silenced. Much more often, however, privacy breaches are misogynistic. In 2016, images of Australian schoolgirls were shared to a pornographic site. When one teenager asked for photos to be removed, she received the response: 'Darling, don't be a slut and you won't end up here. Once a photo is on snapchat or the Internet, it belongs to the Internet.'

This response implies that the internet is another world, where a completely different set of rules and norms applies. Or perhaps, where rules and norms don't apply at all. But the reality is something else altogether.

To say that a revealing photo of an underage schoolgirl 'belongs' to the internet is to make an ethical claim. Further, this claim suggests that the values and norms that apply online differ from those that apply offline. Similarly, various forms of digital vigilantism, such as the activities of Anonymous, suggest that ethical norms should be applied online, but that these norms differ from offline norms. By contrast, the (mistaken) identification of Sunil Tripathi as the Boston bomber suggests that offline ethics and justice *should* prevail online, but that digital citizens must take matters into their own hands because there is insufficient online enforcement of such standards. And so too a moral code applies to doxing, even if that moral code is wildly inconsistent. The point is: ethical norms *are* being applied on the net, and those norms are contradictory and contested.

They may also be shifting. Take 'hurtcore porn', which involves real footage of people, including children, being sexually abused. As one hurtcore user says, 'At first I felt ashamed in myself for being attracted to such a thing, but as time went on I slowly grew more accepting of myself.' Such habituation is terrifying. And in much the same way, there is a risk that privacy norms are shifting not because they should, but because people are behaving according to new norms they wouldn't usually accept, for reasons such as peer pressure. These norms can then become entrenched after a period of habituation. Online, as privacy researchers including Gordon Hull have observed, 'the plasticity of norms' can be problematic.

A MILITARISTIC OPENNESS

What about the internet's *encoded* norms and values?

The internet, in the form of ARPANET, flickered to life on the evening of 29 October 1969, when computer scientists gathered in the engineering building at UCLA to send a message to their computer scientist peers at Stanford, 600 kilometres to the north. Their inaugural message had been intended to read 'LOGIN', but the receiving computer crashed, cutting the message to 'LO'. For a new medium, it was a very Old Testament beginning, just at a time when the Cold War was at its iciest. And like many innovations, it was a military project. Facing a hostile Soviet Union, the United States Defense Department Advanced Research Projects Agency (ARPA, aka DARPA) wanted a communications network that would survive nuclear attack, and so ARPANET was built to link thousands of autonomous computer networks in a seemingly limitless number of ways, thereby circumventing barriers and breakdowns. To suit the military, the network was closed; but even so it was built to be highly decentralised. In these early years, the ability to circumvent obstacles proved a defining characteristic.

When the Iron Curtain came down, the internet stayed up. However, its role changed. In the 1970s and '80s, the net was embraced by scientists and academics, who used it to access information stored on remote computers, and to enable distant colleagues to share their work. By the time the Cold War thawed in the late '80s, the National Science Foundation's NSFNET had replaced the military's ARPANET as the internet's high-speed 'backbone'. As scientists and academics began to unlock the new medium's collaborative potential, an ethic of openness was superimposed onto the net's architecture of decentralisation. Indeed, some argue that the net's academic, peaceful origins are more significant than its military origins. ARPANET, write internet historians Katie Hafner and Matthew Lyon, 'embodied the most peaceful intentions to link computers at scientific laboratories across the country so that researchers might share computer resources. ARPANET and its progeny, the Internet, had nothing to do with supporting or surviving the war – never did.'

The original intention behind the net may well have been more peaceful than martial. Some of the internet's architects argue that any suggestion that the internet was intended to be a nuclear resistant network is merely 'false rumor'. In any case, an architecture of openness came to prevail; the pioneers of the net wanted, writes Manuel Castells, 'to allow the network to evolve as an open system of computer communication, able to reach out to the whole world'.

Next, during the 1970s and 1980s, the values of decentralisation and openness were joined by a third influence, the 'hacker ethic'. This ethic, writes sociologist Thomas Streeter, was eccentric, anti-authoritarian and often libertarian. By the mid-1970s, tens of thousands of the world's brightest microelectronics innovators were working in California's Silicon Valley. These internet pioneers met in loose clubs, such as the Home Brew Computer Club, and their members included Bill Gates, Steve Jobs and Steve Wozniak, who between them created Microsoft, Apple, and 20 more companies.

They blended innovation and invention with informality and irreverence and saw themselves, in a way, as successors to the counterculture of Haight-Ashbury. In the 1960s, San Francisco had been the epicentre of the world's hippie counterculture, complete with its attempts at sexual, gender, racial and other emancipations; by the 1970s, 50 kilometres to the south, Silicon Valley became the epicentre of the world's nascent computer industry. Unsurprisingly, there was overlap in their outlook.

In this context, 'hack' was a complimentary term, with the original hacker spirit built on principles including mistrust of authority, the promotion of decentralisation, and keeping all information free. In 1984, an idealistic Hacker Ethic was codified by technologist Steven Levy, with six precepts that included, 'You can create art and beauty on a computer', and 'Computers can change your life for the better'. The idea was to be playful and probing, and thus to spark a 'benevolent ripple' through society. Today, the hacker spirit persists, coded into the net to protect freedom of information, freedom of speech and the principle of 'net neutrality', which prescribes a free and open internet. That spirit is evident in open-source software, or OSS, and in the work of coder Richard Stallman, who campaigned for *free* software – software that can be used, studied, distributed and modified.

As it evolved in the '70s and '80s, the internet's architecture fostered decentralisation, openness and hacking. Nevertheless, sometimes there was tension. Militaristic imperatives clashed with anti-war ideals. Overwhelmingly, however, the values encoded into the net in its first two decades tended to promote the free flow of data. Openness, collaboration and sharing were encouraged; privacy was not. Just as the net's creators had not foreseen email, social media or location-based apps, neither had they foreseen the *privacy concerns* that would arise from email, social media and location-based apps. On the net, privacy concerns were not initially addressed by design, and could only later be addressed via add-ons.

Then, in the 1990s, the values and norms of companies and governments were superimposed as the internet went mainstream and global. Following the launch of the World Wide Web in 1991, internet service providers (ISPs) started turning the net into a commodity. The internet's free spirit was joined by a spirit of free enterprise. First came the proliferation of commerce-based websites; then, in the 2000s, social media gave rise to 'Web 2.0'. Ever since, the influence of Silicon Valley's tech giants, plus their Chinese counterparts, is hard to overstate. They don't just dominate the net, they dominate our lives. And they certainly dominate the world's markets. As at June 2019, the world's five biggest companies by market capitalisation were *all* tech firms: Microsoft; Amazon; Apple; Alphabet (Google's parent); and Facebook. Also in the top 10 were China's Alibaba and Tencent. The profits of these companies are supersized and seemingly bulletproof. For Facebook, the Cambridge Analytica scandal has barely left a dent. In fact, Facebook's global advertising revenues keep soaring: from $11.8 billion in the first quarter of 2018 to $14.9 billion in the first quarter of 2019.

Companies exist to make profit, and internet companies often build profits on personal data. To this end, companies routinely embed an ethic of openness into their services, and into their privacy settings. On the internet default settings tend to be public, not private. If a user wants privacy – including by avoiding the collection of personal data for targeted advertising – she generally needs to opt out of these public defaults. In May 2018, Zuckerberg announced that Facebook was improving its privacy policies. Soon users would be able to opt out of one of Facebook's key data-gathering practices: its use of people's web-browsing history, which the company uses to sell targeted ads. The fact that users need to opt out of data gathering is telling, and concerning. Unsurprisingly, research shows that users are often apathetic in the face of default settings.

In many ways, including in their default settings, companies are encoding *user popularity* as a core value. In other words, the affordances of digital media have been designed to promote the pursuit of popularity. This is most readily apparent on social media, where influencers reign. Online, a person's worth is measured in friends, followers, likes, shares, favourites, retweets and comments. It's no wonder that, for a small sum, users can buy fake friends from sites such as SocialYup offering 'best quality friends on the market'. People have always connected, revealed and shared. The difference is that on the internet, driven by the embedded value of popularity, users are encouraged to do so with a minimum of discretion and discrimination. The affordances and architecture of social media, and the internet generally, avidly encourage liking, sharing and befriending.

Just as companies have been encoding their values into the internet, governments have been increasingly enacting their values too. This shift has been sometimes hidden (as in the covert surveillance described earlier) and sometimes visible (including in standards and laws that I will come to later). Whereas the spirit of the original internet has been described as anarchic and anti-establishment, today's internet has become highly regulated and controlled. 'The invisible hand of cyberspace is building an architecture that is quite the opposite of its architecture at its birth,' writes tech lawyer Lawrence Lessig. The challenge now, Lessig argues in *Code: Version 2.0*, is not an excess of freedom, but a shortage. One symbol of this is Aaron Swartz, a hacker who co-founded Reddit and Creative Commons. Part of the 'internet free culture movement', he was arrested (and later committed suicide) after publishing and sharing academic articles otherwise available only for a fee.

So while initially decentralisation, openness and the hacker ethic were coded into the net, these have now been joined, and sometimes overrun, by the values of companies and governments, which include profit and surveillance. These values push and pull in various directions. With remarkable consistency, however, they work against privacy.

Admittedly, privacy *has* found a modest home online. Here and there, privacy has been encoded. I have already discussed anonymity, encryption and security. In the '90s, the success of the commerce-driven 'Web 1.0' required an inbuilt level of security to protect users who were handing over credit card details. This security, when effective, brought a degree of privacy. In some cases, however, companies sought to protect user privacy, only for governments to step in. BlackBerry has employed strong encryption, and thus protected privacy, only to be challenged by governments. In India, Russia, Saudi Arabia, the UAE and Indonesia, governments threatened to ban BlackBerry if the company didn't unencrypt its communications. Given that BlackBerry has not been banned, privacy experts have concluded that governments in those countries are now eavesdropping on BlackBerry exchanges. In these cases, companies are working to buttress privacy, while governments are working to weaken it.

Consistently and worryingly, the values and norms encoded into the digital world work against privacy.

NET ETHICS: NON-DETERMINED AND NECESSARY

In the face of all these values and norms, both user-generated and encoded, it can be tempting to surrender to a bleak fatalism. The odds are stacked against privacy, so why waste energy defending it?

Certainly, there is a school of thought that technology determines humanity's future. This is the school of technological determinism. In the hard determinists' vision of the future, write historian

Merritt Smith and Leo Marx, 'we will have technologized our ways to the point where, for better or worse, our technologies permit few alternatives to their inherent dictates'. Techno-utopians and cyber-pessimists are often determinists. Technology will inevitably save us, they say, or doom us. But as sociologist John Tomlinson writes in *The Culture of Speed*, the hard determinist position seems intuitively false. Humans build technology; humans use technology. Surely it is in the building and the usage, not in the technology itself, that outcomes would seem to be decided?

Like Tomlinson, I am not convinced by arguments of technological determinism. However, I am convinced that technology has a *significant* impact on behaviour. Its affordances allow certain behaviours, encourage specific behaviours, and disallow others. As I have described, there are various values and norms that prevail online, which have two sources: some are imposed by users; and some are encoded in technology. Rather than technological determinism, then, I am proposing that people and technology have an effect on each other, just as people and the internet have an effect on each other. In the words of Manuel Castells, there is a 'dialectical interaction between society and technology': 'technology does not determine society: it embodies it. But neither does society determine technological innovation: it uses it.'

Or, as US historian Melvin Kranzberg wrote, in the first of his six succinct laws on technology: 'Technology is neither good nor bad; nor is it neutral.'

The internet too is neither good nor bad; nor is it neutral. Rather, there are powerful values and norms at play. Online, there is a continuation and contestation of norms, some of them user-imposed, some of them embedded in the very architecture of the net and its platforms. And these embedded norms can't be discounted.

And even once we allow for the limiting effect of affordances, it isn't just *our* use of technology that determines *our* privacy. In some cases, surveillance technology is so powerful that we can't evade it. China's facial recognition system, involving hundreds of billions of cameras, is ferociously expansive. China is reportedly building a facial recognition database of all the world's faces. I have no say whatsoever in how this technology is used on me. Sometimes, it is how *others* use technology that impacts and determines *my* privacy. In other words, my privacy is not just determined by how I use technology, but by how others, including the governments of other countries, use that technology.

Unlike countries, the internet itself has no central governance. And in half a century, it has grown into a global, horizontal computer network accessed first by thousands, then millions, now billions of people. The contest of values and norms has grown too. On the net, user-generated ethical claims range from conventional to eccentric, from safe to toxic: the net is utopian; it is dystopian; it is a haven for anarchy; it is a site where digital enforcers and cyber lynch mobs dispense DIY justice. Meanwhile, values and norms have been coded into the internet and its platforms, and these have consistently undermined privacy. As a result, the condition of privacy has been diminished, and the right to privacy has become less clear. A surveilled openness prevails, enabling hackers to phish in the cloud, Acxiom to build extensive dossiers and governments to monitor meticulously.

The internet is not ethics-free; nor should it be. Rather, it's an ethical battleground. All that remains is for us to decide what the prevailing values and norms *ought* to be.

WRITING THE FUTURE

In *The Social Network* (as in real life), Zuckerberg is aided in his efforts to develop Facebook by Sean Parker, who had previously run the file-sharing music service Napster. 'We lived on farms, then we lived in cities, and now we're going to live on the internet,' Parker says, adding that the effects on privacy are devastating. 'Whatever it is that's gonna trip you up, you've done already. Private behaviour is a relic of a time gone by.'

Truth is, privacy still exists. And it can exist online. Overwhelmingly, however, the various values and norms that prevail on the internet tend to undermine it. These include: the decentralisation built into the net's original ARPANET architecture; the collaborative nature of NSFNET; the idealistic hacker ethos of Silicon Valley in the '70s and '80s; the corporatisation of Web 1.0 and Web 2.0 by turning sharing into profits; the burgeoning surveillance practices of governments; and the seductive imperative of popularity.

The future of the internet is not determined, but will be written by how we code it, make it and use it. And in order best to decide how to code, make and use the net, we need to chart an ethical course. As Barry Leiner and various co-inventors of the internet wrote in 2000: 'If the Internet stumbles, it will not be because we lack for technology, vision, or motivation. It will be because we cannot set a direction and march collectively into the future.'

As we emerge blinking from our maze of norms, let's march collectively to Ancient Greece, and then to Königsberg in 1785. For it's in the past that we might find our future.

PRIVACY IS *NOT* ALL
ABOUT CONTROL

A professional photographer and amateur voyeur, L.B. 'Jeff' Jefferies is recuperating after an accident.

Confined to a wheelchair in his Greenwich Village apartment, he looks out his window, fascinated by the antics of his neighbours: a dancer he nicknames 'Miss Torso'; a single woman, 'Miss Lonely-hearts'; and a travelling salesman with a bedridden wife. One night during a storm, glass shatters and a woman screams, 'Don't!' Next, the salesman can be seen acting suspiciously.

Has the salesman murdered his wife? When a neighbour's dog has its neck broken, Jeff wonders: did the salesman do that too?

This is the plot of *Rear Window*, the 1954 thriller directed by Alfred Hitchcock. Immobilised but curious, Jeff (James Stewart) enlists the help of his girlfriend Lisa (Grace Kelly) to break into the salesman's apartment. And inevitably events spin out of control and into violence, as *Rear Window* unfolds to be a film about secrets, and about privacy. It prompts several questions: what is the connection between secrecy and privacy? What control should we have over our privacy? And how does privacy link to our relationships?

In this chapter, I ask one simple question: what is privacy? After providing some etymological, historical and legal context, I show that privacy is slippery. To grasp it, I propose that the best approach is to settle upon a definition based on a conceptual model. With this definition, privacy begins to come into focus, just as Jeff's neighbours do through his telephoto lens.

A DEFINING ISSUE OF OUR TIME – BUT CAN ANYONE DEFINE IT?

'Privacy has become the object of considerable concern,' wrote law scholar Charles Fried in an influential paper published in 1968. With references to 'electronic eavesdropping' and 'the more insidious intrusions of increasingly sophisticated scientific devices into previously untouched areas', Fried was uncannily prescient. Today, headlines routinely herald the hacking of celebrity accounts, the democracy-destabilising work of Cambridge Analytica and various new surveillance capabilities developed by companies and governments. In 1968, Charles Fried argued that privacy is an emerging and significant subject. Today, privacy is a defining issue of our time.

So then, what is privacy?

'The concept of "privacy" is elusive and ill-defined,' says jurist Richard Posner. 'Nobody seems to have any very clear idea what it is,' says philosopher Judith Jarvis Thomson. 'There is little agreement on the most basic questions of its scope and derivation,' says lawyer Jed Rubenfeld.

Scholarly debate has often led to more confusion than clarity. As philosopher Beate Rössler writes, 'The predicate "private" is a complex one, which we can attribute to actions, situations, states of affairs or states of mind, places, and objects alike.'

Philosophers, lawyers and sociologists have constructed a labyrinth of claims and counterclaims. Some have given *descriptive* accounts, describing what in fact counts as private, while others have given *normative* accounts, seeking to delineate privacy's value and the ways in which it might be protected. Some have regarded privacy as an *interest* with its own moral value; others have regarded it as a moral or legal *right* that warrants protection. And many regard privacy as somehow *valuable*, whereas some see it as a duplication of other interests and rights that is, in itself, *worthless*.

There are further debates. What can we say about the distinction between *bodily* privacy and *informational* privacy? Between *personal* and *situational* privacy? And where does *constitutional* privacy fit? And anyway, is privacy a condition? A preference? An interest? A value? A moral right? A legal right? Or all of the above?

At least there is one point of consensus. 'One point on which there seems to be near-unanimous agreement is that privacy is a messy and complex subject,' writes Helen Nissenbaum.

The aim of this chapter is to disentangle these various 'privacies'.

A first point is that the topic of privacy has been tackled by scholars working in a variety of disciplines, who all bring different approaches and agendas. Beate Rössler identifies six types of privacy discourse, which are based in five disciplines: sociology; feminist theory; information technology; the law; and philosophy. In the philosophical discourse, writes Rössler, various strands of the other discourses converge. This book sits within the philosophical discourse.

A second point is that privacy has its detractors. As I've already noted, some feminists argue that privacy can be oppressive. For instance, philosopher Virginia Held argues that the public/private distinction has typically served to privilege 'the points of view of men in the public domains of state and law, and later in the marketplace, and to discount the experience of women'. On this view, the very notion of the modern public sphere depends upon the exclusion of women, with the private sphere merely the necessary and invisible foundation of the public sphere.

According to privacy scholar Anita Allen:

Marriage, motherhood, housekeeping, dependence, and her
own moral ideals of caretaking and belonging have made
many a woman's home life a privacy bane rather than boon …
Women face the problem of overcoming inequitable social and
economic patterns that substitute confinement to the private
sphere for meaningful privacy.

Allen is a privacy advocate, arguing that privacy is required by
the liberal ideals of personhood, and for the participation of citizens as equals. Still, she writes, it can also be a tool of inequity, and
what is required is a liberating, rather than a restrictive, form of
privacy. This will take widespread change: 'Women's abilities to
participate and contribute in the world as equals and on a par with
their capacities are limited where laws and customs deprive them
of opportunities for individual forms of personal privacy.' To have
meaningful privacy, for example, women should have easy access to
contraception and abortion: 'Decisional privacy to choose whether
or not to bear a child affords fertile, younger women a valuable
degree of control over the personal privacy they have at home.'

Allen is arguing that privacy can range from worthwhile to
damaging. From the grave, the murdered wife of *Rear Window*
would probably agree. I certainly do. The challenge is to foster privacy as a good, not an instrument of oppression. This is one of my
central arguments: privacy needs to be valued and protected *appropriately*, not absolutely. It must always be considered in balance with
other values and rights.

Others go much further than Anita Allen. They argue that privacy is worthless. Specifically, they say it's derivative and insignificant. This is the view taken by privacy sceptics and 'reductionists',
including James Moor, who argues that privacy is not a core value:
'The core values are the values that all normal humans and cultures

need for survival ... The core values allow us to make transcultural judgments. The core values are the values we have in common as human beings.'

For Moor, core values include life, happiness, freedom, knowledge, ability, resources and security, and privacy is merely an expression of the core value of security.

Similarly, Judith Jarvis Thomson argues that a person's right to privacy is violated only if there has been a violation of another, more basic right. For Thomson, the right to privacy is in fact a cluster of rights, which always overlap with property rights or rights to bodily security. Hence, given that any privacy violation can be better understood as a violation of a more basic right, there is nothing illuminating about privacy. And Richard Posner proposes that we should simply dispense with privacy altogether, describing it as a mere 'intermediate' value with no utility.

In chapter 1, I distinguished between the condition of privacy and the right to privacy. My condition of privacy is provided at this moment by the clothes I am wearing, the walls around me and the encryption of my emails. My right to privacy, by contrast, denotes the moral or legal entitlements to privacy I currently have. As I write this book, I have a right to privacy under Australian and international law, but also under the social norm that my neighbour will not walk into my home without knocking, even though my door is unlocked.

Discussions about the condition of privacy tend to be descriptive. For instance, philosopher William A. Parent defines privacy as 'the *condition* of not having undocumented personal knowledge about one possessed by others'. Conversely, discussions about the right to privacy tend to be prescriptive, as when philosopher Jeffrey Reiman writes:

If … we think that individuals ought to have others deprived
of access to some of their personal affairs, whether or not a law
says so, then we think that there is something like a moral right
to privacy. And we will want our laws to protect this moral
right by backing it up with an effective legal right.

The distinction between condition and right is often subtle, but
it is crucial. Judith Jarvis Thomson is not arguing that the condition
of privacy is meaningless; rather, she is arguing that we have no need
for the right to privacy, given that the right to privacy is invariably
covered by the right to security. The reductionists aren't arguing
that privacy doesn't exist. They can hardly dispute the condition of
privacy. They can't argue against the existence of the word. Rather,
reductionists argue that there should be no *right* to privacy, given
that what we would seek to cover with such a right is in fact covered
by other rights.

But the majority of privacy scholars disagree, arguing that
the right to privacy is significant in its own right. Among them is
philosopher Ferdinand Schoeman, who provides the example of
sound wave interceptors. Imagine that these come in two varieties:
the first records the speech carried by the sound waves; the second
converts the sound waves into usable energy but makes no record
of the speech. Now suppose I have two neighbours. One trains the
first device on my house, and records every one of my utterances.
The other trains the second device on my house, and records every
sound wave, which is then converted to energy. These two neighbours, argues Schoeman, affect my rights in different ways. The first
breaches my right to privacy; the second does not.

For Thomson, who sees nothing distinctive about privacy, these
two unique instances of recording must presumably be categorised
as morally identical. As Schoeman writes: 'Without reference to
privacy rights specifically we shall not be able to account for the

wrongfulness of certain acts consistent with the innocence of certain others. Without reference to privacy, we will not be able to draw moral distinctions which are important to describe.'

It's a good point. As Schoeman shows, the right to privacy is not always covered by the right to security.

Broadly, then, the arguments I have just summarised reveal two distinct ways to dismiss privacy. The first way is to argue that privacy does not matter, because it has no value. The strong version of this argument is that we would all be better off without privacy. A more nuanced variation of this argument is the feminist position that privacy can be dangerous, and hence that it should be protected only in certain forms, in certain contexts. I return to the issue of privacy's value in the next chapter.

The second way to dismiss privacy is to argue that privacy may well have value, but that the concept is derivative and insignificant, and hence needless. In this chapter, where my goal is to articulate a conceptual definition of privacy, I hope to convince you otherwise.

FROM REALM TO RIGHT: THE WORD, ITS HISTORY, THE LAW

The idea of privacy is old. As the *New Shorter Oxford English Dictionary* tells us, the English word stems from Ancient Rome, from the Latin verb *privare*, meaning 'to deprive', and its past participle, *privatus*, meaning 'withdrawn from public life, peculiar to oneself, a man in private life'.

The notion extended far beyond the Roman Empire, however, with an explicit distinction drawn between 'private' and 'public' realms for at least two-and-a-half millennia in western thought, and also in eastern thought. About 2500 years ago, Confucius recognised privacy and noted its significance when he wrote that 'a private

obligation of a son to care for his father overrides the public obligation to obey the law against theft'. And in Ancient Greece, as philosopher Adam Moore writes, the distinction between public and
private activity was clearly demarcated by the time of Socrates, Plato
and Aristotle. In the fourth century BC, Aristotle made a crucial
distinction: between the *polis*, or the public sphere of politics; and the
oikos, or the domestic sphere of the family. Ever since, the *polis/oikos*
distinction has prompted a demarcation between the public realm of
our life as citizens and the private realm of our domestic lives within
the home, where we tend to our families. In this way, privacy has
traditionally been connected with place.

If the idea of privacy is old, however, the idea of *individual*
privacy is not so old. Individual-based notions of privacy are now
widely assumed, but in the Middle Ages they didn't exist. The privacy of the bedroom and bathroom, with allowances for sexual intimacy and bodily functions, only emerged later, with the spread of
the Enlightenment and liberalism. In 1689, Enlightenment philosopher John Locke linked privacy with self-ownership. In the *Second
Treatise of Government*, Locke argued that in a state of nature all the
world's riches are held in common and are thus public, whereas one
possesses oneself and one's own body, and can acquire property by
mixing into it one's labour, thus transforming it into private property. For Locke, the public/private distinction was used to mark the
limits of justified interference in personal conduct.

So too for John Stuart Mill. In the 1859 essay 'On liberty', Mill
contrasted the realm of governmental authority with the realm of
individual self-regulation. Only with the spread of the Enlightenment and liberalism, as the individual increasingly came to promi-
nence, did privacy begin to be attached to persons, rather than just
to that realm that was not the public realm.

Then, 130 years ago, the association of privacy and the individual culminated with the emergence of a *right* to privacy. In 1890,

an essay published in the *Harvard Law Review* was entitled, simply, 'The right to privacy'. Therein, US jurists Samuel Warren and Louis D. Brandeis examined US law to see whether they could find the existence of any such right, which they described as 'the right to be let alone'. The essay is commonly regarded as the birthplace of modern thinking on privacy, with Ferdinand Schoeman dubbing it 'the first sustained and explicit discussion of privacy'. Admittedly, Warren and Brandeis did not invent the right to privacy, nor even the phrase the 'right to be let alone'. However, as law professor Ruth Gavison notes, their analysis of the common law in search of a right to privacy gave the principle shape and form.

Like this book, the 1890 essay was prompted by concerns about the ethics of new media: Warren and Brandeis had become dismayed by the excesses of photography and newspapers, which were becoming increasingly efficient at spreading malicious rumour. 'To occupy the indolent, column upon column is filled with idle gossip, which can only be procured by intrusion upon the domestic circle,' they wrote, providing a template for 21st-century complaints against phone hacking, long-lensed paparazzi and gossip sites.

After surveying the law of contracts, property, trusts, copyright, trade secrets and torts, Warren and Brandeis concluded that existing US law *did* offer protections for individual privacy, and particularly for the invasion of privacy engendered by the public dissemination of personal details. This general right to privacy would protect the extent to which one's thoughts, sentiments and emotions could be shared with others. And the aim of this right was not to protect intellectual property or the items produced by individuals, but *peace of mind*. They wrote:

> … a principle … may be invoked to protect the privacy of the
> individual from invasion either by the too enterprising press,
> the photographer, or the possessor of any other modern device

for recording or reproducing scenes or sounds ...
[T]he principle which protects personal writings and any
other productions of the intellect or of the emotions, is the
right to privacy.

Their newly identified right, they wrote, was based on a principle of 'inviolate personality' which was analogous to, and connected
with, the prevalent conception of one's home as one's castle.

Before Warren and Brandeis, the *condition* of privacy had been
at issue, whether for Confucius, Aristotle or Mill. After 1890, however, the condition of privacy became complemented by the notion
of privacy as an individual's moral or legal entitlement. In the digital age, any comprehensive account of privacy must look further
than just the notion of a private 'realm', and must address not just
privacy's condition, but also its right. Indeed, the paper's impact on
the law is hard to overstate. In 1954, US lawyer Melville Nimmer
described it as 'perhaps the most famous and certainly the most
influential law review article ever written'.

It did, however, take several decades for privacy to gain a solid
legal footing in the US, as elsewhere. In 1928, now sitting on the
Supreme Court bench, Louis Brandeis delivered a judgment in
Olmstead v United States in which he reiterated the phrase 'the right
to be let alone', describing it as 'the most comprehensive of rights
and the right most valued by civilized man'.

This was a dissenting judgment; but 37 years later, in the 1965
case of *Griswold v Connecticut*, a majority of Supreme Court justices
came to agree with Brandeis, emphatically announcing the right's
arrival with a 7-2 verdict. The majority found that the US Constitution protected a right to privacy, even though the word does not
in fact appear there. Rather, wrote Justice William O. Douglas, the
right was to be found in the 'penumbras' and 'emanations' of various
constitutional provisions. These included the Fourth Amendment to

the Constitution, which defends 'the right of the people to be secure in their persons, houses, papers, and effects, against unreasonable searches and seizures'.

After lying dormant for many decades, the right to privacy roused quickly. Two years later, in *Katz v United States*, the Supreme Court laid down its 'lodestar' precedent for Fourth Amendment cases. *Katz* set the definitive and enduring four-word test: people are entitled to assert their right to privacy only when they have a 'reasonable expectation of privacy'. It remains a key test, though it does encounter difficulties when applied online. Given the extent of digital surveillance, many people have a sense of fatalism. Does this mean that today it is only reasonable to expect very little privacy online? If so, Americans are seemingly entitled only to limited protections of digital privacy under the Fourth Amendment.[1]

Still, since *Katz* US courts have repeatedly solidified the legal right to privacy, invoking it to allow people to dispense contraception, to overturn a ban on interracial marriage and to allow people to possess obscene materials in their own homes. In 1973, in the enduringly controversial case of *Roe v Wade*, the US Supreme Court upheld a woman's right to have an abortion, finding an implied right to privacy in the Fourteenth Amendment, which provides that 'No State shall make or enforce any law which shall … deprive any person of life, liberty, or property, without due process of law'. In cases such as *Roe v Wade*, the connection to conventional understandings of the word 'privacy' is tenuous. They reveal the extent to which US courts have stretched and expanded the right to privacy.

To supplement the case law, a series of statutes has been passed in the US. At a federal level, these acts protect the privacy of medical records, the privacy of students and the privacy of children online. These are supplemented by various state laws. I have already discussed the *Biometric Information Privacy Act* (BIPA) of Illinois, which limits the use of facial recognition and other biometric technologies without informed, opt-in consent. These are further supplemented by municipal ordinances, such as San Francisco's new ban on the use of facial recognition technology by city and county agencies.

Many US laws – from the *bodily* privacy protected by *Roe v Wade* to the *informational* privacy protected by BIPA – are far removed from the *oikos/polis* distinction drawn by Aristotle. They show that today privacy often has nothing to do with place. And these laws are typical of the manner in which privacy has been finding its way into law in the US and many other countries: by legislatures and courts willing to find privacy protections in broad instruments such as the Constitution in response to specific issues. Indeed, it is telling that in the US the 'constitutional' right to privacy is regarded as distinct from 'informational' privacy. This distinction is sometimes confusing and counterintuitive. Since 1890, the legal protection of the right to privacy in the US has been inventive and interstitial.

In Australia, the legal right to privacy is weaker than in the US. It is, to be blunt, frustratingly inadequate, which is being routinely exposed in the digital age. Most obviously, the Australian Constitution has no bill of rights to provide for privacy, either explicitly or in its penumbras and emanations. (Although the state of Victoria does have a Charter of Human Rights and Responsibilities, which includes a protection of the right to privacy and reputation.) Instead, Australia protects privacy in a consistently inconsistent way, via a complex of federal, state and local laws. Tellingly, not one contains a definition of privacy. These laws are then supplemented by case law.

Australian federal instruments include the *Telecommunications Act* 1977, the *National Health Act* 1953 and also the *Privacy Act* 1988 (which establishes principles that constrain the handling of personal data by government agencies and large businesses); state laws deal with topics including health data or image-based abuse; and local government laws tackle specific issues. In 2015, one central Sydney council became the first in Australia to ban drones in parks and public spaces. Meanwhile, courts are plugging the gaps. In Australia, no tort of invasion of privacy exists, unlike in the US, the UK, Canada and New Zealand. However, in 2001 the High Court, in *ABC v Lenah Game Meats*, left the door open for such a cause of action to develop. And in both the Victorian case of *Giller v Procopets* and the Western Australian case of *Wilson v Ferguson*, instances of image-based abuse (or 'revenge porn') led to the award of monetary damages. These decisions, argues lawyer Susan Gatford, reveal the way Australian courts are actively compensating for a lack of a privacy tort. These laws are further supplemented by the civil tort of trespass, which gives the occupier of a property some control over who comes onto her property, which in turn mirrors legislation such as the *Inclosed Lands Protection Act* 1901 in the state of New South Wales. All of this means that privacy is ill-defined and erratically protected in Australian law.

By comparison, Canadian law is more coherent and comprehensive, both in its legislation and its case law. In 1983, the *Privacy Act* came into effect, with the *Personal Information Protection and Electronic Documents Act* (PIPEDA) following in 2000. These general protections are supplemented by specific protections. In 2015, the non-consensual sharing of intimate images was criminalised, with a maximum penalty of five years in prison. The law's reach was broad, with section 162.1 of the *Criminal Code* providing that:

> Everyone who knowingly publishes, distributes, transmits, sells, makes available or advertises an intimate image of a person knowing that the person depicted in the image did not give their consent to that conduct, or being reckless as to whether or not that person gave their consent to that conduct, is guilty.

In 2016, a 29-year-old Winnipeg man became the first to be jailed under the law when he was sentenced to 90 days in prison for posting three naked photos of his ex-partner to Facebook. Further, the man's name was suppressed to protect the privacy of the victim.

Various landmark court cases have further expanded the legal right to privacy. In Ontario in 2012, a common law right to privacy was recognised in *Jones v Tsige*, which involved one bank employee repeatedly accessing the bank account information of another employee. This, the court held, involved a 'tort of intrusion upon seclusion'. More recently, following a case of a man posting an explicit video of an ex-girlfriend to a porn site, a tort of public disclosure of private facts has also emerged. However, as law researcher Sarit Mizrahi wrote in the *Western Journal of Legal Studies* in 2018, 'the privacy torts ... are riddled with uncertainties in their application and leave much to be desired ... these torts have a long way to go in providing adequate protection to digital privacy as a societal value.' This leads Mizrahi to argue that legislative remedies need to be extended.

Arguably the strongest protections for privacy are to be found in Europe. Indeed, Europe presents a marked contrast from jurisdictions such as the US, with law historian James Whitman arguing that the differences in privacy law in the US and Europe arise because two different legal systems with two different histories are protecting two different values. In the US, privacy primarily protects a liberty interest, whereas on the Continent privacy laws are based on French and German notions of personal honour. Certainly, rather than interstitial, Continental law has sought to be general and broad, with the European Court of Human Rights providing explicit protections based on Article 8 of the European Convention on Human Rights, which states: 'Everyone has the right to respect for his private and family life, his home and his correspondence.' Article 8 has been interpreted broadly. In a 1992 case, the court construed the phrase 'private life' to encompass more than simply a private realm. In *Niemietz v Germany*, authorities searched the premises of a lawyer to find the identity of a man who had written insulting letters anonymously, an offence in Germany. The lawyer complained that the search interfered with his private life, and the court agreed. Interpreting the phrase 'private life', the court found:

> it would be too restrictive to limit the notion to an 'inner circle' in which the individual may live his own personal life as he chooses and to exclude therefrom entirely the outside world not encompassed within that circle. Respect for private life must also comprise to a certain degree the right to establish and develop relationships with other human beings.

The court thus held that Article 8 protects the right to make and maintain relationships with other people, including at work, given that it is at work that people often have 'a significant, if not the greatest, opportunity of developing relationships with the outside world'. Hence the court's conception extended far beyond the *oikos* of Aristotle.

Most commonly, European law is concerned with 'data protection', or informational privacy. The extent to which European protections go beyond those of the US or Australia is revealed by the 'right to be forgotten'. In 1998, notices were printed in a Spanish newspaper about the forced sale of properties, including one owned by Mario Costeja González. Much later, and much to his dismay, a Google search of his name returned those same notices. In 2014, the European Court of Justice ruled González was entitled to have these hyperlinks from 1998 removed from Google's returned search results.

On 25 May 2018, the General Data Protection Regulation, or GDPR, came into effect. It codified the right to erasure, as the right to be forgotten is formally known, amid a sweeping raft of privacy protections. Within minutes, privacy campaigner Max Schrems lodged multi-billion euro complaints against Google, Facebook,

WhatsApp and Instagram, accusing them of coercing users into accepting their data collection policies.[2]

The law of privacy varies dramatically between jurisdictions. In part, this reflects the fact that different cultures have vastly different understandings of what privacy is, why it matters and how it ought to be protected. Whereas the people of Norway are renowned for being reserved and private, the concept of *ubuntu* in southern Africa suggests that the collective be prioritised over the personal and private. I return to this point in the next chapter.

One consistent ingredient, however, is that many countries enshrine privacy protections in their constitutions. Brazil's Constitution provides that 'the privacy, private life, honor and image of the people are inviolable'; South Africa's Constitution prescribes that 'everyone has the right to privacy'; and South Korea declares that 'the privacy of no citizen shall be infringed.' The Chinese Constitution protects 'freedom and privacy of correspondence of citizens' as well as the 'personal dignity' of all citizens, with dignity interpreted by Chinese legal scholars as including privacy rights. And the Qatari Constitution provides that the sanctity of human privacy is 'inviolable' and that no interference into the privacy of a person is allowed unless permitted under the law. These are significant provisions, even if they are not always zealously enforced.

Meanwhile, international law has sought to set universal standards for privacy. Indeed, the right to privacy became well established in international law during the 20th century. Its most prominent appearance is in Article 12 of the Universal Declaration of Human Rights, adopted in 1948: 'No one shall be subjected to arbitrary interference with his privacy, family, home or correspondence, nor to attacks upon his honour and reputation. Everyone has the right to the protection of the law against such interference or attacks.'

In this formulation – which forms the basis of Article 8 of the European Convention on Human Rights – privacy is not defined, although an implied meaning is evoked via references to family, home, correspondence, honour and reputation. The same wording then appears in Article 17 of the International Covenant on Civil and Political Rights, which came into force in 1976.

Privacy is a labyrinth. Still, there are some clear conclusions to be drawn from the brief overview I have given of the word itself, the history of the concept and the legal protections afforded in various jurisdictions. First, with the spread of the Enlightenment and liberalism, there has been an increasing association of privacy with the individual. Second, the right to privacy, since emerging in 1890, has become established as a significant ethical and legal principle, explicitly recognised by the law of nations, as well as internationally. Third, the definition of privacy is far from settled. Indeed, the legal definition is often implied and contextual.

And fourth, legal protections take many forms. In Australia, privacy has limited protections from a patchwork of laws, and 'privacy' is never defined in any law. In the US, privacy is emerging interstitially from landmark judgments relying on implied constitutional provisions, as well as specific legislative instruments. In Europe, privacy is codified in the General Data Protection Regulation and elaborated in a weighty body of case law that links privacy to, among other things, family life and the right to establish relationships. And in many countries, privacy enjoys explicit constitutional protection – which may or may not be enforced. Legal protections thus range from the implicit and interstitial to the explicit and expansive.

Privacy protections also target different *types* of privacy. One approach involves the protection of the private realm, as seen in the law of trespass; another involves the protection of privacy that attends the individual whether or not she is in a private space, as recognised in *Niemietz v Germany*; another involves informational privacy, as in Europe's newly recognised 'right to be forgotten'; and yet another involves bodily privacy, as in the landmark abortion case of *Roe v Wade*. Clearly, privacy is contested. It is also expanding. It has extended from *oikos* to the individual to a right to the body. What is understood by 'private' in the 21st century is much broader and more encompassing than in the time of Confucius and Aristotle; these days, 'private' and 'privacy' attach themselves with more subtlety and elasticity to a remarkably wide range of exchanges, activities and attributes.

At the same time, privacy is under threat. Here, then, we see two conflicting trends. Just as it is being more recognised and protected, privacy is increasingly being challenged (and confused) by technology and how it is used. Just as privacy is flourishing, it is also being eroded. More accurately, just as the *right* to privacy is increasingly being protected, the *condition* of privacy is increasingly under threat. Internet users, it would seem, have less privacy even as they acquire more right to it.

WHICH MODEL DID YOU HAVE IN MIND?

Privacy is a conceptual contortionist. Its flexibility is remarkable. My body? My diary? My sexual preferences? The god I worship? My email correspondence? My medical records? The conversation I have with a friend when seated in a public café?

In Ancient Greece, privacy was limited and precise, confined to the realm of the *oikos*. Today, that meaning persists, but privacy is also associated with individuals. It extends into their relationships. It follows them into public spaces. Often, it takes the form of a right, protected in law. Today, the term 'privacy' has transcended its neat and quarantined origins to grow complex and unwieldy. Given this complexity, I am seeking a conceptual account that is narrow enough to be meaningful, yet broad enough to cover the scope and subtlety of modern notions of privacy. It will be broad enough, I am hoping, to apply cross-culturally (I'll return to this). And from this conceptual account, I will then construct a working definition.

Now, my primary focus is *individual* privacy. That is, privacy as it pertains to individual human beings. Privacy can also pertain to couples, or families, or groups. For the clarity of my argument, however, my primary focus is the privacy of individuals.

What's more, I am arguing in the post-Mill tradition of liberalism. As Beate Rössler notes, the distinction between private and public is both fundamental and constitutive for the political and philosophical school of liberalism, given that the private/public distinction seeks to protect individual freedom and autonomy in the face of impermissible interference from the state. Admittedly, liberalism has lost some of its lustre, with philosophers and political scholars increasingly noting the significant inequities and dissatisfaction emerging in liberal democracies. Sure enough, wealth and power are unfairly distributed. In response, it is said, liberalism must be re-imagined in a manner that is less individualistic. And indeed, this is my project. Rather than presenting a conventionally liberal account, I aim to expand on the post-Mill tradition of liberalism by arguing that individual privacy concerns not just the individual in question, but also that individual's relationships, and society too. In other words, I will be giving an account of individual privacy that is more than just individualistic.

Privacy is not just about the individual. We are all beings-in-relation, constituted by the various links that embed us in society. A thorough conception of privacy must take account of all these various links. In this way, my aim is to advance the concept of privacy as *relational*, rather than purely individualistic. Such an account flows logically from the notion of relational autonomy, as developed by philosophers including Catriona Mackenzie, who writes:

Its [relational autonomy's] starting point is the individual as situated in, shaped, and constrained by her socio-relational context in all its complexity; that is, its starting point is non-ideal agents in a non-ideal world, characterized by social oppression, injustice, and inequality.

Similarly, relational privacy begins by acknowledging that an individual exists in a socio-relational context. I expand this idea in the next chapter, including by outlining the collective approaches to privacy taken in South Africa, in Japan and by the First Nations people in Canada. In so doing, my aim is to take a liberalist starting point, and from there to build a conceptual account of relational privacy that applies globally.

To do so, I am going to start by testing a series of models that will potentially enable us to define privacy: the place model; the onion model; the secrecy model; the intimacy model; the relationships model; the contextual integrity model; the control model; and the access model.

I have already raised the link between privacy and place. This is the basis of a first conceptual model, the *place* model, which aligns with the traditional *oikos/polis* distinction. On this account, privacy prevails in a 'private realm', 'private space' or 'private domain'. More than 2300 years after Aristotle, the link between privacy and place remains strong. Homes are considered private; bathrooms and bedrooms are considered especially private. Privacy extends to the activities that occur in those spaces. Going to the toilet is considered private. Sleeping is considered private. Dressing, undressing and physical intimacy are considered private. Even in a digital age, privacy and place remain linked. Working at home on my laptop, I would be surprised and affronted if a man peered in at my family through our living room window. This is in part because we live on the third floor, but it's also because I have an expectation of privacy.

I would be similarly affronted if anyone were eavesdropping on me in my bedroom via my smartphone.

However, sometimes privacy attaches to individuals, and follows them into public spaces. It is a breach of privacy, for instance, to 'upskirt'. In some jurisdictions, the law recognises this. In 2018, a man was sentenced to jail for at least 12 months for filming video up the skirts of women on escalators at Sydney's Central Station; the 59-year-old pleaded guilty to three charges of intentionally recording an intimate image without consent. What's more, as I have been arguing, in a digital age we are often in several places at once, some physical, some virtual, as when we're using social media apps while riding public transport. This complicates questions of private and public, showing that privacy isn't always just about place. An adequate conceptual model of privacy cannot be solely about place.

In a second conceptual model, privacy resembles an *onion*. This seems to be how many people think about privacy. On this view, there are layers of privacy, and whatever is most intimate and personal comprises the innermost layer. Herein lies bodily privacy, say. Within the second layer might be found family and other intimate relationships. Moving outwards, another layer might represent community. Only on the very outside layer is the state, the skin of the onion that is fully public. Again, however, this model seems inadequate.

My body is generally private, shared only with those closest to me, or amid, for instance, the specific etiquette and norms of a gym's changing room, where the expectation is that eyes are averted. Such expectations of privacy shift, however, in a doctor's consultation room, where my body might be thoroughly examined by a complete stranger. This suggests that privacy sometimes hinges on context. What is private in one context may not be private in another. Something that we might think sits at the core of the privacy onion – such as my body – is sometimes not private at all. An adequate conceptual model will need to allow for context.

The onion model is inadequate, so what about *secrecy*? The plot of *Rear Window* suggests privacy and secrecy might be one and the same, but can my bedroom and bathroom activities be described as secret? Not typically. As a human being, I am, to a certain extent, constrained by biology. There is generally little *secrecy* about my activities in bedrooms and bathrooms. And yet I still hope that privacy prevails, so that, unobserved, my dignity will be respected. Sometimes, then, there can be an expectation of privacy that has nothing to do with secrecy. And sometimes there can be secrecy, but no right to privacy. This is particularly clear with criminal acts. A person plotting a murder – as opposed to simply daydreaming about committing one – is likely to be conspiring in secret, but has no right to privacy.

The secrecy model is flawed. Perhaps an *intimacy* model is better, given that philosophers have long argued that privacy cannot be defined without reference to intimacy, and more specifically to notions of vulnerability, the body and the personal. Jurist Charles Fried argues that privacy is necessary for one's development as an individual who is able to trust, love and befriend, and that these social bonds can only be built by a judicious and selective sharing of intimacies. Lawyer Robert Gerstein argues that intimacy is necessary in our communications and relationships for us to fully experience our lives, and that such intimacy can only occur without intrusion or surveillance, so that we can act spontaneously and shamelessly. And for philosopher Julie Inness, intimacy is the defining ingredient in privacy invasions. Intimacy, for Inness, is based on intention, not behaviour, and draws its meaning from love, liking or care. Privacy is what enables a person to be intimate with behaviour or information in a way that fulfils her need to love and care.

As with secrecy, however, the problem seems to be that not all forms of privacy involve intimacy, and not all forms of intimacy involve privacy. The privacy that I demand for my medical records, for example, may or may not be related to intimacy. We could fairly describe gynaecological procedures as intimate. By contrast, receiving a tetanus shot in the arm is unlikely to be an intimate procedure. Nonetheless, I may want details of both to remain private. The privacy of medical records is not always a function of the intimacy of the details they contain. Rather, it may be a function of the potential for embarrassment, my future job prospects or some ill-defined unease with having the world know my medical ailments and history. Conversely, I can have an intimate moment in full public. My wife and I can hold hands or kiss in way that is intimate, even though we do not require or expect any privacy for our exchange of affection. Often, there is a strong link between privacy and intimacy. However, intimacy on its own is an insufficient notion by which to define privacy.

What, then, about *relationships*? While some define privacy in terms of intimacy, there are also those who define privacy in terms of social relations. Sometimes it is difficult to prise apart the two groups. Charles Fried, for instance, argues that privacy is integral for both intimacy and relationships. And in 1975 ethicist James Rachels was even clearer when he proposed that healthy social relations depend on privacy. Rachels argued that privacy is necessary if we are to maintain relationships, and that this is true for both non-intimate relationships and intimate relationships. Privacy is how we determine who knows what about us and who has access to us so that we can make and maintain all our social relations. It's a compelling argument that I'll come back to in the next chapter.

In some cases, however, social relations have nothing to do with privacy. A lawyer, doctor, accountant or bureaucrat may or may not know all manner of private, personal details about me, but our relationship might be distant and impersonal either way. Simply, the giving or withholding of privacies is in itself not enough to account for all our social relations. Apart from privacy, other values, such as affection and respect, contribute to the formation of such ties. In this spirit, Jeffrey Reiman argues that relationships are much more a function of how much people care for one another than how much they know about one another. Further, as James Moor points out, there are people who do not want relationships. Is privacy irrelevant to them? Surely not. Privacy, it seems, must be defined with regard to more than just the relationships it enables.

In the face of these difficulties, perhaps the very attempt to define privacy is futile. It's not that privacy is unimportant. It's just that perhaps the concept is too slippery, so perhaps we should avoid the vexing definitional issue, and simply get on with formulating protections. As law professor Daniel J. Solove writes:

> The quest for a traditional definition of *privacy* has led to
> a rather fruitless and unresolved debate. In the meantime,
> there are real problems that must be addressed, but they
> are either conflated or ignored because they do not fit into
> various prefabricated conceptions of privacy ... In this
> way, conceptions of privacy can prevent the examination of
> problems.

Hence Helen Nissenbaum simply abandons the hunt:

> Attempts to define it [privacy] have been notoriously
> controversial and have been accused of vagueness and internal
> inconsistency – of being overly inclusive, excessively narrow, or
> insufficiently distinct from other value concepts. Believing that
> one must define or provide an account of privacy before one
> can systematically address critical challenges can thwart further
> progress.

Without a definition, Nissenbaum proposes 'contextual integrity' as the key to unlock the issue of online privacy. And here, finally, thanks to its refusal to engage in a definitional debate, is a model that seems sufficiently elastic to accommodate privacy's vast, unwieldy scope.

Contextual integrity, founded on definitional agnosticism, is based on two principles: first, people engage in activities in a 'plurality of realms'; second, each realm has a distinct set of norms governing it. In other words, privacy hinges upon context. It doesn't hinge on the information in question, but on the context in which that information is shared. Similarly, it doesn't hinge just on the body part, or on a decision, or on a situation, but on the context. Online engagements usually have offline analogues, Nissenbaum writes, and the appropriate norms for online engagements can usually be determined by identifying the correct offline analogue. Contextual integrity thus focuses on the *granularity* of privacy, and Nissenbaum's project is to establish which privacy norms should apply in a given online milieu. The approach is proving influential.

However, as Nissenbaum admits, not every online interaction has an offline counterpart. Take Google's search engine. Nissenbaum has proposed that the most appropriate analogue is of a library. Users of Google should thus be able to expect that they are able to search for information privately and without records being kept, just as they are able to do in a physical library. But this analogue is problematic, for a range of reasons: libraries tend to be public institutions, whereas Google is a private company (with a business model predicated on the collection of data); the purpose of Google search is to serve as an index to help users locate information in the vast repository of data that is the web, whereas libraries serve as an index and are themselves the repositories of that data; Google's vast scale dwarfs any pre-existing library; Google personalises itself for every user, offering diverging search results and tailored advertising based on individual profiles; and Google also offers email, maps, music, photos and an expanding list of further services, then links the data collected by those services in ways that are opaque.

Contextual integrity is a promising approach. When it comes to privacy, context matters. The contextual integrity model recognises this. But what I want is something that applies to all cases: a concept that *transcends* context. My goal is to apply a Kantian ethical framework, and for that I'm going to need a working definition of privacy.

THE CONTROL AND ACCESS MODELS

Putting to one side the contextual integrity model, there are two prevailing accounts of privacy among philosophers: the *control* model and the *access* model.

The *control* model is based on scholarship spanning 50 years. In 1967, law professor Alan Westin published *Privacy and Freedom*, which Anita Allen has described as the 'inaugural treatise of the present generation of privacy scholarship'. Westin argued that privacy should be defined as control over information about oneself, and that privacy is 'the claim of individuals, groups, or institutions to determine for themselves when, how, and to what extent information about them is communicated to others'. Further, Westin identified people's right 'to control, edit, manage, and delete information about them'. On this view, the bounds of privacy are determined by each individual (or group).

This view was shared by Charles Fried, who wrote in 1968:

> Privacy is not simply an absence of information about us
> in the minds of others; rather it is the *control* we have over
> information about ourselves. To refer for instance to the
> privacy of a lonely man on a desert island would be to engage

in irony. The person who enjoys privacy is able to grant or
deny access to others.

Note that Fried incorporates the word 'access'. Prising apart
the control and access models is not always easy, as we shall see.
However, at the heart of Fried's definition is the notion of control,
and the way it enables us to determine our privacy by granting or
denying access. Fried refined his definition by stating that privacy
is not just about controlling the quantity of information, but also
about 'modulations in the quality of the knowledge'. Hence you
may willingly allow an acquaintance to know you are sick, but may
feel your privacy has been compromised if that acquaintance learns
of certain specific symptoms of your sickness. What's more, as we
have seen, Fried argued that privacy is intertwined with our relationships. It follows that our relationships depend on the way we
control access to ourselves and information about us. For Fried,
control over access is utterly crucial for us all, as individuals, but also
as social beings.

For many scholars, privacy is indelibly linked with control, and
this control is exercised in the form of consent. For instance, as philosopher Dag Elgesem wrote in 1996: 'To have personal privacy is,
on my account, to have the *ability to consent* to the dissemination of
personal information.' Today, control and consent remain the dominant paradigm for thinking about privacy. When the Cambridge
Analytica scandal broke in 2018, Mark Zuckerberg admitted that
Facebook had breached the trust of users. Between apologies, he
repeated Facebook's commitment to giving users control over their
data. 'You have control over your information,' Zuckerberg said,
referring to Facebook's privacy settings. In his testimony to Congress, Zuckerberg used the word 'control' 45 times, according to the
Washington Post. For Zuckerberg and many others, control is *the*
issue when it comes to privacy.

Control, it seems, reveals something fundamental about privacy. But is it really necessary? Or can we imagine situations where privacy has nothing to do with control?

To find out, I propose a trip to the beach. If I am a man who wants to go swimming, I can choose how much of my body to reveal by bathing in a full-body wetsuit, in board shorts or in the sort of truncated briefs known in Australia as 'budgie smugglers'. ('Budgie' is short for budgerigar, a small parrot.) If I am a woman, I can wear a wetsuit, one-piece or barely-there bikini. In this choice, I have control. However, the notion of control also *lacks* something, I would suggest, because some bathing suit options are closed off to me by convention and by law. By convention, various alternatives are considered acceptable (and, interestingly, these alternatives vary for men and women). And by law, the limits of privacy are affected even more clearly. In Sydney, the law prohibits me from swimming or sunbathing naked, except at a handful of designated beaches. Conversely, on certain French beaches, the modest burqini swimsuit was banned in 2016, leading to curious scenes of fully uniformed police ordering Muslim women to remove clothing at the seaside. In other words, it seems that both my condition of privacy and my right to privacy are not entirely up to me. To some extent, they are out of my control, given they are subject to social norms and the law.

In 2018, Denmark passed a law stating that 'anyone who wears a garment that hides the face in public will be punished with a fine'. Announcing the law, Denmark's Justice Minister said: 'I see a discussion of what kind of society we should have … that we don't cover our face and eyes. We must be able to see each other and we must also be able to see each other's facial expressions.' Critics said the law – which stopped women wearing niqabs and burqas and followed the passing of similar laws in France, Belgium, Austria, Bulgaria and the Netherlands – infringed women's rights. But in 2017 the European Court of Human Rights upheld Belgium's ban.

On this issue, the debate continues. But what is beyond dispute is that the limits of privacy are not always set by an individual's control. As tech reporter Geoffrey A. Fowler wrote in response to Mark Zuckerberg's commitment to giving Facebook users control over their data: 'That's like saying anyone can control a 747 because it has buttons and dials.'

For Judith Jarvis Thomson, *control* of privacy and the *right* to privacy clearly come apart:

> If my neighbor invents an X-ray device which enables him
> to look through walls, then I should imagine I thereby lose
> control over who can look at me: going home and closing the
> doors no longer suffices to prevent others from doing so. But
> my right to privacy is not violated until my neighbor actually
> does train the device on the wall of my house.

Thomson argues that my right to privacy is only violated if I am being spied upon. Until such spying occurs, my neighbour merely has the *potential* to violate my right to privacy. Even when control is lost, the right to privacy can remain intact. Is she right? The question warrants careful consideration, because Thomson's X-ray device makes a fitting metaphor for the internet as a whole.

On the net, it is as if our neighbour *has* invented an X-ray device, because we never know who is watching us. A hacker who has installed malware that accesses footage from our webcam? A social media network that aggregates its data with inferences and data from other sources? A government agency engaging in secret surveillance? At first glance, users seem to have control on the internet. Consent is usually sought; privacy settings can be adjusted. However, this control is often deficient or illusory.

The problematic nature of notice-and-consent provisions has led Helen Nissenbaum to coin the phrase 'transparency paradox', or 'transparency dilemma'. If privacy settings are made simple, brief and intelligible, those settings cannot hope to capture the complexity of online information flows. If, however, privacy settings hope to be sufficiently nuanced to capture the complexity of online flows (if this is even possible), then they need to be so lengthy and labyrinthine that few, if any, users will ever read them, let alone understand them. Many platforms opt for lengthy and labyrinthine. In 2012, journalist Alexis C. Madrigal calculated that it would take 76 workdays to read the privacy policies encountered by the average user in a year.

Earlier, I described the data mining giant Acxiom. In its privacy principles, Acxiom acknowledges the importance of control: 'Acxiom recognizes that individuals should be informed as to how information about them is used and should have choices about the dissemination of that information.' Yet it seems few people know Acxiom exists, let alone that it deals in their data. On the internet, many users *don't* control their privacy in any meaningful sense. Sometimes this lack of control is concerning. At other times, however, it is not concerning at all. In some cases, the limits of privacy ought to be determined not by the individual, but by externally imposed restrictions, including, most obviously, the law.

To put it another way: my privacy is not just about *me* and what *I* want. Nor should it be. Laws ban nudity at Bondi Beach. Are these laws enacted to protect the modesty and dignity of the bathers in question? Perhaps. More directly, however, these laws are designed with respect to others. In the Australian state of New South Wales, nude bathers can be jailed for six months under section 5 of the *Summary Offences Act*, which prescribes that a person shall not 'wilfully and obscenely expose his or her person'. Individual privacy is not just about the individual whose privacy is at issue, but about others too.

The law sometimes asks: if I renounce my privacy, will that adversely affect others? If so, which others? And how badly?

Embedded in these questions is the recognition that privacy, properly understood, is relational. An individual exists not in isolation, but only ever in the context of social ties and relationships. My privacy matters not just for me, but also for others. And hence we do not allow an individual to have all the say about the limits of her privacy, because the rest of society will want a say as well. Control, it seems, is a core component of privacy. However, privacy is sometimes beyond my control. The limits of my privacy are sometimes set by someone other than me, including legislators. And sometimes this is just as it should be.

The shortcomings of the control model bring us to one final contender for a viable concept by which to define privacy: the *access* model. This model holds that my privacy can be defined as restrictions upon access to me and information about me. These restrictions might be imposed by me. That is, they might involve control. Alternatively, they might be externally imposed, including by the law. Such an approach fits with dictionary definitions. The *New Shorter Oxford English Dictionary*, for instance, defines privacy as: '1. The state or condition of being withdrawn from the society of others or from public attention; freedom from disturbance or intrusion; seclusion ... 2. Absence or avoidance of publicity or display; secrecy ...'. The idea of access is encapsulated in the ideas of withdrawal, seclusion and freedom from disturbance. By contrast, the notion of control is nowhere to be found.

Ethicist Sissela Bok is one advocate of the access model. 'Privacy,' wrote Bok in 1982, 'is the condition of being protected from unwarranted access by others – either physical access, personal information, or attention.'

However, the most thorough account of the access model comes from Ruth Gavison. In 1980, Gavison wrote that our privacy is determined by the extent to which others have access to information about us and physical access to us. As such, we have perfect privacy only *when we are perfectly inaccessible to others*. For Gavison, Fried is wrong when he says that it would be ironic to talk of a man on a desert island as having privacy. His inaccessibility gives him tremendous privacy, via his solitude. Gavison argued that privacy can be gained in three ways: secrecy (when others don't have information about me), anonymity (when others don't pay attention to me) and solitude (when others don't have physical access to me).

These three elements of secrecy, anonymity and solitude are distinct and independent, but interrelated, and the complex concept of privacy is richer than any definition centred around only one of them.

Gavison's paper has proved extremely influential. In 1988, Anita Allen presented a restricted access view broader than Gavison's to allow for the feminist recognition that women experience losses of privacy unique to their gender. And in 1990 James Moor wrote:

> The core idea of restricted access accounts is that privacy is a matter of the restricted access to persons or information about persons … By my definition, an individual or group has privacy in a situation if and only if in that situation the individual or group or information related to the individual or group is protected from intrusion, observation, and surveillance by others.

The access model is more complete than the control model. It holds that my privacy concerns the access of others to my person and data about me, and sometimes to my space or possessions. Sometimes this involves my control, sometimes not. This model seems to account for my choice of swimwear, which is not without limits.

Now let's refine this model by exploring what type of access is required. In a scenario I'm borrowing from Adam Moore, imagine someone walking in a park. From this, a wealth of data can be garnered, including the person's image, height, weight, eye colour and general physical abilities. More significantly, biological material such as strands of hair will probably remain behind. Shed in public, this material is accessible to all. Hence the genetic data it contains, the very essence of that person's physiological identity, is accessible to all. Here, there is no restriction upon access whatsoever. Does this mean that all the genetic information that can be garnered from a strand of hair is public, not private? If I walk in public, do I thereby renounce any privacy claims I might have to the information my DNA contains?

Surely not. Yes, someone could find a DNA sample, then have it analysed and the results uploaded to a public database. But surely an expectation of privacy still prevails. We need to be more specific. We must ask: what sort of access is required before privacy is breached? Is *potential* access sometimes enough, or must there be *actual* access?

To answer, we again need to separate the condition of privacy from the right to privacy. Clearly, my condition of privacy is affected as soon as DNA mapping technology is invented. *Potential* access is enough to affect my condition of privacy. What's more, if there is *actual* access and the technology is used to map my DNA, my condition of privacy is affected far more profoundly. As for my right to privacy, it's a different story. If I leave behind a hair in a park, thus giving *potential* access to my DNA, my right to privacy surely remains intact. The mere invention of DNA mapping technology does not mean that my right to privacy has been breached as soon as I leave genetic material in a public space. And if a stranger picks up my hair, puts it in her pocket, but has no intention of analysing its DNA? In that case, there is actual access, but it's to the hair, not the DNA. By contrast, if someone picks up the hair and maps its DNA before posting that data to a public database, we clearly have actual access that amounts to an actual breach. It seems actual access of the DNA, not just the hair, is needed for a breach of the right to privacy.

Out of this discussion, then, let me propose a hypothesis: an actual breach of the right to privacy requires actual access to the relevant information or person. However, not every instance of actual access constitutes a breach, given that some access might be authorised. To put it more formally, actual access is necessary, but not sufficient, for an actual breach of privacy's right. Meanwhile, the condition of privacy can be affected by potential access.

It is the same with Thomson's X-ray device. My condition of privacy is altered as soon as my neighbour invents the X-ray device, whether or not any spying occurs. This is particularly true if I know about the invention of the device. Suddenly, my walls no longer shield me against my neighbour's eyes, and I am potentially as exposed inside my home as outside it. This is even more the case if I happen to know that many people own such devices. Clearly, a world in which such X-ray devices exist (and proliferate) is different from a world without such devices. This ray gun makes me vulnerable, just as the invention of DNA mapping makes me vulnerable. However, there is no breach of the right to privacy simply by virtue of the machine's invention. My right to privacy is breached only once there is actual access.

In a similar way, my condition of privacy is immediately impacted and altered by the development of the various surveillance capabilities that exist on the internet. As soon as a hacker, company or government agency develops the capacity to monitor every single email I draft and receive, my condition of privacy is instantly altered. Obviously, such capacity exists. Hackers, corporations and governments have developed metaphorical X-ray devices. Our condition of privacy has been irrevocably altered and impacted. The potential exists for each user (and non-user) to be watched and intimately profiled at any time. However, that does not mean that the right of privacy of every user (and non-user) has been violated. *Potential* access, which can arise from the invention of new technology, merely constitutes a *potential* breach of the right to privacy.

An added complication involves non-human access. To return to the DNA example, what if it is not a person that collects my hair and analyses its DNA? What if it is an AI-powered machine? And what if the DNA data is collected, analysed and then anonymised, all by machine, so as to be paired with more data in the service of disease prevention and the greater good? Does this non-human analysis constitute actual access? Certainly, there is actual access of a sort, but does it breach the right to privacy? The answer, I suggest, depends on how we want to set the parameters of privacy. If we want stronger protections, then laws can be drafted to define actual access by machine as an actual privacy breach. By contrast, we may resolve that actual access requires access by a conscious agent.

Similarly, is it a breach of the right to privacy if a government surveillance program automatically collects every citizen's emails, but those emails are never read by a person, simply stored so that AI can pick out those containing certain keywords? And what if this system includes significant safeguards, such as ensuring that citizens' emails may only ever be read with a court-ordered warrant based on a well-founded suspicion that a serious crime has been, or will be, committed? Here too it can be argued that there is no breach of privacy. (Although, of course, the converse can also be argued.) The game changes, however, if all emails are secretly collected and made indiscriminately accessible to a wide range of government agency employees for each and every purpose. In the face of the meta-phorical X-ray device that is the internet, there exists a compelling urgency for clarity, including from the law.

My larger point is that each of these scenarios is *not* an effective counterargument against the access model. The notion of restrict-ing access remains definitive. Even though access to my DNA is potentially unlimited if I leave behind a hair in a park, only actual access can constitute a breach of my right to privacy. What's more, to breach my right to privacy that access needs to be *unauthorised*:

unauthorised by my consent; and unauthorised by the law.

Digital technology allows for potentially unlimited access to our privacies. That's the promise of Panopticon 3.0. But as technology increasingly challenges the condition of privacy, the right to privacy is not necessarily affected. What remains for us to do is to define what type of actual access constitutes a breach.

Privacy *sometimes* involves control, but *always* involves access.[3] Sometimes an individual sets the limits; sometimes the limits are set by external forces. Sometimes privacy has to do with the intentions of the person whose privacy is at stake; sometimes it has to do with the intentions of others and society as a whole. The access model fits. A working definition might be worded:

> **The right to privacy is my right that others be deprived of unauthorised access to me and to information about me. In some cases, this right will involve my ability to control such access. The condition of privacy, meanwhile, is the state of others being denied such access.**

To allow for the relational nature of privacy, we might expand this definition to refer to 'access to me or us'.[4] Note also that I have used the phrase 'information about me', rather than the more narrow 'personal information'. Among other things, the former also includes information that can be inferred.

We might add to this working definition, if we care to, that privacy is often connected with secrecy, intimacy and social relations. And we might add that different combinations of ingredients will come to the fore in different contexts. However, these additions are unnecessary. What matters is the recognition that privacy is about access, and that I get to choose which swimmers I wear, even as my choice is circumscribed by the law and other external constraints.

CHOOSE PRIVACY – BUT NOTE THAT
THE CHOICE ISN'T ALWAYS UP TO YOU

Is privacy a condition? A right? If so, is it a descriptive right? A normative right? Or a legal right? And is it a value? An interest? A preference?

Yes.

Privacy is all these things. The concept is versatile and complex. We can have a private realm; we can distinguish bodily privacy from informational privacy; we can prise situational privacy from personal privacy. Further categories have been identified. Privacy is widely, wildly inclusive. It is also contested. Our task of illuminating the ethics of internet privacy involves applying a contested notion in an ethically contested realm. Still, we *can* arrive at a conceptual definition.

When I choose my bathers, I decide how much of my body I want to expose. I can be modest, exhibitionistic, or casually in between. However, the decision is not entirely mine. I cannot legally bathe nude at Bondi Beach. Privacy is all about restricting access. Sometimes access is restricted by my choice; other times, access is restricted by externally imposed limitations, such as the law, or social norms, or whether a wall is soundproof.

In *Rear Window*, Jeff is castigated for his voyeurism by his friend Doyle, a detective.

'That's a secret and private world you're looking into out there,' Doyle says. 'People do a lot of things in private that they couldn't explain in public.'

And when a dog is killed, its owner is distraught. 'You don't know the meaning of the word "neighbours",' she yells out into the courtyard. 'Neighbours like each other, speak to each other, care if anybody lives or dies. But none of you do.' After this, the neighbours run to their windows to see what's going on, except the salesman, who sits silently in a darkened apartment, visible only by the glow of his cigar.

As *Rear Window* shows, privacy is sometimes connected to secrecy, and to relationships. What's more, it shows that privacy is sometimes about control, and sometimes about the law. Sure, residents can draw their curtains; but the murderer is not entitled to keep his crime to himself.

By the film's end, the killer has confessed, and the neighbours have formed new relationships, seemingly with a healthier understanding of privacy, secrecy and social relations. In the closing scene, Jeff rests in his wheelchair, even more injured than in the opening reel. Lisa reclines nearby, reading a novel. As soon as Jeff falls asleep, Lisa puts down the book and opens a glossy magazine. Even from her boyfriend, she has secrets.

The next question is, just why does she value her privacies?

MY PRIVACY IS FOR
YOUR BENEFIT

Truman Burbank is unaware that his whole life is an elaborately constructed illusion.

A chirpy naïf, Truman lives in a coastal town. Or so he thinks. In fact, the 30-year-old lives under a giant dome on a Hollywood set, where every moment of his existence, right from birth, has been filmed as part of a reality TV show. Complete with product placement and choreographed extras, Truman's every waking moment is broadcast live to an audience of billions.

Of course, Truman Burbank is a fictional character. He's the protagonist of Peter Weir's 1998 comedy/drama *The Truman Show*, starring Jim Carrey. The drama raised the question of what life might be like for an individual whose privacy has been taken away entirely, not by a government, but by a corporation. Slowly, as the truth begins to dawn, Truman's quest becomes to escape his faux reality so that he might find his way into a more human world, where privacy (among other things) is still possible. As Truman begins to suspect something is amiss, his millions of viewers become even more enthralled. Will he discover the truth? How will he react? Just how important is his privacy?

In this chapter as in the last, I address a simple question. This time the question is: why does privacy matter?

To start, I propose two imaginary worlds: one with no privacy;

one with absolute privacy. Both are alarming. I then give four justifications for the value of privacy: dignity; autonomy; relationships;
and society and democracy. What's more, privacy is relational. It
constitutes our relationships. While privacy is a means for individuals to separate and withdraw, it's also a means for them to bond and
coalesce.

If we can somehow keep others from reading our thoughts,
then we might just remain free, *and* find a way to save democracy.

'I'M THINKING IN MY HEAD'

Over breakfast one morning, shortly after turning five, my daughter
looked pensive.

'I'm thinking in my head,' she said, finally.

'Oh,' I said, between sips of coffee. 'What are you thinking?'

'That's a secret,' she said. 'A secret only for me.'

Having barely started kindergarten, my daughter already had a
sense of some private part of herself, a part she could choose not to
share. In the previous chapter, I argued that privacy involves restrictions on access. I also argued that there is sometimes a link between
privacy and control. My daughter, it seems, agreed with both these
points.

Our exchange also reveals another point: as long as we can have
our own thoughts, we have a degree of privacy. That is, if others
cannot read our minds, we have a degree of the *condition* of privacy.
As such, it seems that a world without privacy is impossible.

At least, mind-reading is currently impossible. Perhaps the
internet will change that. Individuals may one day be able to transcend their own consciousness, perhaps in a type of singularity, as
described in chapter 1. Indeed, perhaps the internet is already beginning to make it possible to read users' thoughts. We have seen the

way location data can be used to predict user location 24 hours into the future. We have also seen the way Facebook likes can unintentionally reveal supposedly hidden personality traits including sexuality and political views. Meanwhile, 'emotion recognition' software is being used by advertisers to gauge users' latent emotions by analysing facial cues. As computing reporter Rob Matheson wrote in 2014, the goal is to create a 'mood-aware' internet that reads a user's emotions to help shape their content. By deducing facts that users don't even know they're sharing, these developments are arguably types of mind-reading.

This field is advancing quickly. In September 2019, tech writer Kaveh Waddell noted that brain–computer interfaces are being developed by several cashed-up companies. For now, machines that read brain activity are inefficient and inaccurate, but progress is accelerating. Facebook and Elon Musk's startup Neuralink are investing heavily, aiming to enable users to type with their thoughts, or even merge with AI. In the process, the technology may reveal insights about a brain that are unknown even to its user. As neurotechnologist Tim Brown says, 'The sort of future we're looking ahead toward is a world where our neural data – which we don't even have access to – could be used.'

This naturally raises concerns about hidden manipulations. What if our thoughts are in fact *not* our own, but the result of manipulative techniques that override our autonomy? The Cambridge Analytica scandal showed how personal data can be extracted and exploited in a way that leaves people vulnerable to highly personalised content that might change their voting intentions. Earlier, in 2014, research led by Adam Kramer found that emotional states can be transferred between Facebook users via 'emotional contagion'. In this way, emotions can be manipulated too. (The research remains controversial. It was run by Facebook, where Kramer is a data scientist, and it's hard to see how the users whose emotions were manipulated gave meaningful consent to participating in the research. Indeed, it's eerily apt that the researchers used hidden manipulations to reveal the power of hidden manipulations.)

The issue is not just mind-reading, but mind control, as the techniques being employed online involve predictive analytics and behavioural nudges. As Kaveh Waddell writes, marketers and advertisers are increasingly turning to neuroscience to know consumers better than they know themselves. In this way, digital platforms have been accused of 'attention hacking', using sneaky techniques to keep users engaged, and employing 'dark patterns', which shepherds users into choosing, say, sharing over privacy. As technology keeps getting better at reading and manipulating the brain, the challenges to privacy, and to freedom, are deeply concerning.

But I'm getting ahead of myself, and of technology. At least for now, the nature of human existence is such that each individual has his or her separate consciousness, thereby guaranteeing (some degree of) privacy. A person can say one thing while thinking something contradictory. In the absence of mind-reading, in the absence of the ability to transcend individual consciousness, every individual has privacy.

The question is: is this a good thing? For some, individualised consciousness is a nightmare. '*L'enfer, c'est les autres,*' wrote Jean-Paul Sartre in 1944, in a line that translates as 'Hell is other people.' Here, Sartre gives a resolutely pessimistic account of the unknowability of another's thoughts. And some philosophers have unambiguously argued that we'd be better off with no privacy at all. These philosophers propose that people and societies could, and *should*, exist without it.[1] People want privacy, they argue, merely due to the illusion that elements of their lives are embarrassing and unique; the reality is that human lives are essentially universal. On this view, privacy-related embarrassment and uniqueness are feelings that, with sufficient progress, we could and should discard.

Plato is in this camp. While Aristotle distinguished *oikos* from *polis*, his teacher Plato considered privacy an obstacle to the ideal state. In *The Laws*, Plato argued that a state will be truest, best and most exalted in virtue if it contains:

> this communion of women and children and of property, in
> which the private and individual is altogether banished from
> life, and things which are by nature private, such as eyes and
> ears and hands, have become common, and in some way see
> and hear and act in common, and all men express praise and
> blame and feel joy and sorrow on the same occasions, and
> whatever laws there are unite the city to the utmost.

Plato has his supporters. A similar view is presented by Isaac Asimov in his account of Gaia, which I described in the introduction. As Ferdinand Schoeman summarises, 'People who hold this view claim that institutions of privacy are conducive to social hypocrisy, interpersonal exploitation through deception, and even a-social or anti-social loyalties.' On this account, privacy is atavistic and selfish. A world without privacy would be a world of brilliant sunshine. It would be a world without hypocrisy, shame and deception.

Who is right? Plato? Or my five-year-old daughter?

A first point to note is that privacy norms vary dramatically over time, and across cultures. In the ruins of the ancient Greek city of Ephesus, in modern-day Turkey, contemporary tourists can take their position on one of several toilet seats in the public hall. This, writes James Whitman, is where posh Ephesians 'gathered to commune, two thousand years ago, as they collectively emptied their bowels'. I don't know about you, but in the places I frequent, the emptying of bowels tends to be solitary, not collective. The variation in norms is clear too across geography. As Whitman notes, in the US but not Europe, people casually discuss salary and net worth; in Europe but not the US, people casually take off their clothes.

To understand privacy, mid-20th century researchers charted the norms and customs that prevail among Native Americans, Polynesians and Javanese, among many others, only to find that privacy appears to be valued, recognised and institutionalised in all human societies. In the 1960s, anthropologists Robert Murphy and Alan Westin separately concluded that privacy seems to be a cultural universal, necessary for humans to survive as the social animals they are. Privacy exists among the Tuareg and the Tlingit, among Australians and Americans, among islanders and Europeans.[2]

Globally, however, privacy manifests in wildly varying forms. This is revealed by language. Tellingly, some countries have no direct counterpart for the English word 'privacy'. In German, *privat* means 'private', but no word exists for privacy. Instead, there are notions of *Privatleben*, or 'private life and *Privatsphäre*, or 'private sphere', but these are more limited than the elastic concept denoted in English. Similarly, as media scholar Charles Ess notes, Norwegian and Danish also have no direct counterpart, but instead value *privatlivet*, which goes beyond the individual to also accommodate the *intimsfære*. In this way, the notion of the intimate sphere also takes in close relationships, and goes beyond the merely individualistic. French has no word for privacy either, but has *l'intimité*, le secret and *le solitude*, but again these are more specific. Given the absence of a direct counterpart for 'privacy' in many European languages, it's no wonder that European privacy law often concentrates on data protection, rather than protecting privacy per se. What's more, the conception of privacy that prevails in Germany, Norway, Denmark and France diverges from the English conception to align more closely with a relational approach. *Privatsphäre*, *intimsfære* and *l'intimité* all extend beyond the individual to evoke a private life that also encompasses one's closest family and friends.

Sometimes the law doesn't align with common understanding. It can be argued, for instance, that European law tends to approach privacy from an individualistic standpoint, but European languages often approach it from a more communal, relational standpoint. Something similar can be seen in Canada. As legal/computing scholars Megan Vis-Dunbar, James Williams and Jens Weber-Jahnke wrote in 2011, Canadian statutory privacy law is based on an individualistic notion of privacy; however, *Indigenous* notions of privacy in Canada tend to be communal. This creates a tension. For instance, under Canada's Model Code for the Protection of Personal Information, organisations have a prima facie duty to obtain the knowledge and consent of an individual before collecting, using and disclosing personal information. Community interests are not mentioned. However, this account will not satisfy Indigenous notions of privacy. In Canada, First Nations people have synthesised four key information management principles into principles covering ownership, control, access and possession. These principles explicitly acknowledge community. The ownership principle, for instance, states: 'The ownership principle concerns the relationship of a First Nations community to its cultural knowledge and collective information. Certain information is owned collectively, much as an individual owns their personal information.'

Like the First Nations people of Canada, many cultures regard privacy primarily as a collective, rather than an individual, notion. A guiding philosophy in post-apartheid South Africa, for instance, has been *ubuntu*, which emphasises the values of community and connectedness. As law professor Dan Burk wrote in 2006:

Under *ubuntu*, personal identity is dependent upon and defined by the community. Within the group or community, personal information is common to the group, and attempts to withhold or sequester personal information are viewed as abnormal or deviant. While the boundary between groups may be less permeable to information transfer, *ubuntu* lacks any emphasis on individual privacy.

Similarly, writes Charles Ess, many Asian cultures take a collective view of privacy. Rather than the interests of an individual, privacy conventionally concerns the interests of the family vis-à-vis society. And in many cases, the notion of individual privacy is regarded with suspicion, or worse. In Japan's Jodo Shinshu (Pure Land) Buddhist tradition, the idea of 'no-self', or *Musi*, is key to attaining enlightenment. As Ess writes:

> The Buddhist goal of nirvana, or the 'blown-out self', justifies the practice of what from a modern Western perspective amounts to intentionally violating one's 'privacy': in order to purify and thus eliminate one's 'private mind' – thereby achieving Musi, 'no-self' – one should voluntarily share one's most intimate and shameful secrets.

I wonder what Plato would have made of this tradition. Meanwhile, the Chinese word for privacy, *yinsi*, was traditionally associated with something shameful and best hidden. This stems in part from the Confucian emphasis on community. In recent years, however, *yinsi* is beginning to be regarded more positively, with significant new protections under Chinese law. (There are, in fact, two distinct characters for *yinsi*, one translating as 'shameful secrets', the other as 'privacy'.)

Is privacy universally valued by every human culture, as Robert Murphy and Alan Westin argued in the 1960s? Certainly, there is huge variation, as they observed. In some countries and cultures, privacy is construed as highly individualistic. In others, the notion of privacy is regarded as relational and communal, and as an interest that attaches to the family or group. And for some, there are negative associations that attach to privacy, including among Buddhists who propose that enlightenment can be had only by entirely opening up one's private mind and its secrets.

This is a fundamental point. In different cultures, privacy means very different things. It is also valued in different ways and for different reasons. Sometimes, perhaps, it isn't valued at all. Any attempt to come up with a universal standard for privacy must allow for this myriad variation. Is this even possible? To begin to answer this question, let's shift from exploring how privacy *is* valued in various cultures and countries, to exploring how privacy *should* be valued.

And to do that, let's imagine two hypothetical societies that value privacy in very different ways. In one, privacy is not valued at all. In this society, privacy is dismissed as worthless and irrelevant. Only that which is public is valued. In the other, privacy is valued fiercely, just as much as is possible. Here, privacy's value is absolute, or as close to absolute as can be managed. What might these societies look like? What would it be like to live there?

In the first, everything is public that could possibly be public. There are no doors on toilets, no walls on homes and no curtains on windows. There is no ability to control the flow of information, even if sensitive; and there is no restriction upon access to oneself or to information about oneself. Every space is public, all data is public, every body is public. In this world, privacy's condition and right have been eradicated. Each individual inhabits a personal panopticon, where even thoughts are not private. This is, in fact, Panopticon 3.0.

This is the total lack of privacy contained in the notion of an ever-present, omniscient deity. Or in the world inhabited by

Truman Burbank, who is watched over by the godlike TV producer Christof – and an audience of millions. In this world, each one of us is Truman, potentially being watched at any time, at any place. In 2014, it emerged that the ride-sharing service Uber was able to spy on the movements of high-profile politicians, celebrities and ex-spouses of employees. Uber called this capability 'God view'.

What would a total lack of privacy mean for our dignity, our autonomy, our relationships? Surely all three would suffer. If we were able to withhold *nothing*, physically or psychologically, then our dignity would take a blow, it would seem, just as our ability to act freely would be compromised. We would be both exposed and constrained. And how could we forge friendships? Or love? When life must play out fully in public, how can we hope to separate close friends from strangers? And how would democracy fare without the secrecy of the ballot box? This world of full publicity seems so foreign that it is difficult to imagine with any level of detail. That in itself is revealing.

By complete contrast, in our second hypothetical society privacy is worshipped as a supreme value. Every house has its curtains drawn; every property has a fence; and privacy-protecting laws have been drafted to prescribe that one individual cannot take a photo of another, even with consent, and that every person must be fully covered, at all times. Spaces are private; data is private; bodies are private. Secrecy, anonymity and solitude abound. Communication, when it happens, is superficial and restrained, given that anything even remotely connected to the intimate and the secret is taboo. Privacy is afforded absolute value; both its condition and right are privileged over any competing considerations.

This world is perhaps even harder to imagine than the first. One qualified version of this world is that imagined by Margaret Atwood in *The Handmaid's Tale*, where fertile women are cloaked, hooded and chaperoned. Here too, dignity, autonomy and relationships are at risk. How can dignity and autonomy be respected if others cannot come near? And how can meaningful relationships be forged when each person must keep a distance?

Both these worlds appear troubling. In the first, the bright light of full publicity is blinding. Each detail, intimacy and body is exposed. Everything is shared and social, with nothing left for individuals (or couples, or families) to keep to themselves, and to share judiciously. Ironically, although all is shared and social, relationships would be stunted. There would, it seems, be a limit to their depth. And in the second, the light cannot penetrate. Dark and shrouded, this is a place of secrets and shadows. Here, the individual has been isolated at the expense of interaction, community and social engagement.

These two scenarios are both, in contrasting ways, dystopian. 'We start from the obvious fact that both perfect privacy and total loss of privacy are undesirable,' writes Ruth Gavison. 'Privacy thus cannot be said to be a value in the sense that the more people have of it, the better.' Fortunately, both worlds also seem to be impossible, as hinted at by the difficulty of mapping their contours. 'The total loss of privacy is as impossible as perfect privacy,' Gavison adds.

Privacy ought to be valued, but not in the extreme. Countervailing rights and freedoms must be valued too. A balance must be struck. My right to privacy is merely one of several rights, and this must in turn be balanced against your equal rights. After co-writing the 1890 essay 'The right to privacy', Louis Brandeis reportedly planned to write a companion piece on 'The duty of publicity'. He never published this paper, but did pen the famous lines: 'Publicity is justly commended as a remedy for social and industrial diseases. Sunlight is said to be the best of disinfectants; electric light the most efficient policeman'.

For individuals and society to prosper, we need to strike a balance between the light of publicity and the shade of privacy. And to strike this balance, we need to understand with greater clarity why privacy matters.

DIGNITY

One common argument for privacy's value involves dignity and respect. This argument can be traced directly to 1890, and to Warren and Brandeis's proposal that every individual deserves respect for privacy on account of their 'inviolate personality'.

In 1964, philosopher and lawyer Edward Bloustein expanded on their proposal to argue that 'inviolate personality' encompasses dignity, integrity, uniqueness and autonomy. As he wrote: 'I take the principle of "inviolate personality" to posit the individual's independence, dignity and integrity; it defines man's essence as a unique and self-determining being.' Four years later, Charles Fried advanced an account founded on respect. For both jurists, an attack on privacy is potentially an attack upon what it means to be human. They argue that some intrusions upon privacy are violations of dignity.

Fair enough, but what is dignity? As it happens, the term is widely used, but poorly understood.

Philosopher Paul Formosa writes that there are at least five different types of dignity. One is *achievement* dignity, or aspirational dignity. Achievement dignity is what we can earn for ourselves through our actions, appearance, reputation, and so on. This is the dignity we have for our sporting achievements, mathematical proficiency or competence on the flugelhorn.

What I'm interested in is another type of dignity: *status* dignity. Also known as inviolable dignity, status dignity concerns the absolute and irreducible worth of humanity. As Kant wrote in 1785 in the *Groundwork of the Metaphysics of Morals*: 'If [something] is exalted above all price and so admits of no equivalent, then it has a dignity ... [and] morality, and humanity so far as it is capable of morality, is the only thing which has dignity.'

Kant is referring to the dignity that attends the priceless worth of humanity, which has 'an unconditioned and incomparable worth'. Such dignity attaches to rational beings, given that the origin of such dignity is the ability of rational beings to autonomously legislate the universal moral law. This is a deft argument from Kant: that a rational being is free to obey only those laws she herself has legislated; through this process, she makes the universal law.

The necessary complement of dignity is respect. Dignity *demands* respect, in the same way that rights demand duties. And status dignity demands unqualified respect. It requires each person to respect every other and themselves as free beings. As Kant wrote in *The Metaphysics of Morals*:

> a human being regarded as a *person*, that is, as the subject of morally practical reason, is exalted above any price; for as a person he is not to be valued merely as a means to the ends of others or even to his own ends, but as an end in himself, that is, he possesses a *dignity* (an absolute inner worth) by which he exacts *respect* for himself from all other rational beings in the world.

I'll return in the next chapter to that tricky phrase 'and end in himself', and also to Kant's reliance on reason as the basis for human worth. For now, the key point is that Kant builds on his account of reason, dignity and respect to argue that all persons are not just free, but equal. His system of ethics is profoundly egalitarian.

Further, the value of dignity lies not in what it can do for us or others. Rather, dignity is valuable in and of itself. Its value, above all, is *non-instrumental*. Sure, dignity may have instrumental value too. If others respect my dignity, they may be less likely to lie to me or steal from me. Anyone who actively respects dignity will be likely to treat women and men as equals and reject slavery as immoral. These benefits are significant. But dignity mandates that *humanity* is respected, both individually, and globally. To argue that privacy matters for reasons of dignity is to argue that privacy matters for non-instrumental reasons.[3]

For legal scholar William Prosser, this is all too much. In 1960, Prosser argued that privacy has only instrumental value, and privacy violations are founded specifically on injured reputation and emotional distress.

As a counterargument to Prosser, the shadow profiles discussed in chapters 1 and 2 come to mind. Indeed, one recurring strand of arguments for privacy's non-instrumental value invokes cases in which a person's privacy is violated without that person ever knowing. James Moor describes Tom, an unseen voyeur who uses secret cameras and devices to spy on a woman. Let's assume that Tom does no instrumental harm. He doesn't share his footage; he doesn't tell anyone; he certainly doesn't attempt blackmail. The only benefit Tom gains is the fulfilment of his voyeuristic impulses. Is Tom harming this woman, even though she doesn't know she's being spied upon? Moor says yes: 'I think most of us will agree that there is something repugnant about Tom's peeping ... Some people, including myself, regard privacy as intrinsically valuable, not merely instrumentally valuable.' I agree. Even if no instrumental harm is being done, even if the victim is blissfully unaware, there is a breach.

On the internet, unseen voyeurism is commonplace. For the CreepShots website, men secretly take photos, in public, of women's behinds and breasts, then share the images. The site defends itself with the motto 'No harm, no foul'. That is, because these women are none the wiser, no harm can flow. My response is that even if there is no instrumental harm, there has been a foul. Consent has not been sought for actions that, intuitively, require consent. In the process,

there has been a glaring failure of respect. The women whose face-
less body parts are photographed and published are being treated
not as people, and not even just as objects. They're being treated as
commodities, given that their images generate revenue for the website's administrators, who charge US$9.95 for a three-month mem-
bership. These women are being treated as things to be exploited
for entertainment, titillation and enrichment, and as a result something larger occurs: the worth of humanity as a whole is diminished.
By failing to treat women with the respect that all persons are due,
CreepShots is a privacy violation even in the absence of instrumental
harms such as emotional distress or increased risk of sexual assault.

(That said, CreepShots is doing instrumental harm too. Women
who know that websites such as this exist are likely to behave differently and be less free, even if they never know whether or not
they themselves are victims. They will potentially be more anxious.
What's more, incidents of sexual assault and stalking *are* reportedly
on the rise. Citing such instrumental harms, legal scholar Marc Tran
has argued that the practice ought to be criminalised.)

Some privacy violations that threaten dignity involve surrepti-
tious watching. Others involve people at their most vulnerable, as in
the case of women giving birth. Childbirth is universal. Everyone
has attended at least one. Yet it is also a moment of tremendous vulnerability. When in labour, a woman can reasonably expect that she
will be surrounded only by her nearest and dearest, as well as medical professionals, but definitely not random strangers and voyeurs.
Unwanted intrusions upon childbirth can clearly have instrumental
ramifications. These might include a stalled labour, adverse physical health outcomes for mother and/or child and ongoing mental
health issues such as postnatal depression. At the same time, however, an unwanted intrusion upon childbirth also involves a non-
instrumental failure to respect a woman's humanity *for its own sake*.
As Edward Bloustein writes: 'A woman's legal right to bear chil-

dren without unwanted onlookers does not turn on the desire to protect her emotional equanimity, but rather on a desire to enhance her individuality and human dignity.' Failure to respect the privacy of a woman in labour diminishes humanity, not least because such a woman is in the very process of bringing a new person (or persons) into the world.

Bloustein describes the 'spiritual characteristic' of privacy case law. Yes, he writes, sometimes privacy has instrumental value; but it is true also that 'the interest served in the privacy cases is in some sense a spiritual interest rather than an interest in property or reputation'. This spiritual interest turns on the priceless worth of human beings. In cases of secret surveillance such as CreepShots, women (and tellingly it is only women) are being treated as objects, as *things* whose reason, feelings and worth are irrelevant, and certainly not worthy of respect. In cases involving the vulnerable, the story is similar. When a woman's privacy is violated during childbirth, there is something troubling in the way the woman herself, and in the way humanity more widely, has not been afforded due respect, all in the ultimate life-affirming moment that is birth. Similarly, we can imagine many other privacy invasions of the vulnerable (children, the mentally ill, the elderly) that violate dignity. Sometimes privacy violations are egregious simply and precisely because they violate status dignity, nothing more.

This raises the question of whether privacy should *ever* be bought and sold. For 30 years, Truman Burbank was unaware that his every breathing moment was secretly being watched by an audience of millions. It is a telling plot detail that Truman is described as the first baby legally adopted by a corporation. The writers of *The Truman Show* presumably saw a link between an absence of privacy and a dignity-compromising 'ownership' of humans. Status dignity mandates that no human ever be owned. If privacy protects dignity, and if dignity must never be for sale, then perhaps privacy ought never be for sale. Perhaps privacy, or at least those portions of it connected with dignity, should be beyond the market.

Communitarian Michael J. Sandel argues that the market economy has given way to the market society, where an increasing commodification of life is leading to greater inequality. The rich can, for instance, buy their children places in academically elite schools. This is problematic, Sandel argues, because the market inevitably changes the character of the goods it touches, such as sex, friendship, family life, health, education, art and more. This is having a deep effect on democracy, and hampering citizens' ability to share in a common life. And now, as we know, privacy is being bought and sold, by companies including Acxiom and Palantir, and also by some government agencies. On the internet, the commodification of privacy is well-established, so we urgently need to ask ourselves some big questions. Should privacy be commodified? If so, how can we avoid creating a world where the rich are able to afford significantly greater privacy and liberty – via superior software, hardware and IT knowledge – than the poor?

'We need to think through the moral limits of markets,' writes Sandel. 'We need to ask whether there are some things money should not buy.'

To be fair, we should also note that some scholars think dignity isn't a very useful concept after all. In 2008, psychologist Steven Pinker wrote, 'The problem is that "dignity" is a squishy, subjective notion, hardly up to the heavyweight moral demands assigned to it.' Pinker was building on a 2003 editorial by bioethicist Ruth Macklin. In 'Dignity is a useless concept', Macklin argued that bioethics doesn't need the concept of dignity, because the concept of autonomy is sufficient.

Let's turn, then, to autonomy.

AUTONOMY

Most commonly, privacy's value is located in autonomy, via arguments proposing that privacy invasions can restrict our ability to think freely, act freely and express ourselves fully. Privacy invasions, it is argued, can promote adherence to *what is conventionally regarded as right*, rather than a reasoned adherence to *what is right*. These arguments fit the digital context well. As Shannon Vallor writes: 'Surveillance technologies that work too well in making us act "rightly" in the short term may short-change our moral and cultural growth in the long term.'

For Kant, autonomy played an unconditional role in morality, such that individuals should act in such a way as to respect and promote the ability of others to determine their own lives. Indeed, Kant regarded autonomy as the foundation of human dignity: dignity involves observing the moral law, but also being autonomous with respect to it by *self-legislating* one's morality. Herein lies a paradox central to Kant: morality is self-generated, but is also universal and immutable. And for Kant, the antithesis of an autonomous will is the heteronomous will, governed by something other than a self-given law dictated by reason.

Two centuries later, the value of individual autonomy has become so well-established that its role is rarely questioned in applied ethics or legal philosophy. However, there is little consensus as to what the concept means. As philosophers Catriona Mackenzie and Natalie Stoljar note: bioethicists often construe autonomy as informed consent; liberal political theorists consider autonomy in terms of the right to non-interference; and Rawlsian liberals tend to think of autonomy in Kantian terms as the capacity for rational self-legislation. Mackenzie responds to this confusion by proposing three distinct *axes* of autonomy: the self-determination axis identifies external, structural conditions for autonomy; the self-governance axis identifies internal conditions, which comprise having the requisite skills and capacities to choose and to act; and the self-authorisation axis involves regarding oneself as authorised to exercise practical control over one's life. Together, these three causally interdependent axes define free moral agents. On this view, my autonomy is not determined by me alone, but also by external factors. What's more, autonomy is not an 'on' or 'off' proposition. There are degrees of autonomy, just as there are degrees of privacy.

The finer points are up for debate, but in general terms we can think of autonomy as the ability to steer one's own ship.

And the concept figures prominently in the privacy literature. In the 1960s and '70s, jurists and philosophers including Bloustein, Fried and philosopher Stanley Benn all proposed explicitly Kantian justifications for privacy involving autonomy. More recently, Joseph Kupfer has argued that 'privacy is essential to the development and maintenance of an autonomous self'. As Adam Moore writes: 'According to these theorists, privacy is morally valuable because it protects and promotes the sovereign and autonomous actions of individuals – since autonomy is morally valuable privacy must be as well.'

In its strongest form, the argument proposes that there can be no autonomy without privacy. But, as Moor argues, privacy and autonomy come apart: 'Privacy is not an essential condition for autonomy. It is conceivable to have autonomy without privacy.' Some privacy violations, particularly trivial ones, will presumably have no impact on autonomy. A second version of the argument is that people tend to act differently if they think they are being watched. Famously, US politician Hubert Humphrey said: 'If we can never be sure whether or not we are being watched and listened to, all our actions will be altered and our very character will change.' This version of the argument is common and compelling.

I'm going to defend a more qualified version of the argument:

that *some* invasions of privacy compromise autonomy. Earlier, I mentioned CreepShots. On its website, CreepShots says the 'creeps' who surreptitiously take and share photos ought, if challenged, to invoke *their* right to privacy: 'If you see someone trying to catch you by looking over your shoulder at your phone/camera then politely tell him/her to stop invading your privacy.' Presumably, 'creeps' feel that such interruptions curtail their autonomy. I have already mentioned Google Glass, which arguably failed because of concerns about privacy and autonomy. As Chris Edwards wrote in the online magazine *Digerati*:

> Google Glass created an environment where people were
> subjected to the potential for 'always on' recording. Living
> like this, with a constant fear of being caught on camera, alters
> how people behave. Glass also gave prospective stalkers and
> creeps in general the ultimate tool for taking invasive photos of
> women in public without their knowledge.

Edwards is suggesting that the prospect of secret surveillance by Google Glass is wrong because it alters behaviour.

How, exactly?

In 1971, Stanley Benn wrote that invasions of privacy are constraints upon the 'self-creative enterprise' of living. People act differently among others, he noted. When we are alone, we act a certain way; among others, we become conscious that we are being judged from others' perspectives, and hence we are liable to modify our actions. This is so even when we merely *suspect* we are being observed, although in fact we are not. Benn thus argued against non-consensual surveillance (unless there exist strong reasons for it). This includes secret surveillance, which knowingly and deliberately alters the conditions of the person being spied upon, and thus fails to respect them as a person: 'Respect for someone as a person, as a chooser, implies respect for him as one engaged on a kind of self-creative enterprise, which could be disrupted, distorted, or frustrated even by so limited an intrusion as watching.'

Benn argues that watching, and the trespass upon privacy that such watching entails, compromises an individual's autonomy. This seems obvious if the surveillance is known. Yet even if the surveillance is secret, autonomy is being undermined to the extent that a person is no longer able to make informed choices, simply because they are unaware of the surveillance. The self-creative enterprise of living is stunted.

Above, we met Peeping Tom, who is secretly spying on a woman. I argued that even if Tom neither shares nor exploits this footage – aside from satisfying his immediate voyeuristic impulses – her dignity has been violated. To this Benn would add that her autonomy has suffered too, given that she is conducting her life without full knowledge of the prevailing circumstances. The problem becomes clearer when we think of autonomy more broadly, and women generally. If women know that hackers, companies and government agencies are sometimes able to access webcams surreptitiously, they might put sticky tape over their webcams, just as Mark Zuckerberg does. Alternatively, they might modify their behaviour in a way they would prefer not to, but feel is necessary given that their smartphone, laptop and internet-connected fridge all enable covert surveillance. Tom's actions have a direct effect on his victim, and an indirect effect on women generally. If women know that websites such as CreepShots exist, they might dress differently, or avoid public spaces altogether.

In other cases, invasions of privacy compromise autonomy even more directly. If I know my car is being tracked, I may not drive places I would otherwise visit. If all my credit card transactions are being stored, I may avoid certain purchases. If my every click is being recorded, I may not visit websites I would otherwise be keen to frequent. The 'self-creative enterprise' that is my life has been compromised.

Casting life as a self-creative enterprise has a further advantage: it recognises that life is a process of constant change, growth and reinvention. Over time, people may eat different food. They may redraw their politics. They may change gender. In some ways, how-ever, this notion of change runs counter to the spirit of the internet, where all data can be collected and collated. In chapter 1, I described the way that the internet is making it harder for people to be ephem-eral. Increasingly, as more and more of our digital interactions are recorded, we live in a state of 'digital eternity'. Our digital identi-ties can be enduring, even as we ourselves are in flux. To this end, some users are adopting strategies such as automatically deleting old tweets. As @wibbly notes: 'Twitter is not for my permanent writing. My messages here are pruned automatically. I reserve the right to change and develop as a human.'

Of course, it might be argued that my behaviour is likely to *improve* if I think I'm being watched and recorded for eternity. If I know there are surveillance cameras, I may be less likely to swear in public, for instance, and more likely to volunteer for charity. This approach underpins China's social credit system. However, if we value autonomy, our goal surely is that citizens *choose* to refrain from rudeness and *choose* to perform good deeds. If autonomy mat-ters, then it is not enough that citizens act rightfully merely because they fear widespread surveillance. A surveillance society with a minimum of privacy may well be less rude, but it will certainly be less free. (And an important caveat here is that privacy can never rightfully be invoked as a cloak for criminality.)

Privacy gives us the space to be nonconformist. In *On Liberty*, Mill wrote that liberty is a school for character: 'A person whose desires and impulses are his own – are the expression of his own nature, as it has been developed and modified by his own culture

– is said to have a character.' To this, Jeffrey Reiman adds that *privacy* is a school for character, sheltering people from conformity and allowing them to become the sorts of people who are not vulnerable. If our goal is to foster strong-willed citizens who are able to resist social pressures, he writes, then we must first give them privacy, in order that they can gain experience making and acting upon their own judgments. While they are vulnerable, they need privacy in order to become the sorts of people who are less vulnerable to conformity. 'In short, the vast majority of actual people need privacy for free action, and those who do not, needed privacy to become that way,' writes Reiman.

In the same spirit, Ruth Gavison notes that in certain spheres of life, including artistic expression and intellectual development, people need freedom from close and constant scrutiny to flourish. It is privacy that affords people the space, both intellectual and emotional, to contemplate unpopular ideas without the pressure of social disapproval and sanctions: 'Privacy is needed to enable the individual to deliberate and establish his opinions.'

Privacy thus serves as a shield. If a person is gay, then homosexuality is their individual standard. However, that might contradict the prevailing social norm of heterosexuality, even in a liberal society, where beliefs or behaviours that stray from the norm can arouse hostility. This prospect may inhibit a person from forming a gay relationship. It is privacy, Gavison argues, that ensures social norms do not govern such behaviour, which is particularly valuable when social norms are, say, homophobic, racist or misogynistic.

As Charles Fried put it in 1968, privacy helps defend our liberty when it allows us to do or say things that are unpopular or unconventional. Without the freedom of thought that privacy brings, we risk becoming a conformist member of a compliant herd. In the words of Edward Bloustein:

The man who is compelled to live every minute of his
life among others and whose every need, thought, desire,
fancy or gratification is subject to public scrutiny, has been
deprived of his individuality and human dignity. Such an
individual merges with the mass. His opinions, being public,
tend never to be different; his aspirations, being known,
tend always to be conventionally accepted ones; his feelings,
being openly exhibited, tend to lose their quality of unique
personal warmth and to become the feelings of every man.
Such a being, although sentient, is fungible; he is not an
individual.

Subject to public scrutiny? Given Edward Snowden's leaks and
the Cambridge Analytica scandal, internet users can fairly suspect
that every click, drag and interaction is potentially being observed.
As a result, there's the real risk that we're losing what it is that makes
each of us an individual.

Research shows that behaviours are changing. In 2016, Andrea
Peterson reported US Census Bureau data that showed some internet users have stopped expressing their opinions in comment threads
and forums. Also in 2016, research by Elizabeth Stoycheff revealed
that awareness of surveillance practices can stifle the expression of
minority political views. This, she wrote, can have a chilling effect
on democratic discourse: 'Knowing one's online activities are subject
to government interception and believing these surveillance practices are necessary for national security play important roles in influ-
encing conformist behavior.'

The risk here is no less than an infantilised populace. Jeffrey
Reiman notes that a lack of privacy impoverishes people's inner life,
making them vulnerable to external oppression. People without
privacy – infantilised and lacking a vibrant inner life – won't just
be easy to oppress. They won't *need* to be oppressed, because their

one-dimensional outlook will never see the need to be anything but compliant.

Just like Hannah Arendt, Reiman draws a direct link between the loss of privacy and the rise of autocracy. More recently, whistle-blower Edward Snowden has warned of the dangers of surveillance states that spy on their own populations. 'We are building the biggest weapon for oppression in the history of mankind,' Snowden said in the film *Citizenfour*. The fear is that citizens who are subject to pervasive surveillance can have their privacies and weaknesses exploited in a way that renders the government invincible. Such a privacy-obliterating totalitarianism is the dystopian vision described in Orwell's *1984*. Stripped of privacy, citizens are enslaved. They become, to use Kant's language, heteronomous.

In many cases, the value of privacy is interconnected with our autonomy. When our privacy is invaded, we are likely to be less free. Indeed, privacy doesn't just protect freedom, it *constitutes* freedom. Jeffrey Reiman gives the example of driving to destination X at time T. In the digital age this act has become more complex: 'It now becomes driving to X at T and creating a record of driving to X at T.' Hence some freedom has been lost. 'I am no longer free to do the act ... *without leaving a record.*' Attacks on privacy are attacks on our freedom as individuals.

But they are also attacks on us as beings-in-relation, as members of a family, a community, a society.

Traditional conceptions of autonomy posit the individual as atomised and isolated. These conceptions of autonomy, which dominate in the liberal tradition, privilege the individual over the social. Recently, however, scholars have enriched these traditional conceptions by fleshing out notions of relational autonomy. On this account, autonomy is multi-faceted, scaffolded by the observations and judgments of others. As philosophers Andrea Veltman and Mark Piper write, relational autonomy is no idealised abstraction, but allows for, and indeed depends upon, personal connections and social bonds.

In part, relational autonomy is a response to feminist arguments that traditional accounts of autonomy are 'coded masculine' by being individualistic and rationalistic. By contrast, relational conceptions of autonomy allow, in the words of Catriona Mackenzie and Natalie Stoljar, 'that persons are socially embedded and that agents' identities are formed within the context of social relationships and shaped by a complex of intersecting social determinants, such as race, class, gender, and ethnicity'. Autonomy thus aligns with the real world only when allowance is made for these many social determinants.

An adequate conception of relational autonomy recognises, as Catriona Mackenzie writes: that humans are vulnerable and dependent rather than self-sufficient and rational; that persons are embodied and socially, historically and culturally embedded in a way that constitutes their identities; and that social conditions restricting the exercise of self-determination are unjust. To foster autonomy, these conditions must be addressed. In other words, if we want to foster autonomy, we need to look to the bigger picture and wider context.

Relational autonomy provides a better account of the sort of autonomy that should be pursued as an ideal. What's more, relational autonomy chimes more harmoniously with privacy. After all, privacy is one of the key ways in which both a demarcation and a connection are drawn between self and society. Everyone is connected to others. However, these connections are qualified. Individuals are more connected to some than to others. And privacy is a key means by which individuals are constituted socially: it keeps some people at bay, but draws others closer. It informs an individual's identity, strengthening some ties and weakening others. Privacy is a means by which an individual situates herself (control) and is situated (externally limited access) within a society, both apart from it and a part of it.

Which brings us to relational privacy. When I first began researching relational privacy in 2015, inspired by the work of Catriona Mackenzie on relational autonomy, I struggled to find references in the academic literature. That's starting to change. In 2018, communications scholar Sara Bannerman published a paper entitled 'Relational privacy and the networked governance of the self'. Bannerman wrote: 'A relational theory of autonomy goes further than Western liberal notions of autonomy and provides a broader and more fruitful grounding for privacy law and policies.' She went on: 'A relational theory of privacy provides a descriptively and normatively superior foundation for thinking about privacy.'

Indeed, just as we ought to aspire to an autonomy that is relational, so too we ought to conceptualise privacy as relational. This is particularly evident on the internet, where a growing body of research is showing that data revealing one person simultaneously reveals many others. Most obviously, this point is clear from the shadow profiles created by social networks, which depend upon a 'privacy leak factor'. Even if I never go online, my friends will have inadvertently shared enough data about me that many of my private details can be gleaned.

Individual privacy is dependent upon an individual's community, write Emre Sarigol, David Garcia and Frank Schweitzer, and online social networks harness this dependency. Privacy, they suggest, is a 'collective concept': 'In an interlinked community, an individual's privacy is a complex property, where it is in constant mutual relationship with the systemic properties and behavioral patterns of the community at large … [W]e should consider privacy as a collective concept.'

Similarly, Shannon Vallor notes that individual data is, in fact, more than just individual data: 'Information about me is *also* usually information about the others with whom I share my life, and thus to focus only on the question of whether *I* have something to hide is a profoundly solipsistic attitude to privacy concerns.'

Given that my ethical grounding comes from Kant, it may come as a surprise that I am now advocating a relational and collective approach. Truth is, Kant and relationality fit well. While Paul Formosa has argued that Kant's account of autonomy is compatible with modern accounts of relational autonomy, philosopher Sharon Anderson-Gold has mounted a Kantian defence of privacy along relational lines. Traditionally, scholars have assumed that Kant's strict prohibition on lying (which, in any case, I will challenge in the next chapter) was attended by the equally strict necessity of truth-telling. This, it would seem, leaves no room for privacy. However, Anderson-Gold locates a Kantian argument for privacy in 'the duties that we have to respect the humanity of others and to promote the moral development of future generations'. Anderson-Gold then argues that reticence can be a virtue, in the form of non-disclosure about ourselves, and in the form of not responding to the faults of others. Hence it is the public and social aspect of privacy that is valuable: 'A Kantian defence of privacy is not focused so much on individual rights or welfare as it is on the character of our public–social culture.'

Online, perhaps even more than offline, privacy is contingent on those around us. If one individual has her privacy invaded, the privacy of others is thereby invaded too. At the same time, privacy *informs* our relationships with those around us. Without the relational autonomy that relational privacy brings, ours would be a world significantly more homogenous and more heteronomous.

In other words, none of us is fully free. We are all, to some extent, constrained: by our DNA; by our bank balance; by our relationships. Our freedom is necessarily imperfect. It is our imperfect freedom that is meaningful, and worth safeguarding.

RELATIONSHIPS

On Facebook, whenever a friend has a birthday, users are notified via email alerts. 'Today is Jane Roe's birthday. Wish Jane Roe a happy birthday Wednesday, August 10.' For busy people, this is a boon, particularly since anyone with a Facebook account is required to supply a birthdate.

Not everyone is a fan, however, including writer Sam Biddle:

> On Facebook, your birthday is automated and empty because nobody has to devote a single shred of mental energy to remembering or celebrating it ... Your birthday used to be an event – now it's a notification ... The next logical step is having Facebook just post 'happy birthday, buddy!' on your behalf at 12:01 AM every year. The intimacy is gone. The thoughtfulness is gone. And that's sad.

Facebook has rendered automatic something that was once contingent and human. For some people, birthdays are a tight-knit affair. Perhaps they only want a handful of close friends to know their birthdate. Perhaps they don't want to celebrate or mark the occasion. But the default position on Facebook is that birthdays are a public matter. As a result, the distinctions between our various liaisons are in danger of being lost.

I have been arguing that we ought to think of both autonomy and privacy in relational terms, rather than in the individualised terms that have traditionally dominated. In this section, I am going to mount a linked argument: that privacy's value lies in the role it plays in our relationships. Indeed, I'm going to argue that privacy is essential for relationships. It is a mechanism that enables me, on the one hand, to withdraw from others, and, on the other hand, to connect with others. The privacies I withhold matter, but the privacies

I share matter too, and these various privacies are constitutive of my relationships. In a literal way, my argument thus adopts a relational approach, locating privacy's value in our ability to make and keep social ties.

With this argument, I'm in good company. In 1968, Charles Fried wrote that privacy is as necessary for love, trust and friendship as oxygen is for combustion. Fried argued that our relationships depend on the selective, deliberate, discretionary sharing of our inner selves with others. We might share nearly all of ourselves with our lovers; we might share much of ourselves with our friends; we might share a more limited part of ourselves with acquaintances. For Fried, a person who will not share of herself cannot have a friendship or a love relationship. Conversely, a person who shares *all* of herself with everyone without discrimination cannot have friendships or love relationships either, because there would be no way to differentiate close relationships from distant relationships. Fried writes:

> It is my thesis that privacy is not just one possible means among
> others to insure some other value, but that it is necessarily
> related to ends and relations of the most fundamental sort:
> respect, love, friendship and trust. Privacy is not merely a good
> technique for furthering these fundamental relations; rather
> without privacy they are simply inconceivable ... To make
> clear the necessity of privacy as a context for respect, love,
> friendship and trust is to bring out also why a threat to privacy
> seems to threaten our very integrity as persons.

Individualistic conceptions of privacy suggest that one can only have a private life by *escaping* the limitations imposed by social constraints. By contrast, a relational account of privacy sees social 'constraints' as necessary for privacy. Sometimes, ironically, these constraints are liberating. Social ties are not what we need to escape to have privacy; rather, they help to inform and create our privacy. In my family, it may be an unspoken principle that politics is a private matter, not to be discussed in public. This norm matters, both to my condition of privacy, but also to my relationships within my family. Breaching this tacit understanding would involve a breach of trust.

As James Rachels points out, privacy is morally valuable because it enables persons to control the *patterns of behaviour* necessary for them to build stable and meaningful relationships. People behave differently around different people, Rachels writes, and what constitutes appropriate behaviour varies significantly from one relationship to another. A man behaves differently with his wife, his mother-in-law and his boss, and in this there is nothing dishonest or hypocritical.

In response, some have said that it is phony and inauthentic for an individual to have various modes of behaviour, and that all these social 'masks' hide the 'real' person underneath. In 2010, Mark Zuckerberg echoed this view, saying: 'Having two identities for yourself is an example of a lack of integrity.' This suggests that not revealing information about oneself can be the moral equivalent of deception. (Has Zuckerberg changed his mind on this point? I don't know. The nature of 'digital eternity', which I described above, ensures that he is still indelibly associated with these words, whether or not he still believes them.)

People *do* have multiple versions of themselves, and this is evident online. In her book *It's Complicated,* danah boyd writes that we tend to have several digital selves. These can be playful and sometimes experimental, but at a minimum they enable us to differentiate various social situations. It's true offline too. As Rachels writes: 'The different patterns of behaviour are (partly) what define the different relationships.' In each relationship, he writes, there exists an appreciation of what kind of knowledge about one another it is appropriate to share and to know.

Of course, some say that our relationships have nothing to do with privacy. As Jeffrey Reiman writes: 'I think that intimate relations are a function of how much people care about each other, not how much they know about each other'. Reiman says that a person can share intimate, private information with a doctor, and yet have no relationship whatsoever. True enough. Similarly, philosophers Dean Cocking and Jeanette Kennett dismiss what they call the 'secrets view', arguing that friendship is about trust and caring, and not about the sharing of personal information.

Ok, but imagine a close friend of yours decides to get married. She tells others, but not you. Unless there are extenuating circumstances (perhaps she tried to reach you but couldn't; perhaps she was worried about the impact of the news) the failure to share such personal news might dent your relationship. Granted, relationships are indisputably about caring. But relationships are also about knowing. What's more, knowing and caring are linked. It is through the sharing of privacies that care is sometimes expressed, and it is on the sharing of privacies that care is sometimes built.

Further, it is on the sharing (and withholding) of privacies that *trust* is built. If I am in a monogamous relationship, I want my partner to be faithful. One way to monitor such fidelity is to know everything about her by tracking every movement and communication. That, however, would be creepy. And untrusting. It leaves no room for betrayal. It is precisely the prospect of betrayal – made possible by the fact that partners afford one another privacies and other freedoms that enable infidelity – that makes fidelity meaningful, and thereby solidifies a relationship. Privacy is essential for strong ties, thanks both to what is shared and what is not shared.

This argument holds on a larger scale too. In 1997, sociologists Richard Ericson and Kevin Haggerty identified the concept of a 'risk society'. In such a society, institutions that deal with individuals collect data on that individual and her activities, and this data is then compared to profiles of 'trustworthy' and 'untrustworthy', and 'good' and 'bad', so that the institution can modify its treatment of that individual. Such societies are fear-driven: 'Collective fear and foreboding underpin the value system of the unsafe society, perpetuate insecurity, and feed demands for more knowledge of risk.' In a risk society, ironically, increased surveillance doesn't quench fear, but creates new uncertainties which demand yet greater surveillance. Their argument prefigured the upscaling of surveillance in many countries following the terrorism of 11 September 2001.

Invasions of privacy can erode trust, one-on-one, but also society-wide. Conversely, respect for privacy can build trust, and thus foster relationships and society.

In saying that, though, I don't want to evoke the onion model. In the previous chapter, I argued that this model is inadequate to account for privacy. Similarly, I am not arguing here that our closest relationships are at the centre of an onion, and the more we share, the closer we are. Sometimes we keep privacies from those closest to us; sometimes we share privacies with strangers. Sure, a nude portrait is more likely to be private than a clothed portrait. However, the level of privacy of any item or data shifts and changes according to context.

Precisely how privacy builds relationships is difficult to discern. We see that context matters. We can also see that privacy is not the only ingredient needed for love, trust and friendship. For instance, care is crucial (and sometimes respect for privacy can express care). But the important point is the larger one: relationships cannot function without privacy.

This is particularly evident in disagreements. At times, writes Ruth Gavison, people in a relationship will be unable to traverse the gulf of their disagreement. They may even be intolerant of the other's values or behaviour, despite acknowledging the legitimacy of such values or behaviour. In such cases, privacy allows for interaction without the need for addressing the disagreement. In other words, privacy affords *practical* tolerance in lieu of *actual* tolerance. Privacy enables people in important relationships to maintain their individuality. For instance, writes Gavison, a spouse may understand a partner's need to fantasise, even if knowing about those fantasies would be hurtful, and hence 'respect for privacy is a way to force ourselves to be as tolerant as we know we should be'.

In this way, privacy is an individual good. When her privacy is respected, a spouse is afforded the freedom to fantasise. And this is the way privacy is typically defended. As privacy scholar Priscilla Regan wrote in 2016: 'Most of the legal, philosophical, and social science thinking about privacy emphasises its value to the individual with less attention to its value to society.' However, privacy is also a public and social good. It makes the spouse who respects privacy more tolerant, it enables the couple's relationship to function more smoothly, and it contributes to a harmonious society.

Our identities are built on our links with others. We are fathers, sisters, daughters, lovers, friends and more. I do not choose to be my parents' son, and so I do not choose the obligations (and the rights) that attend being a son, and yet I am bound by (and entitled to) them. I am a social being. And the limits of my privacy can only ever be determined in light of my social ties. Privacy (like autonomy) is relational, existing in and through my relationships and social ties. And privacy, in turn, helps to determine and forge my social ties. It enables me to make and maintain relationships.

On the internet, however, things get tricky. The internet (and the way it is used) is challenging privacy, and with it our relationships.

For many, romantic relationships have been transformed by the arrival of platforms including OkCupid (an online dating service that matches users via multiple choice quizzes), Tinder (where one user can chat with another if both swipe right on each other's profile) and Grindr (a location-based hook-up service for gay and bisexual men). That's not to mention Ashley Madison, which exists to enable extramarital liaisons. Its motto: 'Life is short. Have an affair!'

The way people make and maintain relationships on these platforms is in stark contrast to the way people make and maintain relationships offline, which has a lot to do with the way people share their privacies. Offline, people often reveal themselves to prospective partners over time. Online, people can open themselves up at the outset. The multiple choice questions answered by OkCupid users range widely over topics including politics, movies and sex. The topics also include religion, with questions such as: 'How important is religion/God in your life?' Here, exposure happens at the start. The personal is exposed quickly, and widely.

In September 2019, *Wired* writer Jason Parham described the website OnlyFans, where 'influencers' share revealing and risque content. Formed in London in 2016, OnlyFans is a subscription-based service with specific channels that show 'topless bathroom selfies and videos of influencers masturbating or engaging in sexual intercourse. Occasionally they might upload clips of themselves cooking or exercising in the buff.' Parham then describes how he became fascinated with this world, subscribing to several channels.

> I signed up for a few accounts in the name of research; soon
> they became gateways to private fulfilment. I was, I realised,
> getting addicted. But the reason I couldn't look away was
> not just about being turned on. The more I watched these
> influencers, the more I felt drawn to them as people. They
> were opening up; I was reaching toward ... The parameters of
> intimacy and fame were being gradually redrawn in front of
> my eyes.

And the parameters of privacy right along with them. How far would these influencers go? How vulnerable would they make themselves? How exposed would they – and he – be? Parham found himself 'drawn to them as people'. The confessional article illustrates the strong link between privacy and relationships. Or, in this case, faux relationships based on asymmetrical sharing of private content.

On the internet, we are sharing our privacies in completely new ways. These privacies are not merely being shared with prospective partners. They are also being shared with digital services, and hence, in all likelihood, with advertisers, data brokers and governments. In 2014, it was reported that Egypt was using Grindr to locate and arrest gay men. More recent reports revealed that Grindr was sharing data with third parties that included users' HIV status.

Romance and sex are changing. Friendship is changing too. For millennia, philosophers have regarded friendship as vitally important. 'Without friends, no one would choose to live, even if he possessed all other goods,' wrote Aristotle in the *Nicomachean Ethics*. Two millennia later, Kant wrote in *The Metaphysics of Morals* that we have a duty of friendship: 'Human beings have a duty of friendship ... striving for friendship (as a maximum of good disposition toward each other) is a duty set by reason, and no ordinary duty but an honourable one.'

Aristotle and Kant had a lot to say on the subject. Both identified three categories of friendship, arguing that the best friendships are extremely rare. Aristotle called them complete, or perfect, friendships; and Kant called them 'moral friendships', writing that they are marked out by 'the complete confidence of two persons in revealing their secret judgments and feelings to each other, as far as such disclosures are consistent with mutual respect'. On social media, by contrast, it can be difficult to separate categories of friends. Friendships tend to exist on one level. Privacies are often shared with one and all, as our multiple identities are compressed into one. A status update can be seen by a 'friend' one has never met just as it can be seen by a spouse. danah boyd calls this 'context collapse'.

Aristotle further argued that meaningful friendship takes time to build: 'A wish for friendship arises swiftly, but friendship itself does not.' Friendship involves getting to know one another over time. Again, this account runs counter to the digital ethos of sharing one's data widely and quickly.

And Kant argued that friendships require an element of restraint. For Kant, friendship is 'the union of two persons through equal mutual love and respect'. Love and respect act as opposing forces: love is attraction, bidding friends to come closer; respect, by contrast, requires them to keep a proper distance. Unlike love, respect constitutes a 'limitation on intimacy, which is expressed in the rule that even the best of friends should not make themselves too familiar with each other'. Online, however, the friendships that prevail often involve sharing and exposure at the expense of restraint.

There are many other accounts of friendship, of course. But clearly friendships made and maintained online will struggle to satisfy Aristotle's and Kant's prescriptions, particularly for the best of friendships. This has a lot to do with the way privacies are withheld, and not withheld.

In the 1990s, British anthropologist Robin Dunbar argued that our brains as humans ensure that we are able to maintain only 150 stable social relationships. These are people whom we contact at least once a year and whom we know well, including the details of how they relate to others we know. This is why historically all sorts of social groups, from military units to subsistence villages, tended to have about 150 members.

In 2014, however, a study from the Pew Research Center found that the average number of Facebook friends among US users was 338, more than double Dunbar's number. Fifteen per cent of users had more than 500 friends. Subsequent research suggests that the global number is now considerably lower, but not in all age groups. In 2018, Australian Facebook users aged 18 to 30 had an average of almost 400 friends. Facebook sets the limit at 5000.

Perhaps social media is rewriting the rules. Perhaps we can now have more genuine friends and bigger social networks. In 2016, Dunbar explicitly tested this question. After examining two large samples from the UK, Dunbar found that 150 remains the magic number. That's the number of people with whom an individual can have real reciprocated relationships and for whom that individual feels obligations and would willingly do favours. As Dunbar says, 'People can have 500 or even 1000 friends on Facebook, but all they are doing is including people who we would normally call acquaintances or people we just recognise by sight but don't know very well.' Like Aristotle and Kant, Dunbar offers a hierarchy of friendship, and says that very close friends are rare. There are six layers of friends, he says. We tend to have five intimate friends, 15 best friends, 50 good friends, 150 friends, 500 acquaintances and 1500 people we can recognise. Clearly the way Facebook uses the word 'friend' is not how Aristotle, Kant and Dunbar use it.

In response, some internet users deliberately split their online and offline selves. In her book *Alone Together*, MIT sociologist and psychologist Sherry Turkle describes a 16-year-old Facebook user named Audrey who treats the internet like a break from real life, and says that the two ought to be kept separate. In her dealings with classmates, Audrey thinks that what happens on the internet should stay on the internet. If a revelation is made on Facebook, her friends should act in real life as if it never happened. That way, people's real life privacy and dignity can be respected – in appearance if not in fact. For Audrey, this makes for a confusing set of rules about how to behave offline and online.

An extension of this approach, adopted by many of the students I teach, is to cultivate contrasting circles of friends in different social networks. Close friends on Snapchat; a wider circle on Instagram; old high school friends and family on Facebook. On each social network, these students reveal themselves in different ways. This is how they allow for the multiple versions of themselves they wish to present, and it affords them a measure of discretion as to what is shared with whom.

The internet allows us to connect as never before, and the impacts are still emerging. Psychologist Aric Sigman argues that social media undermines social skills and the ability to read body language. Neuroscientist John T. Cacioppo has described the importance of the chemical exchange that attends face-to-face contact, which stimulates the trust-building hormone oxytocin. And Sherry Turkle has spent her career studying the effects of technology on relationships. Initially, she was optimistic, but now she is worried about the effects on both our privacy and our relationships: 'Some would say that we have already completed a forbidden experiment, using ourselves as subjects with no controls, and the unhappy findings are in: we are as connected as we've never been connected before, and we seem to have damaged ourselves in the process.'

Others are more positive, of course. Such negativity is hardly unanimous. But what is clear, I'm suggesting, is that privacy and relationships are intimately linked. Privacy is a prerequisite for love, trust and friendship. It lets me draw some closer, and keep others at a distance. And given how dramatically the internet *is* impacting upon our privacy, it stands to reason that our relationships are also being significantly affected.

SOCIETY AND DEMOCRACY

The final justification for privacy – following on from dignity, autonomy and relationships – involves society and democracy. This stems directly from the key point I have been making: individual privacy transcends the individual. As sociologist Irwin Altman wrote in 1975, privacy is 'an interpersonal event, involving relationships among people'. Or, as law scholars Joshua Fairfield and Christoph Engel wrote 40 years later, in 2015, 'the relevant privacy unit is the group, rather than the individual'.

Genealogy websites that analyse DNA data are a prime example. By submitting a sample, I may reveal that my children are at risk of developing certain congenital conditions. This data would be highly valuable for a health insurer. As Priscilla Regan writes: 'The objective then becomes how to get individuals to realize that their individual behavior affects not only themselves but others as well – and in some cases others whom they care about deeply, for example, family members.'

In early 2019, MIT's *Technology Review* reported that more people in the US purchased consumer DNA tests in 2018 than in all previous years combined. 'The testing frenzy is creating two superpowers — Ancestry of Lehi, Utah, and 23andMe of Menlo Park, California,' wrote Antonio Regalado. 'These privately held companies now have the world's largest collections of human DNA.' The tests involve spitting in a tube or taking a swab of saliva and cost as little as US$59. As more and more people submit samples, the relationships between nearly all Americans are being revealed, including those who never took the test. As Ancestry's privacy statement warns, 'Once discoveries are made, we can't undo them.'

This raises a question about the nature of data. Just what sort of resource is this DNA data, exactly? Is it something I own, like a car? Is it something I own together with others, like a house I bought with a spouse? Or is it something more intangible that resists ownership, like a lake? The answer has a major effect on our entitlements, and also on the value we ascribe to privacy. If it's like a car, I can largely do what I like with it; if it's like a house, then

I will need to allow for the other owners; if it's like a lake, there may well be restrictions that take into account the interests of many other people.

In 2002, Priscilla Regan argued that data fell into the third category. She explained privacy with reference to 'the tragedy of the commons'. Following on from Lawrence Lessig's idea of an 'intellectual commons', which led to the release of 'creative commons' licences for content creators to share their work freely, Regan built an argument for an information ecosystem. Personal information, she argued, is a 'common pool resource' akin to a natural resource such as water: the resource is available to more than one person; other users are hard to exclude; and the possibility of degradation due to overuse exists.

In such an information ecosystem, Regan argued that there can be a series of negative impacts: first, the common pool resource can be overloaded; second, the resource can become polluted by incomplete or inaccurate data; and third, there is the negative impact of overharvesting, as data is shared more and more widely. Once the resource system is degraded, public services including health care and public safety are compromised, and businesses suffer too. What's more, if users believe personal data is being overused and exploited, they will lose trust in data-handling practices more widely. The result can be a vicious circle: less sharing; more surveillance; lower trust; less sharing; more surveillance; lower trust; and so on. This is the 'risk society' described earlier.

It's a compelling argument. Clearly the uses and abuses of data can have adverse effects, including overloading, pollution and overharvesting. Once mined, oil can't be put back. Perhaps it's the same with data, the new oil? In this section, I want to extend the argument I have been making about the collective nature of privacy. I want to argue that privacy is essential for society and democracy to thrive, and that this is particularly evident online.

In this regard, several academics have categorised digital privacy as *networked*. Media scholars Alice Marwick and danah boyd have described our 'networked publics', arguing that we need to start thinking of privacy in a way that moves 'from an individualistic frame to one that is networked'. And it is 'networked privacy' that must be identified and fostered. Whether we describe privacy as relational, collective or networked, the point is the same. Individual privacy is socially constituted and socially meaningful. This means that your privacy is for my benefit, and vice versa.

This point, it turns out, is particularly significant in a democracy. In chapter 2, I described the role of Cambridge Analytica during the US presidential election of 2016. Employed by the Trump campaign, Cambridge Analytica unethically harvested personal data from Facebook. Voters were then targeted with personalised advertising: Democrats were targeted with messaging to keep them away from polling booths; Republicans were encouraged to turn out to vote; and undecided voters were targeted with advertisements tailored to convince them to vote for Trump.

The exact impact of Cambridge Analytica on the 2016 election is impossible to calculate. But before the company was shut down in May 2018, it boasted of its involvement in dozens of elections, in the US, Africa, Europe and beyond. Its parent, SCL Group, boasted of determining a closely run election in Trinidad and Tobago via the 'Do So' campaign, which looked like a grassroots resistance movement generated by young black voters, but was in fact part of a campaign devised to convince young black voters to abstain. Here is the fear raised earlier: that humans can be hacked, and that democracy can be hacked right along with them.

As I've noted, philosophers have long drawn a link between invasions of privacy and totalitarianism. Without privacy, they say, citizens may be reluctant to explore unpopular views. Further, a government that knows too much about its citizens will be able to abuse that knowledge. Cambridge Analytica realised those arguments for a digital age, revealing how data mining and behavioural analytics can be combined with psychological profiling and targeting in a way that renders democracy vulnerable to hidden and exploitative manipulations.

Admittedly, not all nations are democratic. Some are one-party states. Even for these nations, I would argue, privacy is of fundamental value. Sometimes the value of privacy lies in the way it protects dignity and autonomy. Sometimes its value lies in the way it enables relationships. And more often than we might realise its value lies in the way it plays a key role in the functioning of society and democracy. What's more, these justifications overlap, so that different values come to the fore in different circumstances. And in different countries, privacy will be valued in different ways.

Privacy represents something basic and distinctive among values. It exists to protect something important, something that other ethical and legal categories fail to cover satisfactorily. It may well be hard to define, and its value may not always be obvious, but underneath all the debate and disagreement lies a coherent concept of great value. As Ruth Gavison writes: 'The reasons for which we claim privacy in different situations are similar. They are related to the functions privacy has in our lives: the promotion of liberty, autonomy, selfhood, and human relations, and furthering the existence of a free society.'

Your privacy isn't only about you. It's also about you-in-relation, and about society. It's a public as well as an individual good.

Which means it matters for all of us, including Jodo Shinshu Buddhists. Earlier, I described the Jodo Shinshu belief that enlightenment could only be achieved by the attainment of *Musi*, or no-self, which involves relinquishing all privacies. However, even Jodo Shinshu Buddhists cannot relinquish *all* their privacy. There will be external limits upon what they can share, including clothes and walls and doors. And there are laws that insist that bodies stay covered and certain acts be kept out of the public eye. In some jurisdictions, for instance, this manifests as laws against 'indecent exposure' or 'obscene language'.

If every one of the world's inhabitants were a Jodo Shinshu Buddhist, it might be different. But as it stands, not one of us is entitled to relinquish every part of our privacy and live a life that is fully public.

In 2015, UK police announced they were investigating a new crime of 'cyber-flashing', after a female commuter received two images on her phone of an unknown man's penis. Clearly, the victim of this breach of privacy was not the person whose privacy was compromised (the man) but the person who witnessed the compromise (the woman). Here, the value of privacy lay in protecting society at large from one man's desire to expose himself.

Privacy norms exist to protect more than just the person whose privacy is at issue. Complex and complicated as it may be, privacy at heart concerns how individuals relate to others. Paradoxically, it both separates and connects. Sometimes it does both at once. Privacy is relational, collective and networked, and its value lies in its ability to isolate, but also in its power to bind. Without it, society would falter, and democracy would wither.

ESCAPE

Not every small loss of privacy enslaves us. Some such losses will be morally trivial. Other losses will be justified, even desirable. However, a due dose of privacy is required for all individuals and societies to flourish — even, I suggest, Jodo Shinshu Buddhists.

As an unwitting reality TV star, Truman Burbank seems to have no privacy whatsoever. And at first glance, his life seems perfect. Happily cocooned in suburbia, he navigates a quietly satis-fying existence, oblivious to the fact that his neighbours are extras, his wife is paid to be affectionate and an audience of many millions is watching his every move.

Inexorably, though, Truman begins to suspect that his life is playing out entirely in public. His dignity, autonomy and relation-ships are a facade. His society is a sham. He wants more. Seeking to escape, he is thwarted, until finally he encounters Christof, the god-like director of the show that has been a worldwide hit for all the 30 years of his life, and of which he has been the star.

'I know you better than you know yourself,' says Christof, who just happens to guard his own privacy with great zeal.

But Truman has a comeback.

'You never had a camera in my head,' he says.

For Truman, for Christof and for my five-year-old daughter, privacy matters. Even under the faux reality of a Hollywood dome, observed by hundreds of cameras, Truman had a modicum of pri-vacy. Now that he's escaped, he's going to find himself just as much of it as each of us deserves.

6

WHY YOU CANNOT CONSENT TO SELLING YOUR SOUL

Batman doesn't make a habit of trampling on the rights of citizens. To defeat the Joker, however, he deliberately breaches the privacy of millions.

In the 2008 film *The Dark Knight*, Batman is pursuing his nemesis, who has rigged two crowded ferries with explosives. To prevent a mass catastrophe, Batman must locate the Joker, and quickly. So he and his team at Wayne Enterprises design a city-wide surveillance system to intercept the high frequency signals emitted by the smartphones of all Gotham's citizens. Custom-built for mass surveillance, the system makes a neat metaphor for the NSA's clandestine monitoring of US citizens' mobile phones. In this way, Batman can keep watch over the whole city.

'Beautiful, isn't it?' asks Batman, showing off a wall of monitors.

Yes, but Lucius Fox, his chief of research and development, is dismayed.

'Beautiful. Unethical. Dangerous,' says Lucius. 'This is wrong.'

With mumbled gravitas, Batman responds that the database is encrypted and can be accessed by only one person: Lucius himself. Still, Lucius isn't happy.

'This is too much power for one person,' he says. 'Spying on 30 million people isn't part of my job description.'

Of course, soon Lucius relents, but with a caveat.

'I'll help you this one time,' Lucius says. 'But consider this my resignation. As long as this machine is at Wayne Enterprises, I won't be.'

The scene raises key issues about the ethics of privacy and technology. Both Batman and Lucius acknowledge it is unethical to engage in clandestine surveillance. For Lucius, this is wrong, on principle. By contrast, Batman is prepared to breach one ethical principle (respecting citizens' privacy) in order to uphold another (keeping citizens safe). Or perhaps Batman is thinking on consequentialist grounds, weighing up the potential benefits and harms to conclude that, in this case, the right thing to do is to invade people's privacy in order to save lives. In any case, Batman's view ultimately prevails, with the commitment that the technology will then be destroyed.

In effect, Batman has invented a device akin to Judith Jarvis Thomson's X-ray device, as described in chapter 4. And his invention reveals the significance of consent. The key to this breach of privacy, it seems, is that Gotham's residents are unwitting and hence unwilling. If they knew and gave their approval, there would presumably be no problem. Instead, Batman goes ahead, despite their lack of consent, in an act of vigilante justice. Does this lack of consent render Batman's action ethically impermissible? Or is there some larger factor at play that renders consent irrelevant?

Consent is at the heart of Batman's ethical dilemma, and it forms the subject of this chapter.

In chapters 1, 2 and 3, I described the way our internet use is challenging our privacy. In chapters 4 and 5, I argued that privacy matters for reasons including dignity, autonomy, relationships and democracy. In this chapter, I argue that we can remedy many of the problems attending digital privacy by turning to Kant's formula of humanity. Kant's formula enables us to see the issue of internet privacy more clearly. It also enables us to devise effective protections. Applying the formula, I argue, involves applying consent.

Specifically, it involves applying a two-tier model which overlays individual consent with *collective* consent.

First, we must ask: does the individual user consent to sharing her data? However, individual consent can be inadequate, particularly amid the convoluted and confusing notice-and-consent provisions that thrive on the internet. And in some cases, as Batman would argue, moral imperatives render individual consent irrelevant. What we need is another, second level, which we can think of as collective consent. Here we make the transition from ethics to politics to find a second layer of consent that overarches the first layer. This second layer is the law, which is itself drawn from morality.

In this chapter, then, I draw on Kant's ethics and politics to give a normative grounding for how privacy ought to be protected.

IS THE FORMULA OF HUMANITY
A FORMULA FOR PRIVACY?

Immanuel Kant didn't get out much. Born in Königsberg in 1724, he died there not quite 80 years later. In between, he never strayed far from his east Prussian base (which is now Kaliningrad in Russia). He studied at the University of Königsberg; he lectured at the University of Königsberg; he became a professor at the University of Königsberg. And the story goes that every morning he would walk precisely the same route at precisely the same time. So reliable was his morning constitutional that the burghers of Königsberg would set their watches by it.

Kant was a man of routine, not a man of the world. Outwardly, his life doesn't appear very interesting. He never married, never had kids and never became involved in a salacious scandal that shocked his hometown, let alone the world. Don't expect a Hollywood biopic any time soon. As for his *inner* life … Kant lived for philosophy, departing from the empiricism of Scottish thinker David Hume (who was 13 years his senior) to develop arguments that made him famous and influential during his own lifetime. Today, he remains one of the world's most celebrated philosophers – and also one of the most contested. Where his outer life was contained and steady, his inner life was expansive and provocative.

And one of his most significant works is the *Groundwork of the Metaphysics of Morals*, published in 1785. For a small book, it has serious heft. As noted by Oxford philosopher H.J. Paton, who translated the *Groundwork* from German into English in 1947: 'In spite of its horrifying title, Kant's *Groundwork of the Metaphysics of Morals* is one of the small books which are truly great: it has exercised on human thought an influence almost ludicrously disproportionate to its size.'

It is in the *Groundwork* that Kant sketches out his reason-based system of ethics. And at the heart of that system is the formula of humanity, which has been described as the central normative principle of Kantian ethics. It prescribes:

Act in such a way that you treat humanity, whether in your own person or in the person of any other, never simply as a means, but always at the same time as an end.

The formula is at once elementary and radical. It posits absolute moral worth not in an external entity such as a god, nor in a goal such as happiness, nor in a calculation of the greatest good for the greatest number. Rather, it locates the supreme good within ourselves, and within others. It locates the supreme good within *persons*. Today, echoes of the formula can be heard in stock phrases such as 'Don't use people', and 'Treat people with respect'.

In essence, it says that we must never treat persons as *things*, but as reasoning beings with dignity and autonomy who are free to chart their own course. This is captured in part by Kant's use of the term 'end', in the phrase 'treat humanity always as an end'. In this context, 'end' is shorthand for 'end-in-itself'. More accurately, the formula of humanity is known as 'the formula of humanity as end in itself'. The idea is that reasoning beings may never be treated as mere means, but only ever as agents who set ends for themselves by making plans and pursuing projects.

For Kant, the specific value of humanity lies in its rational capacities, because a rational being is able to set ends for her or himself. As Kant writes in the *Groundwork*, 'Rational nature sets itself out from all other things by the fact that it sets itself an end.' And elsewhere: 'Rational beings ... are called *persons* because their nature already marks them out as ends in themselves – that is, as something which ought not to be used merely as a means'. Humans, as rational beings, set ends for themselves; and all rational beings must treat all other rational beings as agents who set themselves ends.

In this way, reason is inextricably interlinked with autonomy and dignity (as I began to explore in the previous chapter). Reason enables a person to be autonomous, and it is reason and autonomy that confer upon a person dignity, the irreducible and absolute worth of humanity. As Kant writes, '*Autonomy* is therefore the ground of the dignity of human nature and of every rational nature.' In other words, reason, dignity and autonomy provide Kant's ethics with its normative grounding. And reason, dignity and autonomy command *respect*. As Kant writes, the rational nature of persons marks them out as *ein Gegenstand der Achtung*, meaning 'an object of respect/attention'. To this there can be no exception.

This is a key point: Kant's ethics are founded on the notion of not making yourself an exception. Rather, in his moral theory, Kant aimed to articulate a supreme moral principle, derived from reason, that holds true for all rational beings, without exception. He called this principle the *categorical imperative*. It is from the categorical imperative, Kant argued, that we can derive all our duties. Indeed, unlike approaches such as consequentialism and virtue ethics, Kant's ethics is duty-based, or 'deontological', a term that stems from the Greek word for duty, *deon*. Working purely by reasoning, Kant then presented his categorical imperative in three main forms: the formula of universal law; the formula of humanity; and the formula of autonomy. These three formulas serve different functions. Universality gives us the *form* of the moral law; rational nature or humanity as an end in itself gives us the *material* of the law; and autonomous legislation, by which the universal moral law is self-given, gives us a harmonious 'realm of ends' (see chapter 8). Intriguingly, Kant also wrote that all three of these versions are equivalent, describing them as 'precisely the same law', without properly justifying the claim. Philosopher Onora O'Neill calls this 'puzzling'. Rather than equivalent, I prefer to think of them as mutually reinforcing.

Kant himself said that his preferred approach for moral judgment involved an application of the formula of universal law, which prescribes: 'Act only on that maxim through which you can at the same time will that it should become a universal law'. But what is the maxim, or motivating principle, that underlies an action? Often, it's hard to say. For this reason and others, the formula of universal law has fallen out of favour among some Kantians.

The formula of humanity, by contrast, is regarded as intuitive and user-friendly. Kant himself described it as a 'supreme practical principle'. And despite Kant's stated preference for the formula of universal law, it turns out that the formula of humanity was his own preferred formula of application. As philosopher Allen Wood's analysis shows, it is from the formula of humanity that Kant derives, among many more, the duty against lying, the duty to develop our natural perfection, and the duties against self-love, contempt and giving scandal. What's more, these duties are all relevant for internet privacy. The formula is, writes Paul Formosa, a 'useable, coherent, and intuitively powerful principle … We can use the formula of humanity as a moral guide to what duties and obligations we have in particular cases.' I couldn't agree more. In fact, I regard the formula of humanity as the most powerful ethical prescription I've encountered.

And as it happens the formula of humanity is particularly well-suited to protecting privacy. As I showed in chapter 5, invasions of privacy can be harmful precisely because they impinge upon dignity and autonomy. In the way that the formula of humanity protects dignity and autonomy, it can protect privacy too. The formula of humanity also allows us to account for *degrees* of wrongness. Generally, the more harm that one intends to do to one's rational capacities, or to the rational capacities of others, the greater the wrong. This is significant for privacy, where some violations are more grievous and systemic than others.

Kant further wrote that the categorical imperative enables us to identify three distinct types of actions. 'An action which is compatible with the autonomy of the will is *permitted*,' writes Kant. 'One which does not harmonize with it is *forbidden*.' And a third category of action is *required* for respecting the autonomy of the will. All our actions thus fall into one of three categories: permitted; forbidden; or required.

On closer inspection, the formula of humanity can be divided into two subsidiary principles. The first is the mere means principle, taken from the command to 'treat humanity never merely as a means'. The second is the ends-in-themselves principle, taken from the phrase 'treat humanity always as an end'. Kant scholars disagree about how exactly these two principles relate to each other. For Onora O'Neill, the mere means principle is a subset of the ends-in-themselves principle. The latter requires more of us. For Paul Formosa, by contrast, the two principles are distinct, and a breach of one is not necessarily a breach of the other. For our purposes, we need note simply that *both* principles must be satisfied for compliance with the formula of humanity.

For its part, the mere means principle sets out what is morally impermissible. As philosopher Samuel Kerstein writes, 'In contemporary Kantian ethics, the mere means principle plays the role of a moral constraint: it limits what we may do, even in the service of promoting the overall good.' The mere means principle gives us what Kant called our *perfect* duties. That is, it can command us to do or not do a specific action. By contrast, the ends-in-themselves principle is open-ended. It gives us our *imperfect* duties by prescribing that we treat others as persons. This asks a good deal: it demands that we harmonise with their dignity, rather than merely fail to disrespect it. And for Kant, the overarching imperfect duties that guide us are asymmetrical. Toward ourselves, we have the duty of self-cultivation. That is, we must develop our own talents. Toward others, however, we have the duty of beneficence, which means we must further their self-given ends. In general terms, we must make others happy.

Unlike the ends-in-themselves principle, the mere means principle sets clear limits. And in what follows, the mere means principle is my focus. The question is: how can we know if we are treating humanity merely as a means? More specifically: how can we tell if we're encroaching on someone's privacy in a way that treats them merely as a means?

The answer lies in consent.

Before we come to consent, however, it's worth noting that Kant's approach has attracted objections. One concerns Kant's focus on *reason* as the source of human dignity and the moral worth of persons. What about the moral worth of animals? Or the environment? Don't they count too? In this vein, Australian philosopher Peter Singer has rejected the 'speciesism' of human dignity. Even Kant's contemporary, Jeremy Bentham, argued on behalf of 'less rational animals', suggesting that we ought not deduce moral worth from the question, 'Can they reason?' but from the question, 'Can they suffer?' These are important points, and there have been persuasive efforts to develop a more inclusive Kantian ethics. In 2013, philosopher Christine Korsgaard argued that animals must also be regarded as ends-in-themselves, given that for them things can be good or bad. As such, our rationality requires us to recognise their moral standing. In any case, for our purposes, these issues are not a key concern. Our focus is *human* privacy, which means that issues of the moral worth of animals or the environment don't arise.

Kant's focus on reason has led to a second objection: that humans are not nearly so rational after all. Science is increasingly demonstrating that humans are often *irrational*. Moral decisions hinge upon circumstances, with experiments showing that we're less likely to do good if we're in a hurry, or if there's a bad smell in the room. 'We're all susceptible to the irresistible pull of irrational behaviour,' write Ori and Rom Brafman in *Sway*, describing how a meticulous senior pilot abandoned all his training to take a risk that killed hundreds simply because he felt rushed. It's likely Kant would have been unsurprised by these findings. Recognising that human reason is flawed, Kant wrote that we are all imperfectly rational, subject to desires and inclinations. Hence Kant contrasted a divine will, which needs no categorical imperative, with the 'subjective imperfection ... of the human will'. Indeed, Kant's ethics are explicitly based on *practical* reason, not pure reason. And on this point, it's worth remembering that the imperfection of our reason is exactly what is being used against us by targeted advertising, and by the darker manipulations of Cambridge Analytica. Here, the task of valuing and bolstering human reason coincides neatly with the goal of eliminating hidden exploitation. Recognising the vulnerabilities of reason only makes nurturing it all the more urgent.

A third objection is that Kant's extensive body of work contains some highly problematic sections and arguments. Notably, Kant wrote that women 'lack civic personality' and should not be able to vote; elsewhere, he wrote about race in a way that presupposes a racial hierarchy, and seems to suggest that slavery and colonialism are tolerable. On some such issues, however, Kant adjusted his position. In his later writings, Kant discounted slavery and racial hierarchies, describing colonialism as barbaric and all races as equivalent in their potential. More importantly, these problematic sections and arguments are contradicted by Kant's larger ethical system. At heart, Kant's system proposes the equal worth of *all* reasoning beings, which means that his project is profoundly feminist, just as it is resolutely anti-racist, and firmly against privileging or subjugating any person or persons based simply on their birth. Criticising Kant for these missteps feels a bit like criticising a modern expert for tweets posted while at college.

Finally, this raises a related objection, which proposes that Kant's universalism necessarily privileges the white, the male, the western. How can a German Enlightenment philosopher from the 18th century possibly articulate the basis of an ethics that ought to hold globally in the 21st century? Isn't this a form of ethical imperialism that will necessarily engender the *oppression* of non-white, non-male, non-western? No, not once we recognise that Kant's starting point is the irreducible worth of humanity.

Which brings me to consent.

INDIVIDUAL CONSENT

Consent is a central principle of modern life. In law, the 'age of consent' is the age at which people are deemed to have the requisite emotional maturity to have sex. In medicine, the notion of 'informed consent' is fundamental for the treatment of patients. And in common parlance, consent is a thread woven into the texture of our day-to-day.

Further, many philosophers have drawn a direct link from the formula of humanity to consent. Philosopher Derek Parfit writes: 'We treat people as ends, Kant claims, and not merely as a means, if we deliberately treat these people only in ways to which they could rationally consent.' Similarly, Christine Korsgaard notes that one way to test the mere means principle is to ask 'whether another can assent to your way of acting'. (And note that Parfit does not write 'do rationally consent', and that Korsgaard does not write 'does assent'. Rather, both construe consent in terms of *possibility*. I will return to this point.)

When Kant says that I must treat others as persons, and never merely as a means, he proposes that I ought not treat people as I do rocks or walls, props or tools. Rather, I must treat people as agents capable of directing their own lives in accordance with their reason. If my proposed project is going to affect others significantly, how can I act such that those others remain self-determining agents? Most obviously, by allowing them to express consent and dissent towards my project, and then by respecting their will. In this way I can enable others, via consent or dissent, to either license or veto my behaviour.

The formula of humanity does not refer to consent, but elsewhere Kant draws an explicit connection. Famously, the connection emerges in a section devoted to perfect duties to others, where Kant writes that we breach the mere means principle when we make a false promise to another for personal gain. When we make such a false promise, Kant writes in the *Groundwork*, we:

> make use of another human being *merely as a means* to an end
> he does not share. For the man whom I seek to use for my own
> purposes by such a promise cannot possibly agree to my way

of behaving to him, and so cannot himself share the end of the action.

In this passage, Kant sets out two criteria by which the false promisor breaches the mere means principle: first, by precluding the possibility of consent ('cannot possibly agree'); and second, by precluding the other from sharing one's end. Are these criteria the same? There is some dispute among scholars. But clearly a failure to obtain requisite consent signals a breach of the mere means principle, and hence the formula of humanity.

Imagine I say to you, 'Please do my anonymous survey, because I am researching digital privacy.' Now imagine that your responses are not anonymous, and that I sell my completed surveys, containing highly sensitive personal information, to data brokers. Without being properly informed, you cannot possibly consent to my action. (Nor, by the by, can you share in my ends.) There has been a breach of the mere means principle, and hence the formula of humanity. The formula of humanity requires us not to treat others as mere means, but to respect their reason, dignity and autonomy. To do so, we must respect their consent and dissent. This may well not be the only thing we must do to satisfy the formula. If we fail this test, however, we are acting unethically.

The good news is that consent is much easier to define than privacy. Clearly and simply, it is 'voluntary agreement in light of relevant information'. This is sometimes compressed into the phrase 'informed consent'. In medicine, the orthodox view is that morality and law both *require* that no medical procedures be performed upon competent adults without informed consent. This means giving patients an adequate understanding of treatment options and their risks.

The bad news is that 'informed consent' is easier said than obtained. Ever since the 1950s, when courts started grappling with issues of informed consent in medicine, two main questions have arisen. One, whose consent is required? Two, when is consent adequate?

These break down into more detailed questions. Which patients are competent to consent? What sort of information must be given so that a patient's consent will be informed? And when is consent voluntary, and not the result of undue influence, particularly in light of the unequal relationship of doctor and patient? These difficulties have crystallised into specific issues, including: whether implicit consent counts; whether silence can constitute consent; and the impacts of mental illness on consent.

Unsurprisingly, scholars have noted that consent has significant limitations in a medical context. Similarly, scholars have identified the limitations of consent for protecting privacy on the internet. For the moment, though, individual consent remains the go-to principle, both for medicine and digital privacy, and for good reason. But what sort of consent will serve us best?

Actual consent

Earlier, I argued that privacy is partly about control. When it comes to internet privacy, however, some users feel as if they've lost control. As communications scholars Joseph Turow, Michael Hennessy and Nora Draper found in 2015 regarding corporate surveillance: 'Rather than feeling able to make choices, Americans believe it is futile to manage what companies can learn about them. Our study reveals that more than half do not want to lose control over their information but also believe this loss of control has already happened.'

Users want control, but feel they have lost it, and with it much of their privacy. Consent, it would seem, is a way to reinstate that control. And what could be better than *actual* consent? If a social media site wants to share my contact list with a third party, should it not ask me if I consent in language that is clear and plain?

The complication is that human understanding is flawed. None of us is a perfectly rational and fully informed being with a complete grasp of every relevant fact in every situation. How can I properly assess the import of sharing my contact list, even if – and this is a big if – that import is clearly and succinctly described? For Onora O'Neill, the nub of the problem is the 'opacity of intentionality':

> When we consent to another's proposals, we consent, even
> when 'fully' informed, only to some specific formulation of
> what the other has it in mind to do. We may remain ignorant
> of further, perhaps equally pertinent, accounts of what is
> proposed, including some to which we would not consent.

This is especially evident online, where data flows in ways that are unforeseen and complex, and where it can then be combined with yet more data, some of it not shared, but simply inferred.

O'Neill classifies the difficulties with actual consent into three categories.

The first is that in many cases it is unclear precisely what constitutes consent, and hence what has been consented to. The clearest instances of actual consent exist in legal and institutional contexts involving explicit formal procedures, such as signatures and oaths. Even here, however, there can be ignorance, misrepresentation, duress and pressure. The consent of a marriage, for instance, is a ratified legal bond, formalised with oaths and signatures. But even a marriage can be annulled if one party is already married, or was coerced, or was under the influence of alcohol or drugs during the wedding.

Sometimes formal procedures mask moral issues, as in colonial treaties signed with native peoples. In 1840, New Zealand's Treaty of Waitangi was 'signed' by many (but not all) Māori chiefs, making

New Zealand a British colony. Ostensibly, we have formal consent. Closer examination, however, reveals that the Māori had an oral culture and many were, at this stage, less than fully literate. As sociologist Donald McKenzie has written, various' versions of the treaty exist, and many chiefs believed the oral conditions they discussed during negotiations were more binding than the printed document(s). For the English, the treaty legitimised government of the Māori; for the Māori, the signatures meant less. And when there are no formal procedures in place, it is even harder to determine what constitutes consent. Many nurses, for instance, administer care without seeking verbal or written consent, claiming that their patient's consent is implied.

What constitutes consent? What exactly has been consented to? The boundaries of consent are often unclear, especially in a digital context.

The second category of difficulties for actual consent arises with hidden coercion. Imagine an underpaid seamstress at an exploitative workplace in a developing nation. Ostensibly, she consents to the conditions of her work. Ethically, however, her consent is questionable. Can she consent *not* to take this job? Similarly, women cannot choose *not* to be affected by their socially prescribed gender roles. As O'Neill writes: 'The outward contractual form masks an underlying coercion ... A choice between marriage partners does not show that the married life has been chosen. The outward forms of market economies and of unarranged marriages may mask how trivial the range of dissent and consent is.'

In 1781, Jeremy Bentham invoked the phrase 'false consciousness' to describe the situation when a person 'believes or imagines that certain circumstances exist, which in truth do not'. The phrase is now common in philosophy, sociology and social psychology, referring to people who construct their lives on suspect reasoning, unaware of their true place in society or history.

Under hidden coercion and false consciousness, people believe themselves to be – and often outwardly seem to be – autonomous, even as they are in fact constrained and exploited. The challenge lies in identifying which cases are morally problematic. If an impoverished father donates a kidney to feed his family, is his consent morally justifying? And in personal relationships, coercion can be particularly layered and refined. If I slam a door to win a marital argument, is that coercion? What if my slamming doors has in the past prefigured verbal abuse and violence? Certainly, coercion is distinct from economic pressure and mere manipulation. In law and medicine, coercion is distinguished from 'constrained consent'. Of course, drawing that distinction is often difficult.

When all my friends are on Instagram and Snapchat, I may join in despite serious reservations about my privacy. Like the factory worker and her job, I might feel that I cannot reasonably choose *not* to be on Facebook. Is this drive to be on social media hidden coercion? Or is it constrained consent? Probably the latter, but it is important that we identify any underlying pressures, particularly on vulnerable groups such as children.

On the subject of children, O'Neill's third range of difficulties with actual consent concerns people whose abilities to consent or dissent are limited. Such people include children and the mentally ill, or those whose command of language is rudimentary. Such difficulties arise often in medical ethics, and sometimes the law steps in to assist. In the UK, for instance, the *Mental Capacity Act* 2005 addresses this issue by presuming that every adult has the capacity to consent, but also by protecting vulnerable people deemed unable to make their own decisions. The Act specifies who can make decisions, in which situations, and how. Indeed, *many* patients are limited in their capacity to consent. In a medical context, writes O'Neill, 'consent may be spurious even when based on average understanding and a standard ability to make decisions'. In a sense, questions of consent are more straightforward in cases of heavy impairment. In such cases, paternalism isn't just permitted, but required. For children, the mentally ill and others whose rational capacities are immature or impaired, we need to think about scaffolded consent, and in terms of competence to consent, which I will come to.

As in medicine, such difficulties arise often in the case of internet privacy, where children can masquerade as adults, drunks can feign sobriety and schizophrenics can mask symptoms. As a model, actual consent is less satisfactory than it first appears. It doesn't allow for the frailty, vulnerability and irrationality of human beings. Actual consent is part of the story, but something is missing.

Hypothetical consent

If actual consent has flaws, what about hypothetical consent? Instead of asking whether actual consent has been obtained, hypothetical consent demands that we ask whether a *fully rational* person *would* consent to a similar proposal. Theoretically, the inquiry then becomes straightforward: if a fully rational person would consent to my proposed action, then I can proceed to perform that action secure in the knowledge that I am not merely using others as means.

There are clear advantages to such an approach: it removes the possibility of an actual person misunderstanding what she has consented to; it prevents persons from acting against their own best interest; and it means that people cannot consent without knowing or caring what they are consenting to.

This type of approach addresses the three types of difficulties with actual consent identified above, but the problem is that none of us is a fully rational being, and none of us is infallibly reasonable. This matters because the irrational, unreasonable in us is, in a significant way, what defines us as human beings. If we invoke hypothetical consent, then we are talking about consent divorced from real life. It becomes theoretical and largely meaningless. Indeed, surely it is the *particularity* of our individual rationality that is apposite. If hypothetical consent is the test, then each person's own specific humanity becomes insignificant. To ask, 'Did she consent?' is problematic, as we have seen, but at least it allows for a specific 'she'. To ask, 'Would she have consented, were she fully rational?' is to override that person's self-determination with a sort of moral tyranny. Via hypothetical consent, we might override actual dissent, coercing a person against their will.

Possible consent

If actual consent suffers from the opacity of intentionality and hypothetical consent suffers from moral tyranny, can we do better?

The solution lies in possible consent. If our goal is to treat others not merely as a means (which usually overlaps with our goal to treat them as persons), then this view suggests that we are required to give those others the *possibility* of consent or dissent whenever our proposed actions significantly affect them. As O'Neill writes: 'The morally significant aspect of treating others as persons may lie in making their consent or dissent *possible*, rather than in what they actually consent to or would hypothetically consent to if fully rational.' Or, as Korsgaard writes, 'The question whether another can assent to your way of acting can serve as a criterion of judging whether you are treating her as a mere means.'

This makes for a profound change in focus. From the issue of *does* the other assent, or *would* the other assent, we have shifted to the issue of *can* the other assent.

Kant himself uses the language of possibility in his example of the false promisor. When I make a false promise to another for financial gain, writes Kant in the *Groundwork*, I 'make use of another human being merely as a means to an end … For, he whom I want to use for my purpose by such a promise *cannot possibly agree* to my way of behaving toward him.'

The lender cannot *possibly* agree (or consent) to my action. Kant prefers possible, not actual, consent.

What does this mean in practice?

First of all, when is consent required? Clearly, morally signifi-cant consent is not consent to every aspect of another's proposals that may affect me. To avoid using someone as a mere means, we need to separate morally significant from morally trivial. To borrow an example from philosopher Samuel Kerstein: if a jogger in a park hears a stranger singing and enjoys the melody, does the jogger need the stranger's consent to keep listening? Conversely, does the singer need the jogger's consent to keep singing? Though each affects the other, neither has power of veto. It seems we only have this power over *some* actions that affect us.

If I intend to punch you, or lie to you, or steal from you, the requirement for consent generally provides power of veto. But what about noise levels? If I want to livestream a concert at a low volume, does my neighbour have power of veto? No. But what if I'm plan-ning an all-night jam with my Marshall stacks turned to 11? As For-mosa writes:

> Intuitively it seems that in such cases the other's consent is
> needed only if the noise-making is not, at least depending on
> the context, merely annoying, but far more intrusive or even,
> at the extreme, constitutes a significant harm (a sonic assault on
> you akin to a punch to the ears).

In cases of noise-making, there appears to be some vague point, somewhere between mere annoyance and sonic battery, where the requirement to obtain others' consent kicks in. This vagueness does not doom the formula of humanity. In various jurisdictions, regulations set precise decibel limits for neighbourly noise. These limits can vary according to the time of day, and whether it is a weekday or weekend. In Australia, for instance, these regulations contain exceptions for air conditioning units during heatwaves.

Digital privacy raises similar issues. Some intrusions will be trivial, whereas others will be unacceptable. But how do we draw the line? How can we identify the *morally significant* aspect of proposed plans? (Putting aside for the moment the added complication that digital intrusions upon privacy are cumulative, meaning that even trivial intrusions can become highly significant when aggregated with other data. I return to this point in the next chapter.)

Where, for instance, do we draw the line for photography in public places? If I am on the steps of the Sydney Opera House with my children and want to take a photo, must I seek the consent of everyone in the background? That would be absurd, even if I plan to upload the photo to social media, potentially for a vast audience. By contrast, however, if a company or government agency applies facial recognition software to everyone pictured in my posted photograph, that would be a different story. Facial recognition software is clearly morally significant for our privacy. The company or government agency requires consent.

But what's this? Later that evening, I notice that in the background of my photo a young couple is kissing passionately. When I crop the image, I have a modern version of Robert Doisneau's famous photo, *Le baiser de l'hôtel de ville* (*Kiss by the Hotel de Ville*). I call it *Kiss at the Sydney Opera House*, and it's a masterpiece, I'm sure of it. I want to exhibit, publish and sell it. Do I need the consent of the couple, who are clearly recognisable? Is their consent morally significant?

The power of Doisneau's image – the frisson of desire and risk – lies partly in the tension between public and private. In central

Paris, the town hall square is busy and public, but the kiss is intimate and personal. This is, in fact, analogous to the confusion of public and private that occurs routinely on the internet, where place can be multiplied. If I flirt on my smartphone while commuting on a crowded train, this can be exciting, and disorienting, as I am simultaneously in public and in private.

Doisneau took his photo in 1950, and for decades it was assumed that he'd captured an unguarded moment. As a feted chronicler of street life, Doisneau encouraged this belief, including by keeping the couple's identity secret. In 1992, however, Doisneau was sued by a pair falsely claiming to be the lovers, and so finally admitted that his image was posed. As Agnès Poirier has written, the pair were young actor friends, whom Doisneau followed as they ambled and flirted their way through the city of love. He would not have photographed strangers. 'I would never have dared to photograph people like that,' he said. 'Lovers kissing in the street, those couples are rarely legitimate.'

What's more, had Doisneau shot without consent, he would have been breaking French law. The law prescribes that persons in public may be photographed, but that no photograph may be published that focuses on them as individuals, unless they consent. In this way, French law accords with the formula of humanity. And while Doisneau did obtain the consent of the couple, he did not obtain consent from passers-by, at least one of whom is clearly recognisable. The distinction comes down to moral significance. The couple was engaged in an act often considered private; the passers-by were merely ambling in public.

What does this mean for my accidental masterpiece? Well, it might be hard to identify the couple in *Kiss at the Sydney Opera House*, but it seems that I ought to try. The young couple ought to be given the chance to consent or dissent. Imagine that they are having an extramarital affair. Or that they want to keep their affection secret, because their families disapprove. To avoid treating them merely as a means, I ought to seek their consent. By contrast, however, there is no ethical requirement to seek the consent of those in the background (unless they too happen to be engaged in some sort of private moment). As O'Neill writes, consent is required when the connection between the act and the person acted upon is direct and significant, not tangential and trivial. If I want to publish, exhibit or sell *Kiss at the Sydney Opera House*, the couple's consent is required. By contrast, their consent is not required as to whether I crop them in portrait or landscape format.

The extreme version of my accidental masterpiece is Google Street View. Here are the same issues, on an industrial and global scale. It too involves the nonconsensual collection of images taken in public that incidentally include people, sometimes in situations that are private. However, Street View is anything but accidental. Launched in 2007, Street View is an addition to Google Maps offering 360 degree views of cities and rural areas worldwide. The images are taken by car, but also by walkers, boats and snowmobiles. The results are panoramas of stitched images. In many countries, the rollout of Street View prompted government investigations and regulation. Responses varied, write media scholars James Meese and Rowan Wilken. Australia, Canada and the UK required Google to blur faces and licence plates; Italy ordered Google to publicise the itineraries of its cameras; and Switzerland demanded 100 per cent anonymisation of all content. Meanwhile, Spain and the Netherlands commenced legal proceedings and Germany made it an opt-out service.

In the US, images were published featuring men entering a cannabis club, a man urinating in public and scantily clad women working at a car wash. In Canada, a woman was photographed with 'part of her breast exposed' by a Street View car while sitting outside her house. She sued, and Google was ordered to pay C$2250 plus court costs, failing to make its case that it had merely taken photos of public activities. And in Australia, write Meese and Wilken, even facial blurring wasn't enough to protect privacy in all cases. Among those who were identifiable during Street View's first week of operation in 2008 were a 'cheating spouse', a 'lying neighbour' and a 'man sleeping on the job'. In these cases, consent ought to have been obtained, but wasn't. As Meese and Wilken write: 'Google instead assumed consent and placed the onus on individuals to manage their own privacy after the fact, through privacy self-management.'

(These privacy issues were eclipsed in 2010 when it was revealed Google had also been collecting wifi data from their Street View cars in order to enhance their 'location based products'. Initially, Google denied collecting 'payload data', but an audit by the Data Protection Authority in Hamburg, Germany, revealed Google had been collecting emails, passwords and other sensitive information from non-password protected wifi networks. Investigations were opened in 20 countries.)

For mechanised public photography conducted en masse, it may well be impossible to obtain the informed consent of all those who appear. The facts of Street View resemble the facts of my Opera House image, but the scale and automation make Google's process considerably more invasive. An individual wielding a camera in public can use individual judgment to decide whether taking a photo of a specific subject is permissible. A Street View car doesn't blink. It takes a photo, then stitches it with billions of others. The seeming impossibility of obtaining individual consent in each case means that the obvious solution is for the collective consent of the law to play a defining role. Nonetheless, I would argue that for Street View individual consent *is* sometimes required. When, exactly? Often, the answer will be obvious, such as when an identifiable man is standing outside a strip club, or an identifiable woman has part of her breast exposed. There will, however, be hard cases. To help, we can invoke a heuristic: is this person at risk of being treated merely as a means? And generally, it is better that we cast the net too widely than too narrowly. Ethically, it is better to catch too many cases than too few.

For *Kiss at the Sydney Opera House*, what if I try but cannot identify the amorous couple? Here too the collective consent of the law can provide clarity. Is a reasonable effort enough? Or must we try harder? In this way, personal judgment together with the law can help us decide when consent is required, and what efforts ought to be made to obtain it.

Now that we know consent must be *possible*, and now that we can determine *when* consent is required, how can we account for deception and coercion?

Deception and coercion

'If we coerce or deceive others, their dissent, and so their genuine consent, is in principle ruled out,' writes O'Neill. 'Here we do indeed use others, treating them as mere props or tools in our own projects.' In the face of deception or coercion, it seems, the possibility of giving consent is ruled out. Adopting the principle of informed consent shows a resolute commitment to the principle that people be neither deceived nor coerced. As Christine Korsgaard notes, 'According to the formula of humanity, coercion and deception are the most fundamental forms of wrong-doing to others.'

However, Derek Parfit notes that there are clear exceptions. If someone is unconscious, they cannot consent to life-saving surgery. Presumably, however, such surgery is ethical, even though coerced. People might also freely consent to being later coerced, as was necessary ahead of painful surgery in pre-anaesthetic times. Moreover, people freely consent to being legally coerced. We (mostly) agree, under threat of punishment, to pay taxes, obey speed limits and refrain from indiscriminate killing. Not all coercion is wrong, whether by other individuals or the state.

Perhaps deception isn't always wrong either. If I can lie to save your life, the deception is surely permissible. As Parfit writes: 'My life-saving lie would be like life-saving surgery on some unconscious person.'

On this point, Kant has proved controversial. In the essay 'On a supposed right to lie from philanthropy', Kant gave the example of the killer at the door. You are at home with a friend who has taken refuge from a killer when you hear a knock. Opening the door, you find the killer, who asks if your friend is inside. Answer honestly, and the killer will presumably murder your friend. Lie, and your friend will be spared. Is lying permissible here?

Kant's answer was no, because we have an unconditional duty not to lie. This has prompted outrage, even among Kantians such as Paul Formosa:

> This seems like a 'clean hands' policy gone mad. Do your
> duty, tell the truth (and if you don't you will be held legally
> accountable), and morally wipe your hands of the outcome
> (even if that outcome is the murder of a friend to whom you
> have offered refuge). Such a view seems morally repugnant.

It's easy to make the hypothetical more real. What if the year is 1942 and you are a conscientious German hiding a Jewish family in your attic, when a Gestapo officer knocks on your door? Here, clearly, lying is permissible, if not required. How then do we account for Kant's position? By acknowledging he got it wrong. He misapplied his own theory. Indeed, elsewhere in his work Kant argued that lying is sometimes permissible.

When a killer appears at your door asking for the whereabouts of your friend, the right thing to do is to lie. As Formosa wrote in

2008, 'respect for humanity sometimes *requires* that we lie'. If a lie expresses respect for the value of human dignity, as lying to avert a murder does, then such a lie is mandatory. After all, it is dignity, not truthfulness, that has absolute worth. However, such lying is permissible only in response to a *direct and imminent* threat. Here we need to set a strict test. We are talking about seemingly (but not actually) making exceptions to the categorical imperative. We are talking about lying and overriding consent. This can only be justified in exceptional circumstances, such as when a life is directly and imminently at risk. Only a direct and imminent threat can justify some sort of action that would otherwise be unwarranted. A vague, generalised threat is not enough. (And some unwarranted actions, such as torturing children, say, can never become warranted.)

Sometimes coercion and deception are permissible. This would suggest that coercive or deceptive intrusions upon digital privacy are sometimes justified. This then has the potential, for instance, to validate certain secret surveillance practices conducted by government agencies – albeit only in the face of a direct and imminent threat to reason, dignity and autonomy. It will not, however, justify the use of coercion or deception *merely for profit* by data brokers, social networks and other digital platforms.

The model of individual consent we are constructing needs to recognise that coercion and deception are sometimes warranted. It also needs to take into account the element of competence.

Competence

What can children consent to? Is drunk oversharing problematic? What about cases of mental illness? On the internet, where people routinely present distorted versions of themselves, and where digital platforms often have financial incentives to encourage sharing, competence raises difficult and urgent questions. In fact, competence is a threshold issue for individual consent, and hence for the formula of humanity.

As we have seen, the wellspring of the categorical imperative is human reason. Logically, if the formula of humanity demands respect for reason, then it surely demands respect for the *competence* to reason. For instance, one basic principle demanded by the categorical imperative is that I must not render someone incompetent to reason. If I give someone a stupefying drug, for instance, I am treating her merely as a means, even if I do so with her consent. There are exceptions, including administering anaesthesia before surgery. Generally, however, I must not stupefy others, and I mustn't stupefy myself either, such as by taking recreational drugs. As Kant writes, we must not render useless our own rational powers. While praising the moderate consumption of alcohol as a social lubricant, Kant wrote that we must not drink to the point of stupefaction, because by doing so we temporarily destroy the reason that is the source of our dignity.

Competence to reason, and hence competence to consent, is crucial for any application of the formula of humanity. But what is it, exactly? In plain terms, competence denotes an ability to manage oneself and one's affairs. More formally, the *New Shorter Oxford English Dictionary* defines it as: 'Power, ability, capacity, (*to do*, *for* a task, etc.)'. In medicine, competence is a key component of patient consent. A vast medical literature covers the competence to consent of the elderly, schizophrenics and HIV patients, among others. Approaches vary in different domains. In the law, writes jurist Peter Skegg, competence to consent is widely presumed. In medicine, by contrast, this is not always the case. In an emergency room, for instance, it would be dangerous to presume a survivor of a suicide attempt is competent, even if she is lucid and coherent.

Although the specifics are contested, competence is often significant, and sometimes decisive, for consent. Without accommodating it, we cannot hope to address issues of digital privacy in any comprehensive way.

What should we do when our proposed action will significantly affect someone who is incompetent to consent? That depends on the circumstances. Either we wait until they become competent, as when someone is concussed, or drunk. If a person is concussed or drunk and we propose to encroach upon their privacy, or borrow their car, or have sex, we ought to wait.

However, if a person is in mortal danger, we cannot wait. When waiting for competence is unreasonable, then hypothetical consent is required. A bystander can consent on behalf of a citizen in peril; a parent can consent on behalf of a child; a carer can consent on behalf of a mentally ill adult. They can ask: what would this child/person do if fully rational? Actual consent and possible consent are out of the question. In such cases of incompetence, hypothetical consent is the appropriate test.

Imagine that, while out for an early morning stroll, you stumble upon a jogger who has passed out. He has a pulse, but isn't breathing. With no one around, you administer cardiopulmonary resuscitation and save his life. Clearly, there has been no actual consent, and you haven't offered the possibility of consent. Does this mean that you are using the jogger merely as a means? Surely not. As Samuel Kerstein writes, 'it seems wildly implausible to contend that your attempt to save him was morally impermissible.'

Once we recognise that the jogger is incompetent to consent, hypothetical consent becomes a threshold issue. In this case, you can't wait for him to regain consciousness. Time is of the essence. You have to give consent for life-saving treatment on his behalf.

Ethically required and forbidden

But there is an even more compelling reason to perform life-saving CPR. And that's because it's *required by the moral law*. The dignity of human life means that you have a moral duty to provide aid. Sometimes the formula of humanity renders consent and dissent irrelevant.

We can see this more clearly once we realise that coercion and deception are sometimes permissible, and even required, in cases of *competence*. On a sunny afternoon, you're at Circular Quay in Sydney when a woman steps off the footpath and into the path of a fast-moving bus. She's a tourist from Toronto, unaccustomed to traffic keeping left and absorbed in her smartphone. She's about to become a casualty of the doubling of place. Naturally, though, you grab her arm and pull her to safety. Have you used her merely as a means? Of course not. Despite the lack of consent, and the fact that you never offered her the possibility of consent, you have saved her life, and in the process you have expressed and enacted respect for life in line with the formula of humanity.

This is true even if she had stepped out intentionally. In *The Metaphysics of Morals*, Kant writes that we have a perfect duty not to kill ourselves. For Kant, committing suicide involves treating oneself as a mere means. Intervening to prevent a suicide is perhaps not just permissible, but required, just as the formula of humanity requires me to lie to the killer at the door asking about the whereabouts of my friend. (And let's separate out euthanasia as a distinct issue.)

At first glance, I am treating the killer as a mere means by lying; on closer inspection, I am expressing respect for humanity, and specifically the humanity in my endangered friend, in the face of a direct and imminent threat to her life.

We can imagine similar scenarios involving privacy. Visiting a friend, I find her collapsed, unconscious. Immediately, I suspect an overdose, or perhaps anaphylaxis. Am I justified in rummaging through her medicine cabinet or personal effects, if I suspect that might help save her life? Clearly, obtaining consent is impossible. She is incompetent to consent, and so I must supply consent on her behalf. But the issue of competence is eclipsed by the moral law, given such an invasion of privacy is required by the formula of humanity.

Now imagine that, over a casual meal, you meet a woman planning what she proudly calls the perfect murder. The victim has been selected; the location is determined; the plotting has been meticulous. And she's covered her tracks. The planning has been done on an encrypted smartphone app. Smiling confidently, she says the murder will take place right after dessert. What she doesn't know, however, is that you're an adept hacker. Surreptitiously, you can hack into her phone, unencrypt her plans and warn the victim before telling police. Should you? Should you invade the privacy of a would-be killer to thwart imminent bloodshed? Yes! Such intervention is ethically required. The consent of the would-be killer is irrelevant. In the face of a direct and imminent threat to human life, the formula of humanity demands that you express respect for rational nature by doing what you can to thwart her murderous intentions.

We are starting to home in on a robust model of consent. After accounting for competence to consent as a threshold issue, our model will further take into account whether there are any ethically required or forbidden conditions that render consent irrelevant. In this way, consent will be *possible*.

Of course, other approaches have been suggested. Not all philosophers emphasise the role of consent and autonomy, especially in life and death situations. One alternative approach involves foregrounding trust, including in medicine. As O'Neill writes: 'Autonomy has been a leading idea in philosophical writing on bioethics; trust has been marginal. This strikes me as surprising ... Trust is surely more important, and particularly so for any ethically adequate practice of medicine.'

She's right. Trust warrants careful consideration, particularly in regard to privacy. When we grant others the space to act autonomously and the scope to maintain privacy, we do so knowing that these others may well behave in such a way that causes us harm. We open the possibility that they will abuse our trust by invading our privacy. Francis Fukuyama, Philip Pettit and Onora O'Neill are among the scholars who have shown that trust is crucial for the flourishing of both individuals and societies. Unfortunately, recent research has shown that general levels of trust in many countries are worryingly low. It is no coincidence that these low trust levels coincide with ongoing encroachments upon individual privacy. This is the notion of the 'risk society' described in chapter 5. Certainly, more work needs to be done into the role of trust, and the connection between trust and privacy. Fostering trust, it strikes me, goes hand in hand with fostering privacy. Meanwhile, care-based ethics, which focuses on how we care for one another in our interpersonal relationships, is another approach with tremendous potential for protecting privacy.

However, consent remains a crucial mechanism, and rightfully so. With the collapsed jogger and the killer at the door, there is no possibility of consent. These acts of coercion and deception seem to violate the mere means principle. However, by applying a competence test and an ethically required/forbidden test, we find that the formula of humanity compels us to save the jogger and deceive the killer, just as it compels us to breach the privacy of our collapsed friend and the killer with an encrypted smartphone app.

Actual consent that incorporates possible consent

That still leaves us with a vast number of interactions. These are interactions where consent is required, where parties are competent to consent, and where there are no ethically required or forbidden conditions that render consent irrelevant. In such cases, which version of consent do we apply?

The answer involves a blend of actual and possible consent. In these cases, we apply actual consent, *so defined as to incorporate the possibility of consent*. We can state this model of individual consent as follows: if consent is required because a morally significant privacy issue is at stake, if there is competence to consent, and if there are no relevant conditions that are ethically required or forbidden, then actual individual consent must be obtained. All that's missing from this formulation is the law, which has a major role to play, and which I will come to shortly.

The model is surprisingly intuitive. The overarching query is, has morally satisfying consent been obtained? This breaks down into more specific questions. Is consent needed? Is there competence? Is there an overriding ethical imperative? Once these questions are answered, we can explore the nature of the actual consent at issue.

And with this model we can address O'Neill's three objections to actual consent: that it is unclear precisely what constitutes consent and precisely what has been consented to; that there are instances of hidden coercion; and that problems attend the limited capacity to consent.

Recall that an example of the first objection is the Treaty of Waitangi. Given they were illiterate, many of the Māori chiefs who signed the treaty were seemingly incompetent to consent. What's more, the terms were unclear, containing various oral provisions and promises. This calls into question whether the genuine possibility of consent was ever offered. If the chiefs were not properly apprised of the treaty's terms and its ramifications, it's a stretch to say they gave their actual consent. And the Treaty of Waitangi makes a neat analogy for the privacy terms and conditions offered by some digital platforms. As we have seen, notice-and-consent provisions for privacy are often confusing, if not labyrinthine. As a result, they are rarely read. In 2010, the online gaming store GameStation inserted a new clause in its terms and conditions, which read:

> By placing an order via this Web site on the first day of the fourth month of the year 2010 Anno Domini, you agree to grant Us a non transferable option to claim, for now and for ever more, your immortal soul. Should We wish to exercise this option, you agree to surrender your immortal soul, and any claim you may have on it, within 5 (five) working days of receiving written notification from gamestation.co.uk or one of its duly authorized minions.

In all, 7500 shoppers sold their souls. This despite the fact that the terms offered an opt-out hyperlink, which read 'click here to nullify your soul transfer'. Only 12 per cent of shoppers opted out. It was an April Fools' prank that made a serious point. And in research published in 2016, Jonathan Obar and Anne Oeldorf-Hirsch found that internet users casually agreed to terms that stipulated they must give up their firstborn child. Studies consistently show that digital privacy policies are unread, unreadable and incomprehensible. In many cases, notice-and-consent provisions don't offer the genuine possibility of consent. And where consent is obtained, it's frequently hard to construe it as morally justifying. Ethically, such consent is all too often worthless.

We then come to the second objection, hidden coercion. Above, I cited factory workers labouring under exploitative conditions as an example. For digital privacy, a relevant example is someone who has been bullied and harassed into sharing compromising pictures on social media. These cases turn on exploitation. If consent in these contexts is morally unsatisfactory, that is not because the people involved are incompetent to consent, like children. (Unless they are children.) Rather, it may be because they have no real options. They are constrained to make a choice that they would rather avoid. The genuine possibility of consent was never offered.

Above, I noted that for some people it may be difficult *not* to sign up for online services, given the consistent pressure to sign up for services that others have signed up for. Services from Google, Facebook, Amazon and Apple, and from Alibaba, Tencent, Microsoft, Twitter and Netflix have become so popular that there exist strong pressures to use them, and to share widely with them and through them. This is the 'network effect': the more users digital platforms attract, the better their services can become, and the more users they can attract. In response, some media scholars have described digital platforms as inherently monopolistic. Communications professor Terry Flew identifies 'the rise of network monopolies and oligopolies'; digital economist Nick Srnicek writes that platforms are 'monopolies with centralized control over increasingly vast numbers of users and the data they generate'; and 'information civilization' expert Shoshana Zuboff describes Google, Facebook, Twitter, Alibaba and others as 'hyperscale businesses' that are reconstituting our western economies as an oppressive form of 'surveillance capitalism'. However we categorise the power of digital platforms, the pressure to sign up and to share is strong, and it is vital that we scrutinise these services to distinguish ethically unacceptable hidden coercion from ethically acceptable manipulation and pressure.

Consider microtargeting. If a shoe company releases a new range of sneakers, and if that company also knows every user's favourite colour, is it permissible to microtarget ads for users such that everyone sees that sneaker in their favourite colour? Sure. (Assuming they found out each user's favourite colour via ethical means.) But what if a political candidate uses the same tactic, rendering an ad's background in each voter's favourite colour? And what if the candidate further personalises advertising based also on each voters' personality type (anxious? hot-headed? disengaged?), daily habits (most persuadable at 9 am? 5 pm? 10 pm?), and hidden biases (sexism? racism? homophobia?). We can extend this to include further sensitive attributes such as ethnicity, voting history, sexual orientation, and more.

This describes Cambridge Analytica, the defunct data analytics firm I detailed earlier. Ethically, Cambridge Analytica committed two distinct breaches. The first concerns obtaining personal data. Cambridge Analytica did not have the consent that authorised them to obtain the data of 87 million Facebook users, accessed surreptitiously from 270 000 users of the This Is Your Digital Life app. Here Facebook shoulders some of the blame. Unsurprisingly, major investigations were launched.

The second issue concerns hidden manipulations, and here the ethics are murkier. Cambridge Analytica worked surreptitiously to change the behaviour of voters. What sort of hidden manipulations are we prepared to allow during an election? When does acceptable persuasion become hidden coercion? This question demands urgent attention. One obvious response is to implement a higher level of transparency in political advertising. As I argue in the next chapter, transparency is a fundamental principle that attends the handling of personal and sensitive data. Transparency can mitigate hidden manipulations and expose hidden coercion.

Finally, O'Neill's third objection, concerning limited capacity to consent, is neatly addressed by the introduction of a threshold issue of competence. Online, the issue of competence to consent is crucial for people who are drunk, young, mentally ill or not fully literate, among many others.

Three criteria to help ensure consent is genuine

Actual consent, I have said, must be defined so as to incorporate the *possibility* of consent. In practice, though, what does this mean? Three criteria can help here. First, we must focus on the intention of the person seeking the consent, rather than the intention of the person whose consent is sought. Second, actual consent must take account of the specific personhood of the consenter. And third, we must recognise that questions of consent tend to be iterative and layered, rather than simplistic and singular.

First, the relevant moral test hinges on the intention of the person seeking the consent, rather than the consenter. This is a crucial way in which actual consent can incorporate possible consent. If I am seeking consent, what has been my action? What has been my intention? One heuristic is to ask: have I offered the possibility of consent *to the best of my knowledge*? Or, has a digital platform or government agency offered the possibility of consent to the best of its knowledge? By this test, a cursory notification won't do. If you lend me your phone, that doesn't authorise me to look for intimate images. If I run a digital platform, plain English is better than legalese for my terms and conditions. And if I am a government agency, consent to use data collected for one purpose does not allow further re-use. What we are seeking, paradoxically, is *actual* possible consent. This prohibits wilful ignorance on the part of the person (or body) seeking consent. It means that consent will not be morally justifying unless, for one thing, my proposed action has been described in such a way as to spell out its salient features.

In this way, actual consent steps away from a *caveat emptor* approach, in which the consenter must be unfailingly diligent in giving or withholding consent. The model I am proposing invokes *caveat venditor*. In this model, it is the seller (the person proposing the action) and not the buyer (the person who will be affected by the action) who has the moral responsibility to ensure that consent is more than a mere formality. This is particularly relevant on the internet, where data use and re-use is complex and unpredictable. The onus is on companies, for instance, to obtain the actual consent of users, and this actual consent must contain the genuine possibility of consent.

The second criterion is that actual consent must take into account the particularities of the person whose consent is being sought. If my neighbour is a fanatic greenthumb who curates every leaf and bloom with forensic precision, and I want to chop down a tree that straddles our properties, then the onus upon me is considerably higher than if she were botanophobic. If a woman admits to a low tolerance for alcohol and then, after two drinks, begins slurring and stumbling, it will be difficult to offer the possibility of consent. This is crucial if we want to act in accordance with the formula of humanity. It matters if my proposed action will affect a stranger, a barely known colleague, my close friend or my wife. It matters because in each case our relationship is different, and in each case what I know about this other is relevant.

We must take account of the fact that we know someone is hard of hearing, or struggles to read English, or is in the manic phase of bipolar disorder. To avoid treating another as a mere means, I can only offer the possibility of consent while bearing in mind a person's quirks and eccentricities, strengths and weaknesses. Again, this is relevant online, where consent must be offered in a manner appropriate to users, be they children, or internet novices, or people with poor literacy.

Finally, a third criterion is that genuine consent must be iterative and layered as required. To be morally justifying, consent usually demands an ongoing process, rather than a dialogue box to be ticked once only. Sex is illustrative. For a sexual encounter, consent is rarely an explicit answer to a straightforward proposal; rather, it takes the form of subtle cues, implicit signals and explicit declarations, all of which can be revoked with any of a number of expressions of dissent. Even once I have actual consent, I need to *keep offering* the possibility of consent and dissent. After an initial consent, it would be wrong to insert earplugs to avoid hearing any subsequent reversal.

Is ongoing consent relevant online? Yes, to a degree that we must fight to defend. Online, change is a constant. Google emerged as an advertising-free search engine; it now offers email (Gmail), a browser (Chrome), maps (Google Maps), photos (Google Photos) and cloud-based document services (Google Docs, Google Drive), among many other services, while engaging in sophisticated personalised advertising that relies on secret algorithms and users' browsing histories. And when Google bought Fitbit in late 2019, it gained access to a vast range of personal health data. For Google to offer the genuine possibility of consent it must enable its users to keep re-consenting as its services change, and as its use of individuals' data changes.

What's more, issues of consent are often layered. If I am reading the *New York Times* inside Facebook's Instant Articles application, both companies' privacy provisions and consent policies will be relevant, even as they interlock in ways that are difficult to discern and understand. Consider another example: I am using the Duck-DuckGo search engine, not Google search, but I am doing so on a Google Chrome browser. These are contrasting services from contrasting companies. DuckDuckGo is a search engine founded on the principle of protecting user privacy, whereas Google says, 'Our mission is to organise the world's information and make it universally accessible and useful.' I am using DuckDuckGo because I care about privacy, but does its privacy policy prevail? Or does Google's? Who is tracking me, installing cookies and/or storing my search history? The answer is unclear. A web search (via Google) leads me to a series of discussion forums and blogs, which claim that browsers such as Google Chrome access and track web searches, even when conducted via DuckDuckGo. Further digging suggests that I can prevent such tracking by adjusting my browser settings.

Here, the principle of consent has been rendered largely meaningless. My actions suggest I want my privacy safeguarded. Nonetheless, it seems I need to take further steps to inform myself and to prevent tracking. And in any case, how can I be sure that these steps are enough? Any adequate model of consent must recognise the iterative and layered nature of digital privacy, and seek to minimise opportunities for hidden tracking and secondary surveillance. Perhaps it would help to recognise that there is a *primary* purpose for many of our web engagements. And it is this primary purpose that ought to dictate terms. If I read the *Times* on Facebook, my terms of engagement should be set by my relationship with the *Times*, a relationship that Facebook ought to respect. (Although this arguably changes when I share and react to that content, whereupon the primary purpose becomes social.) By contrast, the use of a privacy-respecting search engine signals that I do not consent to being tracked, and should override any blanket consent I have somehow given for the installation of cookies and the retention of my search history.

If actual consent is required, three criteria can help ensure such consent is genuine: first, the focus should be on the intention of the person (or body) seeking consent; second, the vulnerabilities and specificities of the person (or class of persons) whose consent is sought ought to be considered; and third, there must be adequate recognition that consent tends to be iterative and layered, especially online. With that, we now have a robust model of individual consent. So, what else do we need?

COLLECTIVE CONSENT

Stephen Gough is a former Royal Marine whose abiding love of public nudity and long walks have earned him the nickname the Naked Rambler.

In 2003 and 2004, Gough walked the length of Great Britain wearing only boots, socks and a hat. Two years later, while repeating his cross-country trek, he was arrested. Ever since, he has spent most of his time in prison. His life now follows a rhythm as regular as the seasons: public nudity, arrest, court, jail; public nudity, arrest, court, jail; and so on.

Gough argues that it is his human right to be naked in public. Indeed, under British law, public nudity is not a crime. However, authorities imposed an anti-social behaviour order, or ASBO, making it unlawful for Gough to be naked in public. As one barrister noted: 'The result is that the only person in the country who actually wants to wander naked around the streets of Winchester is also the only man in the country who commits a crime by doing so.'

Putting to one side the ethics of public nudity, I merely want to make the point that Gough himself does not have sole say in determining where the limits of his own privacy are to be drawn. Willingly, Gough has brought his naked body, the acme of what is usually considered private, out into the public sphere. He has consented to his own public exposure, thus implicitly consenting to others looking at his naked body. Through his actions, he has sought to diminish his condition of privacy and to relinquish some of his right to privacy. Unfortunately for him, however, UK legislators, regulators and judges have decided that he is not entitled to do so. On the limits of his personal privacy, Gough's individual determination has been overridden by a collective pronouncement.

So far in this chapter, I have been seeking to apply the formula of humanity by developing a robust model of individual consent.

Indeed, it seems logical that the limits of individual privacy be set by the exercise of individual choice, as expressed by consent and dissent. However, as the case of the Naked Rambler reveals, the limits of privacy are not always to be set by the individual whose privacy is in question. Sometimes individual consent is irrelevant. Just as privacy isn't all about control, so too individual consent is inadequate to protect privacy on its own.

This is the same point I made in chapter 4: that the decision on which swimsuit I can wear is not entirely up to me. Other prescriptions sit over and above individual standards. And these prescriptions include laws, which amount to 'collective consent'.

Most obviously, collective consent has a role to play in bolstering individual consent. The law can prescribe an outline of the sorts of situations involving privacy for which individual consent is required. The law can clarify issues around competence, prescribing who is and isn't competent, and what steps need to be taken in cases of competence and incompetence. The law can specify and enforce ethically required and forbidden conditions. And the law can define genuine consent in a way that incorporates the possibility of consent, including by prescribing the three criteria detailed above. But collective consent doesn't merely bolster individual consent. In other cases, it can qualify, amend, invalidate or otherwise affect individual consent. The key point is simply that collective consent overarches individual consent.

This is true generally. The law trumps individual will. And online, collective consent has an especially vital role to play. In March 2015, following the bankruptcy of US retail chain RadioShack, the company's assets went to auction. These assets included 13 million email addresses and 65 million customer names and physical address files. Presumably RadioShack's notice-and-consent provisions did not cover such a sale. Notice-and-consent provisions are problematic on the internet, where greased data moves with an unpredictable complexity of primary and secondary uses. Not only that, but today's tech will be outdated tomorrow, meaning that today's notice-and-consent provisions may also be outdated. As we've seen, individual consent has an important role to play in protecting individual privacy. On the internet, however, individual consent is especially vulnerable, which means that we must turn our attention from dignity and individual consent to the law and collective consent.

Luckily, the shift in focus is smooth and logical. For Kant, the law is founded in morality. This is in contrast to realist political philosophers such as Nicolò Machiavelli and Carl Schmitt, who argued that the political realm should not be bound by concepts that can be traced back to good and evil. For Kant, politicians are invariably answerable to standards of right or justice in their exercise of public duties. As he wrote, 'all politics must bend its knee before right', and 'right must never be accommodated to politics, but politics must always be accommodated to right'. The state, after all, has powers of coercion, and these must conform with morality.

For Kant, we are all subject to two kinds of constraints: internal and external. Internal constraints, comprising the moral law that all persons legislate for themselves, are required by the categorical imperative. They are founded on dignity. This internal legislation is then supplemented by external legislation enacted by the state. And in this way, external legislation must not contradict the moral law. The external law cannot, for instance, legitimately implement slavery, or apartheid. In this way, the moral law is supported by the collective consent of the external law. It is the external law that empowers a police officer to make an arrest, just as it is the external law that reinforces morality by forbidding slavery and human trafficking.

This brings us to the distinction between virtues and rights. For Kant, both virtues and rights are concerned with morality. While *virtues* pertain to the morality of individuals and their behaviour, *rights* (or more accurately, legal rights) are what individuals are given by the state to protect them, including against others acting in a way that improperly impinges upon their autonomy. The only natural right is that of freedom itself:

> *There is only one innate right. Freedom* (independence from being constrained by another's choice), insofar as it can coexist with the freedom of every other in accordance with a universal law, is the only original right belonging to every man by virtue of his humanity.

Right, for Kant, is the sum of the conditions under which the choice of one can be united with the choice of another, in accordance with the universal law of freedom.

This means that freedom cannot be unfettered. If the freedom of one is to coexist with the freedom of every other, constraint is required. This is the constraint provided by internal and external legislation. At the heart of Kant's politics, then, sits a paradox: freedom requires constraint. According to the formula of humanity, there are limits to the ways in which I ought to behave, just as identical limits prescribe the ways in which you ought to behave. The formula commands that I, you and every other rational creature ought never to treat any person as a mere means, but always as an autonomous agent who sets herself ends. This is the moral law, which I can regard myself as self-legislating. Meanwhile, the state has, and should have, the power to coerce individuals to behave in a manner that aligns with the formula to promote individual freedom. State coercion should thus have as its highest goal the promulgation of an order wherein justice – and hence mutual freedom – prevails. As Kant wrote in 1797:

> Coercion is a hindrance or resistance to freedom. Therefore, if a certain use of freedom is itself a hindrance to freedom in

accordance with universal laws (ie, wrong), coercion that is opposed to this (as a hindering of a hindrance to freedom) is consistent with freedom in accordance with universal laws, that is, it is right.

It's a challenging, intimidating passage. Once deciphered, it reveals Kant's point that laws embodying the united will of the people can rightfully coerce citizens to behave in some ways and not in other ways, in the service of *freedom*.

It comes down to the 'general will', or 'united will', to which Kant refers often. In the essay 'Theory and practice', Kant writes that the sovereign must recognise that he is obliged by the social contract to 'give his laws in such a way that they could have arisen from the united will of a whole people and to regard each subject, insofar as he wants to be a citizen, as if he has joined in voting for such a will'.

The general will can, for instance, extend to revenue raising. As Kant writes, a national leader (*Oberbefehlshaber*) can levy taxes to provide for the poor and to fund orphanages. After all, writes Kant, people submit to the state willingly to help look after those unable to look after themselves. Property rights are also an expression of the common will. In the law we can thus locate a second layer of consent that overarches the first layer of individual consent. This law operates as an expression of collective consent, which can qualify, buttress, amend, invalidate or otherwise affect individual consent. This applies for privacy too.

But this law must be legitimate. That is, it must be *just*. Only a just law can qualify as the united will of the people. Following the political philosopher Montesquieu, Kant wrote that the 'general united will' consists of three persons: legislator; executive; and judiciary. Of these, it is the legislator who can embody the 'concurring and united will of all'. But this does not mean that Kant is suggesting the legislator requires the *actual* consent of every citizen to pass a law. Rather, as with individual consent, Kant returns to the notion of *possible* consent, writing in 'Theory and practice' that no law may be promulgated that 'a whole people could not possibly give its consent to'. Instead of empirically gleaned consent, Kant advocates a *rational possible unanimity*.

For example, argues Kant, a law would be unjust if it provided hereditary privileges only to a certain class of subjects. As dignified rational beings, all persons have equal moral standing. However, such a law would suggest that some have less worth than others due to birth, and then seek to perpetuate such inequality. Those excluded from such privileges could not possibly assent to it. By contrast, a law imposing a war tax could be just, even if many citizens openly disagree with it, as such a tax does not assail the irreducible dignity of all persons.

The key point is that a law, merely by its enactment, does not necessarily embody the united will of the people. A law is not just simply because it is a law. At times, the legislature will make mistakes, passing laws to which the populace could not possibly have assented. Or it may seek to pass laws that contravene morality, such as laws that promote racism, allow slavery or implement apartheid. All these laws are unjust and illegitimate.

For internet privacy, the issue of what constitutes a just law arises in the case of domestic surveillance by government agencies. The larger question is, exactly what sort of domestic surveillance is a government ethically entitled to conduct? It helps if we break down the issue into more specific questions.

Is the government acting unlawfully? First, the legality of the government's practices needs to be addressed. If the government is acting illegally, then it is, on the face of it, acting unethically. (I say 'on the face of it', because a government may still be acting ethically if it is breaking a law that is unjust, or if there is an ethical imperative authorising it to act illegally, such as if there is an imminent act of mass violence.) If, for instance, the NSA is acting in contravention of the US Constitution, it is likely to be acting unethically.

The lawfulness of NSA surveillance remains contested. 'Is this legal?' asked Bruce Schneier in 2015. 'The real answer is that we don't know.'

Certainly, US courts have declared *some* of the NSA's practices illegal. In the 2015 case of *ACLU v Clapper*, the US Court of Appeals found that the bulk collection of telephone metadata was illegal. The plaintiffs, as customers of Verizon, successfully argued that such bulk collection violated their Fourth Amendment rights. This followed the 2013 case of *Klayman v Obama*, in which federal judge Richard Leon described the bulk collection of phone metadata as 'almost Orwellian', and found, 'Surely, such a program infringes on "that degree of privacy" that the founders enshrined in the Fourth Amendment.' In some of its practices, the NSA has been found to be acting illegally. The same is likely to be true of intelligence agencies in other countries. At other times, it seems, government agencies have been acting entirely in the absence of relevant laws. This too is problematic.

Can any law authorising domestic surveillance be just? To answer, Kant would ask whether the law was one the whole populace could possibly have assented to. The fact that it might be unpopular or adversely affect people is of little consequence. However, if a law attacks the dignity and equal moral standing of citizens, then it is unjust. A law implementing slavery or granting hereditary privilege is necessarily unjust, but with privacy the answer is not so readily apparent. My entitlement to privacy is considerably more subtle and conditional than my entitlement not to be enslaved or disadvantaged by birth.

If a surveillance law effectively privileges the rights of one group of people over another – those, say, of a particular race, or religion, or socio-economic status – then it is necessarily unjust. This invalidates, for instance, a law enabling the implementation of a nationwide facial recognition system to surveil and oppress a minority. What's more, if a law is indiscriminately a violation of the dignity of humanity, it is also unjust. As I detailed in chapter 2, whistle-blower Edward Snowden revealed that the NSA's mantra was to 'collect it all'. In Snowden's words:

> The NSA specifically targets the communications of everyone. It ingests them by default. It collects them in its system, and it filters them, and it analyzes them, and it measures them, and it stores them for periods of time, simply because that's the easiest, most efficient and most valuable way to achieve these ends. So while they may be intending to target someone associated with a foreign government or someone that they suspect of terrorism, they're collecting your communications to do so. Any analyst at any time can target anyone.

This is potentially an indiscriminate violation of the dignity of humanity.

As Kant wrote, if a law is framed such that a whole people could agree to it, then the people have a duty to regard that law as just, even if, on their current way of thinking, they would probably refuse to agree. This leaves considerable room for interpretation. Some domestic surveillance laws and practices are no doubt just, but some are patently unjust, according to Kant's model.

Finally, the question of just law must also take into account the non-domestic aspect of such surveillance. The Chinese government, as I have mentioned, is reportedly building a *global* facial recognition database. Have those outside China assented to this? No. Could they? Not likely. 'There's a good chance that Beijing already has your face in its enormous database,' wrote Peter Hartcher in the

Sydney Morning Herald in October 2019. Similarly, the NSA does not restrict itself to US borders or citizens. The internet is international, and the surveillance of non-domestic populations significantly complicates the question of whether the law authorising it qualifies as an expression of collective consent. Theoretically, a global legislative body could pass such a just global law. In the next chapter, I will argue that only a globally minded solution can hope to be effective.

What type of access constitutes an invasion of privacy? A further issue concerns the *type* of access involved. Will this access to people's data be conducted by people, or by machines? If a domestic surveillance law provides that AI can collect all citizens' data, but that a human agent can only access such data under strictly circumscribed conditions, including a judicial warrant, then it is more likely to be a just law than a domestic surveillance law that prescribes collecting all citizens' digital data for indiscriminate human analysis. Who is granted access? Under what conditions? These are crucial questions in determining whether a domestic surveillance law is just. (On this issue, see also chapter 4.)

What about the secrecy of these laws, policies and practices? For Kant, a fundamental principle of politics is that laws ought to be public. More specifically, Kant wrote that government policies ought not be incompatible with publicity. Allen Wood writes: 'A political maxim of policy is known to be unjust when it is possible for the politician to foresee, before implementing it, that its being made public would arouse such public opposition that the aims of the policy would be defeated.'

This is Kant's first principle of publicity. It does not settle once and for all whether a policy accords with right, but if a policy breaches this principle, it cannot be just. The general policy, if not the program specifics, ought to be capable of being made public.

What was the NSA's 'political maxim of policy'? What was, and is, the principle that underpins its policy? That maxim might be expressed: *We reserve the right to inspect anyone's communications and data if we deem them relevant to national security, and this includes the right to store and record everyone's communications and data, because we don't know what might be relevant in the future.* Is this incompatible with publicity?

According to Kant, governments need not act entirely in the full spotlight of publicity. Governments, like individuals, need to know that not every detail of their deliberations and operations will be made public. It follows that some elements of a national security program can justifiably be kept secret. However, transparency ought to be the default, secrecy the exception, and some laws and policies under which government agencies have been conducting domestic surveillance breach the first principle of publicity. That is, had they been made public, they may well have aroused such opposition that their aims would have been defeated.

Journalist John Oliver made this point with comic precision in 2015. In an interview with Edward Snowden, Oliver asked about the government's collection of intimate photos, including 'dick pics'. Oliver showed Snowden prerecorded footage of Americans responding to the idea of such a surveillance program.

'The government should not be able to look at dick pictures,' said one young woman, and several others echoed the sentiment. 'If my husband sent me a picture of his penis and the government could access it I would want that program shut down,' said another woman.

'The good news is there's no program named the "dick pic program",' responded Snowden. 'The bad news is they are still collecting everyone's information, including your dick pics. If you have your email somewhere like Gmail, hosted on servers overseas or transferred overseas, or [if it] at any time crosses over borders outside the United States, your junk ends up on the database.'

Programs of domestic surveillance have generally not been aired and debated before implementation. In the US, writes Bruce

Schneier, the NSA worked largely in secret, under the authority of executive orders, laws and court decisions that were sometimes covert. Had US citizens been made aware, they may well have shown an overwhelming support. However, they may well have objected, as the above quotes suggest. As it happened, following Snowden's revelations, the governments of the US, the UK, Germany and Canada announced a review of their intelligence services. In the US, the *USA FREEDOM Act* was passed in 2015 to scale back domestic surveillance capabilities. Its name is an acronym for *Uniting and Strengthening America by Fulfilling Rights and Ending Eavesdropping, Dragnet-collection and Online Monitoring Act*, and it aimed, among other things, to end bulk collection of phone metadata, of the sort at issue in *ACLU v Clapper* and *Klayman v Obama*. This response suggests these laws and policies were incompatible with publicity, and hence unjust.

Some governments might argue that the very act of making public a surveillance program would nullify its efficacy. By contrast, I am arguing that governments have a duty to subject the parameters (if not all specifics) of their surveillance laws and policies to the scrutiny of the public.

Are they good laws? The 'just law' test merely sets a minimum standard. It prompts us to ask which laws are unjust, and hence should be abandoned. However, it does not tell us which laws are *good*. It does not tell us which laws we should adopt. Whether the laws and policies underpinning surveillance by government agencies such as the NSA are good laws and policies is a question that requires further deliberation. As well as considering whether a surveillance program is based on just laws and policies, we need to consider whether a government *ought* to adopt these laws and policies. This involves a consideration of the effectiveness of domestic surveillance in achieving its aims.

In 2006, psychologist Floyd Rudmin conducted statistical analysis to declare that mass surveillance is doomed to fail: 'Mass surveillance of an entire population cannot find terrorists. It is a probabilistic impossibility. It cannot work.' More recently, in 2015, computer scientist Ray Corrigan wrote that 'mass surveillance makes the job of the security services more difficult and the rest of us less secure'. More research and discussion are needed. If mass surveillance programs are indeed ineffective at realising their chief goal of preventing terrorism and serious crimes, then they ought to be abandoned. The right to privacy should not be violated for merely speculative and ineffective ends. However, if these programs are shown to be effective, then further public discussion is needed, including about the nature of the threat the laws are intended to counter. Only in this way can the government be confident it is acting with genuine collective consent.

Do governments have a conflict of interest? On the one hand, governments collect data in the interests of effective governance. Specifically, they collect data for the oversight of national security, as well as public health, educational policy, infrastructure planning and more. For these purposes, the more data the better. A government with deep knowledge of its populace will recognise, for instance, which diseases are likely to become more prevalent, and hence how the hospital system should adapt. A government might also use data for less altruistic purposes, including being re-elected. On the other hand, governments are responsible for protecting the privacy interests of individuals. In a digital age, as we have seen, the power of consent is limited, and needs to be bolstered by the collective consent of the law. Hence governments must enact and enforce regulation to protect individual privacy.

How can governments reconcile their conflicting interests for collection and for non-collection?

To an extent, this conflict of interest also applies to governments aiming to regulate digital platforms. If access to corporate data can benefit a government, then why would a government want to limit its access to such data? Included among Snowden's revelations was the PRISM program, under which the NSA collected citizens' internet communications from at least nine companies, including Google, Apple and Facebook. By several accounts, PRISM is at the very heart of the NSA's data-gathering programs. We need to account for this potential conflict of interest when it comes to the collection of personal data. Again, increased transparency would help.

The issue of government surveillance is hard. By contrast, the issue of public nudity is easier. Let us presume that Stephen Gough's naked rambling is neither forbidden nor commanded by the moral law. Rather, it is ethically permissible. However, *external* law has forbidden his behaviour. As such, Gough has spent most of the past two decades in jail. During his naked ramblings, Gough flew a white flag from his backpack bearing the hand-scrawled slogan 'The Freedom to be Yourself'. Kant's formula protects the freedom to be yourself. But it also limits that freedom, by taking account of the freedoms of others. Freedoms are offset by obligations (to respect others' freedoms). Rights are offset by duties (to respect others' rights). Gough's freedom to be himself is offset by the collective pronouncement that privates stay private.

The only outstanding issue is whether the laws and regulations by which Gough has been imprisoned are unjust. Unfortunately for Gough, they aren't. These are laws to which every person could possibly assent. Many people might disagree with these laws, but that doesn't make them unjust. In the UK, they set the standard, without discriminating. And so, in the matter of setting aside Gough's bodily privacy, *collective dissent overrides individual consent*.

Consider another case, a hypothetical. While on holiday in Melbourne, I'm dining with my wife in a quiet suburban restaurant. The only other party comprises two men deep in a whispered conversation. Due to a quirk of acoustics, however, my wife and I can overhear every word. Normally, I would respect this party's privacy.

I wouldn't tell anyone what they're saying. Otherwise, I'd be treating them merely as a means. If, however, I overhear that these men host a child pornography website, under Victorian state law I face a maximum penalty of three years in prison if I *don't* report their conversation. Again, the individual limits of privacy have been overridden by a collective pronouncement. And in this case, *collective consent overrides individual dissent* (or, more specifically, absence of required consent).

Collective consent overarches individual consent. I may wish to keep my financial dealings to myself, but the law compels me to share them with the tax office. I may prefer to be naked at the beach, but the law obliges me to cover up.

The same is true for net privacy. Laws affirm individual consent in cases of spyware and 'revenge porn'; laws specify the individual consent required before companies can share and sell user information; and laws authorise governments to store and monitor digital data, irrespective of consent. As long as these laws are just, they are legitimate.

And the larger point is that collective consent *trumps* individual consent. When it mandates a breath test of a driver's blood alcohol reading, collective consent *nullifies* the role of individual consent. When it prescribes that those under a certain age may not use certain services, collective consent *specifies* who may consent, and who may not. When it provides that individuals may not non-consensually share intimate images of another, collective consent *reinforces* individual consent.

The 'united will of the people' stands over and above, overarching and overseeing individual consent. Whenever collective consent is silent, individual consent reigns. But when individual consent must be tempered by justice, that justice is contained in collective consent. It is in collective consent that we find the *legal right* to privacy.

A SUMMARY OF THE MODEL

Combining all the above, the application of our model of consent involves asking a series of questions:

- Is consent required because a morally significant privacy issue is at stake?
- Is there competence to consent? If not, hypothetical consent may be required, unless it is reasonable to wait for competency to commence or return.
- If there is competence, has actual individual consent been properly obtained? This involves a focus on the intention of the person seeking consent; taking account of the specificities of the person whose consent is sought; and a recognition that consent ought to be adequately iterative and layered.
- Is consent rendered irrelevant due to an ethically required or forbidden condition?
- Does the collective consent of just law prescribe any further conditions?

These questions follow a logical sequence, but they don't necessarily need to be addressed in this order. What's more, sometimes some of these questions will clearly be irrelevant.

Let's test the model with my inadvertent masterpiece, *Kiss at the Sydney Opera House*. First, is consent required? Are the couple significantly affected? If I am planning to publish and sell the image, then yes. If I am planning to exhibit a print in a friend's art gallery, perhaps not.

Second, are they competent to consent? Or are they drunk? Or children? Or mentally impaired? If so, I must wait until they become competent, or have someone competent consent on their behalf. If they are drunk, I can wait. If they are children, or mentally impaired, a guardian or parent can decide on their behalf.

Third, if they are competent, I must obtain their actual consent. In doing so, I must also offer them the genuine possibility of consent. This involves satisfying the three criteria I have just elaborated: that consent be a bona fide case of *caveat venditor*, with a focus on my intention; that consent take account of the specificities of the couple; and that consent must be iterative and layered, as appropriate. If I am a famous photographer with a reputation for bullying, or if I omit to mention that I plan to exhibit and sell, it is unlikely I will satisfy the first criterion. If the couple have a limited grasp of English, or hail from a culture where it is impolite to say no, then I may well fail criterion two. And if initially I had planned to exhibit in a gallery, but now also intend to generate viral memes, then I ought to seek their re-consent.

Fourth, is there a moral imperative that applies? Is there a direct and imminent threat to someone's humanity? Clearly this is unlike the case of the unconscious jogger, or the killer at the door. Hence, no. If, however, it turns out that the couple are very young, perhaps even parental consent would not authorise me to publish in certain contexts.

Finally, what does the collective consent of the law say? Different countries have different laws for such cases. French law is more prohibitive than Australian law, or US law. And hard legal issues remain. Can silence be construed as consent? What if I cannot locate the couple? Nonetheless, the law can help by setting parameters. Individual consent enables us to apply the formula of humanity. Especially when it comes to digital privacy, however, individual consent must be generously supplemented by the collective consent of the law.

All the while, we need to construe both autonomy and privacy in relational terms. We are all embodied and embedded. We are all socially constituted: none of us is a being simpliciter; we are all beings-in-relation. In some cases, systemic pressures can unfairly compromise autonomy and privacy, including by undermining consent. In response, we need not aim for an idealised autonomy and privacy, free from interference and compromise. Rather, we need to address the underlying inequities that create the preconditions for oppression and exploitation, both offline and online. In a digital context, for instance, this includes identifying the hidden biases coded into algorithms and artificial intelligence, a point I discuss in the next chapter.

As Catriona Mackenzie writes, an agent cannot be self-determining unless structural socio-relational conditions are in place. If agents stand in relations of subordination, subservience, deference, or economic or psychological dependence, they may well not be autonomous, even if the agents themselves endorse these subordinate, subservient or dependent positions. Only once fair and equitable conditions prevail can consent become more comprehensively morally justifying.

A further point is that the *two-tier model of consent* outlined above aligns with the *access model of privacy*. In chapter 4, I argued that privacy is *always* about restrictions on access. Sometimes these restrictions can involve our control. At other times, however, these restrictions will be the result of externally imposed limitations on access to us and information about us. Individual consent equates to control; and collective consent equates to externally imposed restrictions upon access. Just as control must be complemented by externally imposed restrictions on access, so too individual consent must be complemented by collective consent.

Individual consent can be regarded as a rule of virtue. Collective consent, by contrast, is the rule of right. As Paul Formosa notes, it is only when the coerced rule of right is coupled with the non-coerced rule of virtue that 'humanity's end of an enlightened age of peace' can be realised.

A DIRECT AND IMMINENT THREAT

Towards the end of *The Dark Knight*, Lucius Fox types in his name, and the surveillance apparatus designed by Wayne Enterprises self-destructs.

'Sometimes people deserve to have their faith rewarded,' mumbles Batman.

The Joker is defeated; innocent lives are saved; the surveillance system is history. Of course, that's not to say Batman, or someone with fewer scruples, won't build another just like it. This is no uncomplicated happy ending. Have Lucius and Batman jettisoned ethical principles and civil rights to prevent a calamity? First, Lucius condemns the surveillance apparatus and its power; then he and Batman use it to thwart the Joker's terrorist plot. Are they right to do so?

I have been arguing that an application of Kant's formula of humanity, which exhorts us never to use someone merely as a means, can illuminate the ethics of internet privacy. And to apply the formula, we must abide by the consent and dissent of those significantly affected by our actions. But Batman never sought the consent of Gotham's citizens. With their elaborate surveillance apparatus, Lucius and Batman were ostensibly using the citizens of Gotham merely as a means to capture the Joker. How does this fit with the two-tier model of consent I have been describing?

Clearly, a morally significant privacy issue was at stake. It's also fair to assume that many citizens would have been competent to consent. It's also fair to assume that Batman and Lucius were not authorised by a just law. Lucius admits as much. Instead, they were acting as vigilantes, imposing an ad hoc, extra-judicial justice. They failed to obtain the individual consent of citizens, and they were not authorised by collective consent. It seems that they were not entitled to engage in such surveillance.

However, there is one more consideration, and that is whether there is an ethical imperative that renders consent irrelevant. As it happens, there is. The moral law (to use Kant's phrase) *demands* that Batman spy. Batman is *ethically required* to save the citizens on the ferries, whom the Joker is about to kill. The requirement for consent is nullified by the requirement to save lives in imminent danger. Rather than using the citizens merely as a means, he is expressing respect for humanity by spying on all of them to save some of them. A government would be similarly entitled in the face of a direct and imminent threat.

Batman has an advantage. He's a superhero. In his absence, we'll need to rely for protection on two levels of consent.

7

HOW TO REGULATE
FOR DIGNITY

Whenever I talk to students about privacy and digital media, the pop culture reference they raise more than any other is *Black Mirror*. 'Oh, that reminds me of the episode where ...', they'll say, before describing a scene or a character.

Set in the near future, *Black Mirror* is a science fiction series consisting of self-contained episodes, each one an hour or so in length. The scenarios are unconventional and provocative. And their vision is often bleak, suggesting that today's mediated and tech-heavy lives have us on a dangerous trajectory.

One early episode, *The Entire History of You*, is the story of an ambitious lawyer named Liam. Like other well-to-do young people, Liam has a 'grain' implanted behind his ear. This grain records everything he sees and hears, enabling him to watch a replay, or 're-do', of any past moment, either directly on his eye, or on an external screen.

The episode opens when Liam returns from a work trip to find his wife Ffion in full swing at a dinner party. One of the guests is someone unfamiliar named Jonas, and Liam soon grows suspicious. Is Ffion being unfaithful? The temptation, of course, is to try to access the re-dos captured on Ffion's grain, and also on Jonas's grain. But how can Liam access their grains? And should he? Or would everyone involved be better off without one? Trouble is, removing them can lead to loss of vision or brain damage.

Like the internet, the grain can have a significant impact on the privacy of those who use it, and those around them. What's more, it can have a significant impact on their relationships. In close relationships, we ought to trust one another. This involves privacy, which requires sharing intimacies, and also respecting one another's secrets.

In this chapter, I offer practical solutions in the shape of legal and extra-legal measures that can implement the theory I've been building. In the first section, I outline the legal solutions that can be derived from my theoretical framework. In the second section, I propose complementary extra-legal measures, such as digital literacy education, market-based strategies and coding.

In this way, I propose a global solution intended to prevent a future as bleak as *Black Mirror*.

LEGAL PROTECTIONS

The processes of digital consent have been significantly refined in recent years.

Google, for instance, now offers users a 'Dashboard', a single page which links to all the products and services on which their information is stored. From the Dashboard, users can download their data, including from Google Maps, Google News, Google Photos, Google Hangouts, Google Home, Google Play, Google Drive and YouTube, among other products and services. 'Your account, your data,' says the site, at takeout.google.com. 'Export a copy of content in your Google Account if you want to back it up or use it with a service outside of Google.' And in September 2019, Google released its Android 10 operating system for Pixel devices, which involved giving users more detailed information, including about the data that third party apps are able to access. For instance, users are alerted if an app operating in the background – such as a news site – is tracking the user's location.

Increasingly, consent is being tailored for our modern media habits, including for the small screens of our mobile devices. Companies are working hard to make notice-and-consent provisions as crisp and concise as possible. 'Mobile is the ultimate test,' Google's global privacy counsel, Peter Fleischer, told the Amsterdam Privacy Conference back in 2015. 'We need to get notices down to a sentence. A 10-page notice form is a catastrophe.' Since then, his words have become even more salient.

As we have seen, however, individual consent is simply inadequate to fully protect privacy online. Out of sight, data is collected, inferred and aggregated in ways that are far beyond the reach of control and consent. When I am on a tennis court, I cannot choose to go surfing. And when I am on the internet, I cannot effectively choose to avoid all privacy invasions by individuals, companies and governments. On the internet and its platforms, my behaviour is constrained by the prevailing parameters. Certain activities are possible; others are not. Google doesn't have a button that allows me to turn off all tracking. Facebook doesn't give me the option to reset all my data to zero. And what control do I have over government surveillance? As a result, we need collective consent in the form of robust legal protections to complement individual consent.

This is vitally important. As historian Yuval Noah Harari writes in *21 Lessons for the 21st Century*:

> Over the past two centuries we have become extremely
> sophisticated in regulating the ownership of industry; thus
> today I can own a piece of General Motors and a bit of Toyota
> by buying their shares. But we don't have much experience
> in regulating the ownership of data, which is inherently a far

more difficult task, because unlike land and machines, data is everywhere and nowhere at the same time, it can move at the speed of light, and you can create as many copies of it as you want ... So we had better call upon our lawyers, politicians, philosophers and even poets to turn their attention to this conundrum: how do you regulate the ownership of data? This may well be the most important political question of our era. If we cannot answer this question soon, our sociopolitical system might collapse.

For the sake of our sociopolitical systems, we need legal protections. The challenge lies in sketching out what form they ought to take.

Protecting *relational* privacy

For a start, the focus of privacy laws must extend beyond the individual. As data and society researcher Linnet Taylor wrote in 2017, data injustice is increasingly occurring on a collective level: 'New technologies tend to sort, profile and inform action based on group rather than individual characteristics and behaviour, so that in order to operationalize any concept of data justice, it is inevitably going to be necessary to look beyond the individual level.'

I've already cited the example of DNA databases. If a woman sends off a swab of saliva to a genealogy website for DNA analysis, the results might inadvertently reveal that the man she had thought was her biological father is in fact no relation. Or that her family is predisposed to cancer. Does this mean that she ought to obtain the consent of the man she calls her father? The consent of all her relatives? Are insurance companies entitled to buy this information?

In the US in 2018, Democrat politician Elizabeth Warren released details of her DNA analysis to show she had 'a Native

American ancestor'. Increasingly, however, First Nations peoples are questioning the notion of such testing, arguing that it is wrong to conflate DNA ancestry with identity and culture. As Native American geneticists Krystal Tsosie and Matthew Anderson write, 'the distinction is an important one – "Native American" is not just an ethnic term but it is a cultural and political designation.' They note that the Navajo Nation, among others, has long-standing moratoriums on genetics research. There is a realisation that individual DNA tests can have significant effects on the wider community, making abuse and exploitation possible. Hence individual consent ought to be qualified by group consent.

As I noted in chapter 4, classic notions of autonomy and personhood are founded on liberal political theory, under which the law's role is to protect the individual from unwarranted intrusions by the state and other individuals. By contrast, I have been arguing that autonomy is circumscribed by social relations. Autonomy is impacted by external factors, such as my job and my family, and internal factors, such as my personality and habits. In other words, autonomy is relational. And so too privacy. This means that in some cases I ought, for privacy reasons, to obtain the consent of *others* before I submit my sample to a genealogy website. And the law can help to identify which cases these are. The law, including Navajo law, has a significant role to play.

On a relational view, 'people are not self-made'. Rather, writes law professor Jennifer Nedelsky, 'we come into being in a social context that is literally constitutive of us'. This directly impacts the law. As James Meese writes, 'A relational analysis carries direct implications on how subjectivity is constituted and understood in law ... No longer do autonomous individuals, wholly separate from society, possess legal rights. Instead legal rights are viewed as vehicles through which relationships are constructed between actors.'

In this light, laws that protect procedural autonomy are a start.

Such laws might specify, for instance, that the personal information of someone under 13 can only be collected with the consent of
a parent or guardian. However, also needed are laws that protect
substantive autonomy. Sara Bannerman writes: 'A more substantive
form of autonomy could be fostered by privacy governance that
fosters self-respect, self-worth, and input and control over the
options and possibilities available in the networked configuration of
the self.'

Bit by bit, the law has been adopting a relational approach to
privacy. In chapter 4, I mentioned the case of *Niemietz v Germany*,
decided by the European Court of Human Rights in 1992. There,
the court found that the legally imposed respect for 'private life'
includes the right to establish and develop relationships with other
human beings. And as Charles Ess writes, the Norwegian Constitution protects the rights of the 'mature human being', who sits
somewhere between an individualistic conception (in which the
individual takes precedence over the community) and a collectiv-
istic conception (in which the community takes precedence over
the individual). In 2013, Ess and fellow ethicist Hallvard Fossheim
described this conception as an 'individual–relational self'.

There are still clearer examples of the law taking an individ-
ualistic/relational approach. Ess cites Norway's *allemannsretten*, or
'everyone's right', as an example of the balance between individual
and collective notions of property. The *allemannsretten* entitles all
persons to access private property, including cultivated land, for
purposes of hunting, camping and picnicking. The key point, argues
Ess, is that property is regarded as *inclusive*, rather than *exclusive*. A
variation involves the 'copyleft' schemes of the Creative Commons,
which acknowledge the primary rights of the author, but entitle
others to copy, share and remix. As Ess writes, 'Conceptions of property as inclusive property are affiliated with more relational senses of
selfhood and in contrast with modern property rights as *exclusive*.'

To return to the discussion of chapter 5, this suggests that we need to think of data less as something I own, like a car, and more as something that resists ownership, like a lake.

My general point here is that laws need to be drafted to protect relational privacy and relational autonomy more effectively. Privacy is, in many contexts, inclusive rather than exclusive, and the law needs to enable and encourage this. My DNA doesn't just reveal me. It reveals others too. Hence the law needs to take account of the interests of these others. In part, these interests can be captured in the law's allowance for the 'public interest', but that's just the start.

A relational approach to privacy can also be fostered by the law's recognition that public and private are not binary. The *allemannsretten* and copyleft protections do not give owners exclusive and total rights at the expense of non-owners. Rather, public and private are usually interwoven, involving a layering of entitlements. As I have described, digital media enables an unprecedented multiplication of place. All at once, I can be in public (on Twitter) in private (wearing earbuds, absorbed in my screen) in public (on the bus). The law needs to recognise that privacy is often not merely a yes/no proposition. It is increasingly layered, requiring fine-grained and versatile protections. To start with, as jurists including Lindsey A. Strachan and Andrew Lavoie have separately argued, the law must explicitly recognise a notion of 'public privacy'.

GDPR: the European exemplar

Good law will take due account of the relationality of privacy. It will also emulate the General Data Protection Regulation, or GDPR, of the European Union. In March 2019, the United Nations' Special Rapporteur on Privacy released his annual report. Unequivocally, he recommended that *all* countries make it a priority to adopt 'provisions equivalent or superior to the GDPR'.

The GDPR, which has bound all member states since 25 May 2018, largely dovetails with the ethical approach I have been advocating. Notably it imposes exacting requirements for consent (among other things). Article 4 provides: 'Consent of the data subject means: any freely given, specific, informed and unambiguous indication of the data subject's wishes by which he or she, by a statement or by a clear affirmative action, signifies agreement to the processing of personal data relating to him or her.' We can see how this wording begins to align with the model of individual consent described in chapter 6. What's more, under Article 7, written consent must be presented 'in an intelligible and easily accessible form, using clear and plain language', and Article 7(3) provides that 'Data subjects must be allowed to withdraw this consent at any time, and the process must not be harder than it was to opt in'. There is also a move to a *caveat venditor* approach. As jurists Marc Rotenberg and David Jacobs write, the GDPR shifts the burden of responsibility and accountability from users of data to 'controllers' of data. Under Article 6, 'processing [of data] shall be lawful only if and to the extent that … the data subject has given consent'.

Under the GDPR, competence to consent plays a key role too. The issue of children's competence is addressed in Article 8. Under the original draft of the GDPR, the processing of personal data of a child under 13 required parental or guardian consent. In the final GDPR, however, the threshold age was raised to 16. 'Where the child is below the age of 16 years, such processing shall be lawful only if and to the extent that consent is given or authorised by the holder of parental responsibility over the child.' EU member states may lower that threshold, but not below 13. The bar has been set high.

The demands made by the GDPR are onerous. And they are having an effect far beyond Europe. First, its provisions apply to non-European companies who process the data of EU citizens.

Second, as law professor Graham Greenleaf wrote in 2012, European privacy laws and standards have been highly influential in determining the data protection regimes of a long list of countries globally. European laws, led by the GDPR, ought to be even more influential internationally. And here we currently have an opportunity, given that tech platform executives have consistently started speaking out for globally uniform privacy regulations in line with the GDPR.

The EU's GDPR provides the best, and perhaps the only, viable template for a global regulatory framework.

The right to be forgotten

Among the GDPR's protections is the 'right to be forgotten', or 'right to erasure', which allows for individuals to request that entities such as Google remove specified links to URLs from its search results. As Tim Dwyer writes, 'The "right to be forgotten" is in some senses the 21st century version of the "right to be let alone".'

The right derives from *Google v Mario Costeja González*, a 2014 case that pitted a Spanish man against Google. As I noted in chapter 4, González objected to the fact that whenever someone Googled his name, the search results included links to two newspaper notices from 1998, describing real estate auctions prompted by proceedings to recover his social security debts. In 2010, González lodged a complaint with the Spanish data protection authority against the newspaper and against Google, requesting the links be removed from search results, citing the European Parliament's Data Protection Directive 95/46/EC on the protection of individuals with regard to processing of personal data.

After Spanish courts had considered the case, the European Court of Justice found in his favour, acknowledging that a balance needed to be struck: between the right of the user demanding privacy, and the right of internet users to information. The court noted:

> That balance may ... depend, in specific cases, on the nature
> of the information in question and its sensitivity for the data
> subject's private life and on the interest of the public in having
> that information, an interest which may vary, in particular,
> according to the role played by the data subject in public life.

The court also noted that accurate data that is lawful initially may over time become unlawful. In such cases, links should be erased. The court then found that González fell into this category. He had a right to be forgotten, and Google was required to remove the links. As Google's Peter Fleischer said in 2015, 'We were defending the principle that as long as content is legal on the web, you should be able to find it through a search index. The court disagreed.'

The results were dramatic. Within 18 months of the verdict, Google had received nearly 350000 right-to-be-forgotten requests to remove 1.2 million links. In all, 42 per cent of those URLs were removed from search results. And the key point is that when requests are approved, links are not erased from the web. Rather, the relevant links do not appear in search results. This means that, to erase the links more extensively, Gonzáles would have needed to approach other search engines.

In May 2018, the 'right to erasure' was codified in European Union law as Article 17 of the GDPR. However, there have been criticisms. One is that the right to be forgotten is unwarranted censorship that enables the rewriting of history. Given that the right involves delisting links, not deleting them, this criticism is easily dismissed. A second is that companies shouldn't police themselves. That is, Google shouldn't decide whether a complainant has a valid claim for links to be removed from Google. Fair enough, but the current system is better than nothing, and offers avenues for appeal to a judge. A third is that the binary approach of 'forgetting' versus 'remembering' is too narrow. Law scholars Sylvia de Mars and Patrick O'Callaghan argue that it could be improved by allowing for a more nuanced approach, which also enables 'reordering'. True enough. As I have noted, privacy is anything but binary. It is complex, particularly on the internet. In our digital interactions, the distinction between public and private is marked by subtleties and layering.

The right to be forgotten is a promising response, particularly against breaches by companies. It re-empowers individual consent, but also limits individual consent by balancing it against other salient rights and interests.

Wait, we have privacy laws!

Brian is an American college student whose Facebook profile kept getting hacked. The first time, the hacker altered Brian's 'interested in' to insinuate that Brian was gay. Brian laughed off the episode, changed his password and 'went on with everyday life'. Unfortunately, the hacker struck again, changing Brian's profile completely, including switching his profile picture to an image of Brian's head on a porn star's body. The hacker also changed Brian's relationship status to 'I'm having a hard time coming out of the closet right now'.

Brian was one of the subjects of a 2009 study led by media ethicist Bernhard Debatin, and his story doesn't end there. Next Brian deleted his profile and stayed off Facebook for three months, only to rejoin with a new email address. Six months later, his profile was hacked again. The hacker posted the same manipulated profile picture, but added the Donkey character from the film *Shrek*, tagging Donkey as Brian's girlfriend. This prompted Brian to delete his Facebook yet again, and to set up another new account with another email and strict privacy settings, something he hadn't previously realised he could do. Not surprisingly, he told the researchers he was upset by the hacks.

This case illustrates the complexity surrounding digital privacy. Brian was not gay. As such, his *invented* privacies were exposed. And yet this feels very much like a privacy invasion. Rather than an unauthorised revelation, this is unauthorised access enabling a misrepresentation of private matters concerning sexuality and relationships.

How does the law deal with such a case? How should it deal with such a case? Clearly Brian did not consent to this invasion; clearly he was treated merely as a means.

In many jurisdictions, this type of hacking is a criminal offence, prohibited by long-standing legislation. In Australia, the hacker could have been prosecuted under the federal *Criminal Code Act*, which proscribes 'any unauthorised access to data held in a computer; or any unauthorised modification of data held in a computer; or any unauthorised impairment of electronic communication to or from a computer'. In the US, similar provisions apply. In 2016, following a celebrity nude hack of Hollywood actresses, a Pennsylvania man was sentenced to 18 months in jail. Under the federal *Computer Fraud and Abuse Act* 1986, he was convicted of unauthorised access to a computer to obtain information. Similarly, Cassidy Wolf's hacker was convicted of unauthorised access (as well as extortion), and sentenced to 18 months in prison. Convictions of other hackers followed.

These cases reveal an important point. Before we draft new laws, we must reflect on existing laws. What is their role? Are they adequate? How can they be improved?

Internationally, there are already reams of privacy laws, and they're multiplying. This is particularly true for data privacy. In 1973, Sweden was first to pass a data privacy law; by December 2016, a total of 120 countries had enacted data privacy laws. And that proliferation is accelerating. As Graham Greenleaf wrote in 2017, 'Since 2010, the average number of new laws per year has increased dramatically.'

These laws take many forms, and have been interpreted in many ways. For instance, many laws protect 'personal data'. But what counts as personal data? Should the phrase be defined narrowly? Or broadly? In Australia, following the 2017 decision in *Privacy Commissioner v Telstra Corporation Limited*, a narrow approach has been taken to the interpretation of personal data as protected by the *Privacy Act*. A much broader approach has been recommended in the UK by the House of Commons Digital, Culture, Media and Sport Committee. In 2019, its report into 'fake news' recommended that even *inferred* data be protected. Meanwhile, the EU's GDPR defines personal information as 'information *relating to* an identified or identifiable natural person'. Here, as elsewhere, the GDPR sets a good benchmark that more accurately reflects the reality of data flows than Australia's narrow interpretation.

Jurisdictions need to conduct a thorough stocktake of existing laws, and of how those laws are interpreted. This ought to take in all laws that touch on privacy to determine how various layers of regulation interconnect. This means the net needs to be cast wide. For instance, libel, slander and defamation are clearly relevant. Weak defamation laws can jeopardise privacy; strong defamation laws can protect privacy. Also relevant are laws of trespass and intrusion. As we have seen, the law of privacy has several strands, which vary from country to country. These include: information privacy and data protection; personal privacy; bodily privacy; and constitutional privacy. These strands need to be interrogated too.

Internationally, such a stocktake would reveal a vast disparity, and glaring gaps. In many countries, the word 'privacy' isn't defined in a single statute. And almost everywhere, privacy would be better served by regulation that is more coherent and codified. As I've already noted, a sensible legal template for data protection would be Europe's GDPR. Another sensible approach would be the inclusion in legislation of an access-based definition of privacy.

In many countries, the coverage of privacy laws remains patchy and incoherent. Existing laws need to be reviewed and, where necessary, improved. For instance, to allow for the realities of modern data-gathering, any definition of personal data ought to include inferred data. Even so, in most jurisdictions, new laws are needed.

We need new laws

In 2017, an Australian woman swimming naked in her backyard pool was distressed to see a drone hovering overhead. 'My fences are really high and secure and there's big trees around the backyard, so it's the last place you'd think your privacy would be able to be invaded,' she said. In Australia, it's generally lawful for a person to film what they can see from a public space, including from the sky. This is one area where new laws are needed.

The most obvious function for the collective consent of the law is to reinstate and reinforce individual consent. That is, the law can clarify and buttress individual consent by helping to delineate the circumstances in which consent is required, by specifying who is competent to consent, and by defining what constitutes legally valid consent. New laws restricting the use of drones fall into this category.

So too laws against image-based abuse. Digital technology has enabled a new range of such abuses, including upskirting and 'revenge porn'. Jurisdictions including Japan, Canada, the UK and Australia, as well as states including California (in the US) and New South Wales (in Australia) have criminalised such image-based abuse. In the UK, a 2015 law made it illegal to disclose a 'private sexual photograph or film' without the consent of the person depicted, and with the intent to cause distress. The penalties included a maximum of two years in prison. Previously, the scope existed for prosecutions under existing obscenity laws, but few prosecutions were initiated.

In Canada too, the non-consensual sharing of intimate images was criminalised in 2015. As I noted in chapter 4, in 2016 a 29-year-old man from Winnipeg was jailed for posting three naked photos of his ex-partner to Facebook. There were two noteworthy aspects of the decision. One, the relational nature of privacy was revealed when the *man's* name was suppressed to protect the privacy of the victim. And two, the offence consists of 'knowingly' sharing an intimate image, and 'knowing' that the person depicted did not consent, or being reckless in this regard. Here the law aligns with a *caveat venditor*, rather than *caveat emptor*, approach. This Canadian prohibition has been supplemented by provincial laws that give victims the right to launch civil lawsuits. In 2018, a Saskatchewan law that enabled victims to sue put the burden of proof on the distributor of the image. That is, the distributor *needs to show evidence* he obtained consent to share the image.

Old laws need to be supplemented with new laws, and some of these new laws will have specific targets, such as drones or image-based abuse. At other times, however, new laws ought to be more general. One clear instance concerns default settings. Across the web, default privacy settings tend to be for sharing. If I want privacy, I generally need to actively adjust my settings, and doing so is sometimes difficult and counterintuitive. Here the law ought to step in, prescribing that the default position for data collection must be for privacy, not sharing. Or, in the words of the Australian Competition and Consumer Commission's Final Report of its 2019 Digital Platforms Inquiry, legislation ought to ensure 'that any settings for data practices relying on consent must be pre-selected to "off" and that different purposes of data collection, use or disclosure must not be bundled'.

A right of action

In the United States, individuals have been successfully suing for breaches of privacy for more than a century. In 1905, a man sued successfully for an invasion of privacy after his image was used in an advertisement without his permission. As Judge Cobb wrote in *Pavesich v New England Life Insurance Co.*:

> Liberty includes the right to live as one will, so long as that will does not interfere with the rights of another or of the public. One may wish to live a life of seclusion; another may desire to live a life of publicity; still another may wish to live a life of privacy as to certain matters and of publicity as to others.

More than a century after *Pavesich*, Terry Bollea, aka wrestler Hulk Hogan, was awarded US$140 million after suing the Gawker website for posting footage of him having sex with a friend's wife. After Gawker Media declared bankruptcy in 2016, Bollea settled for $31 million. The website's fans declared a dark day for free speech and press freedom; privacy advocates cheered.

Civil remedies are imperfect. Above all, they are notoriously expensive, favouring rich claimants. Bollea's action was bankrolled by Peter Thiel, the billionaire co-founder of PayPal. (To complicate matters, Thiel is also founder of Palantir, the secretive data analytics company that collaborates with US police departments and immigration authorities.) However, civil suits can serve as a crucial support for other laws and remedies. For one thing, rights of action can compensate for damage that other categories of law often neglect, including emotional injury and psychic distress. More importantly, rights of action provide general protections, which makes them well-suited to adapting to new technologies.

Currently, the US, the UK, New Zealand, Canada and many

other jurisdictions have a tort of privacy. In the UK, a tort of privacy crystallised only recently. Following the enactment of the *Human Rights Act* 1998, which incorporated provisions of the European Convention on Human Rights into domestic law, courts extended the equitable action of breach of confidence. However, there was disagreement as to whether the action had in fact coalesced into a tort until the 2015 case of *Google Inc. v Judith Vidal-Hall*, in which three parties successfully sued Google for the misuse of private information by its use of internet cookies, given that the cookies were installed without consent. This contradicted Google's claims that user-generated content could not be tracked without the user's permission.

In Canada, a common law right to privacy emerged from the landmark 2012 decision of *Jones v Tsige*, which involved the tort of intrusion upon seclusion. More recently, a tort of public disclosure of private facts has also emerged in Canada. The extent of these laws remains uncertain. Clarifying legislation would help.

By contrast, Australia has no right of action, even though federal and state law reform bodies have consistently and stridently recommended one. In the 2014 report *Serious Invasions of Privacy in the Digital Era*, the Australian Law Reform Commission (ALRC) recommended a statutory civil cause of action that would be: 'directed at invasions of privacy that are serious, committed intentionally or recklessly, and that cannot be justified in the public interest. It is also confined to invasions of privacy either by intrusion upon seclusion or by misuse of private information.'

In its 2019 report into the impact of digital platforms, the Australian Competition and Consumer Commission backed the ALRC's position. The ALRC partly based its recommendation for a tort on the principle that privacy laws should be adaptable to technological change.

The ALRC also recommended that a balancing exercise be front and centre. Specifically, the ALRC proposed a law that requires:

a crucial 'balancing exercise', in which courts weigh privacy against other important public interests, such as freedom of speech, freedom of the media, public health and safety, and national security … A plaintiff should not be able to claim that a wrong has been committed – that their privacy has been seriously invaded – where there are strong public interest grounds justifying the invasion of privacy.

In this way, a right of action for invasions of privacy would also have the benefit of specifying different criteria and remedies in the face of threats from individuals, companies and governments. After all, not all encroachments are equal. A vast difference exists between a hacker gaining unauthorised access to a webcam for personal gain and an AI system employed by the government for national security that automatically records webcam footage no human will ever see, unless a court orders otherwise. The formula of humanity recognises degrees of wrongness; so should the law of privacy.

Legal protections modelled on consumer law

In 1980, Ruth Gavison wrote that privacy is a coherent value, but that there is a lack of coherence in judicial decisions about privacy. In response, she had a proposal: 'There is much to be said for making an explicit legal commitment to privacy. Such a commitment would affirm that privacy is not just a convenient label, but a central value.'

Admittedly, much has changed since 1980. In Canada, the *Privacy Act* came into effect in 1983, and the *Personal Information Protection and Electronic Documents Act* followed in 2000. In Australia, the *Privacy Act* landed in 1988, while New Zealand's *Privacy Act* was passed in 1993. Most dramatically, the far-reaching provisions of the EU's GDPR came into effect in 2018. Early in 2019, France's data protection watchdog fined Google €50 million for breaching the GDPR by failing to give users transparent and understandable information on its data use policies.

Since 1980, many explicit legal commitments to privacy have been made. In some cases, these commitments reveal that privacy is a central value. In many jurisdictions, however, legal commitments to privacy fall short. Indeed, outside Europe privacy protections tend to remain incoherent and inadequate. This includes the US, where no general federal law exists to protect privacy. (That said, there are more specific federal laws, including the *Health Insurance Portability and Accountability Act* of 1996 and the *Children's Online Privacy Protection Act* of 1998.) Most jurisdictions have not yet gone far enough with their legal commitments to privacy, particularly in the face of the significant challenges to privacy that arise in the digital era.

In this chapter, I have been making several interconnected arguments about the types of laws that can help to create a coherent and adequate framework for protecting privacy that aligns with the formula of humanity. To these points I want to add one final argument. That is: in each jurisdiction, the law of privacy ought to be underpinned by a series of general principles enshrined in legislation.

Of course, privacy principles already exist, in many forms, including in legislation. Accordingly, in some jurisdictions, the principles I am proposing might inform the refinement of existing law, such as Australia's *Privacy Act*. Or, as in the case of the US, adoption of the principles would require the enactment of entirely new law. My goal is merely to outline the principles that accord with a Kantian approach. And as with a right of action, one major benefit of adopting such principles is that they would effectively accommodate new advances in technology. As Australia's former privacy commissioner, Timothy Pilgrim, told me in 2015, general prescriptions can provide much-needed flexibility: 'I think that's the only way ... for allowing a law to not have to be changed too regularly, because it's almost impossible to change laws regularly.'

And we don't need to start from scratch. Rather, these general protections can take their cue from consumer law. This is the approach advocated by legal scholar James Grimmelmann: 'some of the lessons the law has learned in dealing with product safety could usefully be applied to the analogous problem of privacy safety.' Grimmelmann is writing specifically about social media, but the approach can extend to protection of privacy generally. Indeed, Viktor Mayer-Schönberger makes a similar argument. He proposes that regulation is needed to introduce ex-ante protections, rather than the ex-post remedies that individuals currently try to invoke only once there is a problem. Hence Mayer-Schönberger envisages a prescriptive and preventative model rather than a reactive and punitive model. This is, after all, what society has already done by mandating seat belts for cars, and by introducing regulatory schemes to oversee food safety and drug safety. To enforce such a scheme, a regulator is required, just as a regulators exist for food, drug and car safety.

Five privacy principles to form a cornerstone of privacy law

My normative starting point has been a Kantian prohibition on treating others merely as means. As such, I propose that general legal protections ought to begin with the judicious application of individual consent. We can think of this as **the consent principle**, and it might be expressed: **For any act or process that significantly impacts a person's privacy, that person's consent ought to be sought and respected.**

Alternatively, to accommodate the relational nature of privacy, this principle might be better and more fully expressed as: **For any act or process that significantly impacts a person's or a group of persons' privacy, that person's or group's consent ought to be sought**

and respected. The subsequent privacy principles might be extended in the same way. As it stands, I have expressly accommodated the relational nature of privacy in principle five, the balancing principle.

The consent principle would form a powerful base for legislative provisions that extend to privacy issues generally, rather than merely to data protection. Enacted via statute, such a principle would explicitly reinforce user control. In this way, it would reinforce the dignity and autonomy of users. This principle could be further supplemented with clear provisions regarding competence to consent, as well as the three conditions detailed in chapter 6: consent must be to the best of the knowledge of the person or entity seeking consent; consent ought to take into account the particularities of the person whose consent is sought; and consent ought to be iterative and layered, as required.

Image-based abuse is a breach of the consent principle, as is the hidden transfer of data among third parties, such as data brokers. And clearly such a principle would invalidate the creation of shadow profiles of people who do not use a service. It would also prohibit Google Buzz, a social networking tool launched by Google in 2010. Google Buzz automatically revealed the Gmail contacts with whom each user frequently communicated. It was abandoned in 2011. And in 2019, the *Wall Street Journal* reported that 11 apps were sharing personal data with Facebook – including the data of people without Facebook accounts. Following the report, five of the apps stopped sharing data. In these cases, clearly, users were never given the proper chance to consent.

A second principle, linking with the formula of humanity's prima facie prohibition on deception, would mandate transparency and fairness. Here we have a great irony: transparency is a key principle for the protection of privacy. As James Moor puts it, privacy norms must be public. This applies broadly, including to the data management practices of, say, search engines. As digital media scholar Alexander Halavais writes in *Search Engine Society*:

> The clickstreams and other data generated by individuals using the web are valuable, and when the trade is transparent, many people will be willing to exchange it for services. But when search engines and social platforms collect data without clearly explaining how they will make use of it, and to whom they will release it, it represents an unjust imbalance of power.

A commitment to transparency can address power imbalances, particularly when coupled with a commitment to fairness. And in fact, this seems to be what many internet users want. In research published in 2017, focus groups in Norway, Spain and the UK expressed an overriding concern for fairness in data mining practices. As Helen Kennedy, Dag Elgesem and Cristina Miguel argued, this concern for fairness 'can be understood ... as part of broader concerns about well-being and social justice'.

A **transparency and fairness principle** might be worded: **Individuals, organisations and governments must be transparent and fair in their dealings regarding a person's privacy, including in the collection and sharing of information about a person, with particular regard to personal and sensitive data.** Of course, here there is significant overlap with the consent principle. If companies use your private data without consent, there is a good chance there has been a failure of either fairness or transparency. Without fairness and transparency, it is likely that the possibility of consent has not been offered.

This second principle would mandate a degree of transparency in the workings of algorithms employed by digital platforms. These algorithms determine much of the content we see on the internet. They determine the posts we see on social media, the stories recommended for us when we visit news sites, and the results we get when we use a search engine. The workings of these algorithms tend to be highly opaque, and digital platforms tend to be fiercely protective of this opacity. But what specific signals are these algorithms employing? Are they using only data obtained consensually, ethically and legally? How can we know? A reasonable degree of mandatory transparency would help. (And, I would suggest, more targeted legislation might help too, such as legislation to establish an algorithmic regulator.)

This second principle (as well as the first) would also require that privacy provisions be delivered in 'readable' terms. Studies show that standard consumer contracts are as dense as academic papers. 'Currently, the law neglects to impose on companies a clear and operational duty to draft readable contracts,' writes business law scholar Samuel Becher, who studied the readability of the 500 most popular 'sign-in-wrap contracts' in the US. 'Without a clear incentive, companies will continue to use unreadable texts as their contracts.' A transparency and fairness principle would also have caught the Facebook advertising system Beacon, which was launched in 2007 and shared users' off-Facebook purchase data with other users, but gave no clear way to opt out.

Julie Brill, the former US Federal Trade Commissioner, has said data brokers such as Acxiom ought at the least to tell people about the data they collect, how they collect it, who they share it with and how it is used. The same goes for loyalty schemes and frequent flyer programs, many of which are paired with data brokers. 'We need to figure out what the rules should be as a society,' Brill has said. For instance, what are the rules regarding children? Can Acxiom begin building individual profiles at birth? Even earlier? Or should there be a blanket provision, tied into our prescription for fairness, that harvesting children's data is unlawful?

From this second principle, a third would follow directly, outlawing conduct that is misleading or deceptive. This **anti-deception** principle might provide that: **Individuals, organisations and governments must refrain from conduct that is misleading or deceptive in their dealings regarding a person's privacy, including in the collection and sharing of information about a person, with particular regard to personal and sensitive data.**

Here again, there is a clear link to the consent principle. No one could possibly consent, it would seem, in the face of misleading or deceptive conduct (or claims). Such a principle would apply in cases of misrepresentation, where data is being collected for one stated purpose, but is also being used for a different, hidden purpose. The principle would apply in the common scenario that occurs when users visit websites with content from a third party, and that third party then tracks the users' browsing across the web, as described in research by computer scientists Jonathan Mayer and John Mitchell.

A fourth and related privacy principle would defend against coercion. This **anti-coercion principle** might be worded: **Individuals, organisations and governments must refrain from conduct that is coercive in their dealings regarding a person's privacy, including in the collection and sharing of information about a person, with particular regard to personal and sensitive data.**

Coercion can manifest in many forms. When a large company such as Apple, Google, Facebook, Amazon, Microsoft, Tencent or Alibaba changes its privacy policy, a user may feel compelled to agree, even if she would really rather not. If many of my personal and work documents are stored at OneDrive, but then Microsoft alters its privacy provisions in a way I find unacceptable, I may still feel compelled to accept these new provisions in order to maintain access to my documents. Is this constrained consent or is it coercion? It's a fine line, and courts are well placed to decide what is legal and what is not.

Other cases are easier. Imagine I want to use Google and Facebook. Imagine further that I fully accept the terms and conditions of their privacy policies. My consent to their privacy practices is informed and iterative. However, imagine that I also know government agencies are actively monitoring my Google searches and Facebook activities. To this, I do not wish to consent, but what choice do I have? A principle that explicitly targets coercion is one way of identifying and invalidating practices and policies when the pressure to agree becomes unacceptable.

And finally, we need a fifth principle. Our four general prescriptions require a general exception. Privacy, as we have seen, cannot be absolute, but exists in the contexts of other rights, obligations and freedoms. As Ruth Gavison writes: 'It is obvious that privacy will have to give way, at times, to important interests in law enforcement, freedom of expression, research and verification of data. The result is limits on the scope of legal protection of privacy.' A balancing act must be struck between, on the one hand, people's right to privacy and, on the other hand, the rule of law, the people's right to security and the public interest generally, among other things.

A fifth privacy principle, then, is a **balancing principle**, which would provide: **The right to privacy is not absolute, but exists in the context of other rights, obligations and freedoms. These include, but are not limited to: the right to personal security; the right to be connected; the right to free speech; freedom of the press; and freedom of information. The right to privacy must be balanced against these other rights, obligations and freedoms. This balancing act must take into account the public interest. It must also take into account that an individual's privacy does not just matter for the sake of the individual whose privacy is at stake, but for other persons too.** In this way, this fifth balancing principle recognises and allows for the relational nature of privacy. Indeed, it embeds this relationality in the law as a consideration. The judiciary can then apply the appropriate balancing act, determining just how much weight the right to privacy deserves in any given circumstance.

(Bearing in mind that in several jurisdictions, including Australia, many of these rights are protected only in limited and piecemeal ways.)

Amitai Etzioni argues that different societies are perfectly entitled to approach this balancing act in different ways. One society may value individual rights more highly; another may value the common good (or public interest) more highly. Consider a politician having an affair. Would it be an invasion of privacy to reveal her liaison? In the US, the law of 'public figures' ensures their right to privacy is much more limited than that of the ordinary person. In Europe, the UK and Australia, by contrast, private matters of public figures are generally considered off limits, by law and by etiquette. For Etzioni, it's perfectly acceptable that different societies take different approaches.

Enshrined in legislation, these five general principles would serve to police against improper encroachments to privacy. What's more, the fifth can serve to differentiate challenges from individuals, companies and governments. The balancing act will change if data is being used for voyeurism, for profit or for national security.

Minimum viable legislation to protect citizens

Unfortunately, legislative reform is slow. Reform of Australia's *Privacy Act* took nine years, from 2005 to 2014. To this, Microsoft president Brad Smith has an intriguing suggestion: lawmakers should act more like coders. When designing software, coders realise that perfection is an unrealistic goal. Hence the practice is to release a 'minimum viable software product'. Developers well know that such software can, and will, be significantly improved. During a talk at Sydney University in March 2019, Smith argued that legislators ought to take the same approach. Rather than aiming to draft *perfect* law, they ought to pass *good* law quickly. This, he said, is the approach being taken in Washington State, where legislators are moving quickly on laws to target data collection and facial recognition technology. Here, says Smith, lawmakers are moving at internet speed.

It is worth noting that in several jurisdictions existing consumer law already enforces privacy principles. Indeed, the US consumer watchdog, the Federal Trade Commission (FTC), is the country's main privacy regulator. Specifically, the FTC's Bureau of Consumer Protection targets unfair, deceptive and fraudulent business practices. These 'fair information practices', as they are known, are not binding law; nonetheless, the FTC has imposed penalties including a US$22.5 million fine on Google in 2012 for placing advertising tracking cookies in the browsers of Safari users, despite assurances from Google it would not do so. The fine was imposed not because Google breached fair information practices, but because it breached a previous order in which Google promised to the FTC not to misrepresent its privacy policies to consumers.

This $22.5 million fine remained the largest civil penalty in an order violation until July 2019, when it was put in the shade by a US$5 billion penalty for Facebook in the wake of the Cambridge Analytica scandal. Again, the fine was for breaching a previous FTC order. As Commissioner Rebecca Kelly Slaughter wrote in her decision:

> For years, when Facebook asked you 'who do you want to see your post?' and you chose to share your information only with your 'friends', Facebook provided that data not only to your friends, but also to any of the millions of third-party apps that those friends used. This was precisely the type of misleading conduct that the Federal Trade Commission's 2012 order sought to prevent. Yet evidence suggests that Facebook's practices violated the order early and often.

It is worth noting that Slaughter's statement was dissenting. In the 3-2 decision, she and Commissioner Rohit Chopra argued that a $5 billion settlement *wasn't enough*, given the severity and extent of the privacy breaches.

This case reveals an interesting development. Globally, *competition* regulators are becoming defenders of privacy, as they investigate whether digital platforms use data in ways that give them an unfair market advantage, among other market issues. In February 2019, the German competition regulator, the Bundeskartellamt, found that Facebook could not legally combine the data obtained on Facebook with the data obtained on Instagram, WhatsApp and elsewhere without the explicit consent of users. The Bundeskartellamt ruled that Facebook was exploiting consumers by requiring them to agree to this kind of data collection. A *Wired* article about the ruling was headlined, 'German regulators just outlawed Facebook's whole ad business'.

In October 2019, the Australian Competition and Consumer Commission (ACCC) sued Google for allegedly misleading customers over its collection of location data. Consumers who turned off 'Location History' still had their location tracked, said the ACCC, unless they changed their settings in 'Web & App Activity'. 'We allege that as a result of these on-screen representations, Google has collected, kept and used highly sensitive and valuable personal information about consumers' location without them making an informed choice,' said ACCC chair Rod Sims. The lawsuit followed an 18-month investigation into the impact of Google, Facebook and other digital platforms, which culminated in a 600-page report recommending a suite of far-ranging reforms. And even though the ACCC had not explicitly been charged to investigate issues concerning data, many of its final recommendations involved strengthening the legal right to privacy.

In its final report, the ACCC noted the overlap between data protection, competition and consumer protection considerations. More specifically, the ACCC noted that digital platforms owe their significant market power to data about consumers:

> The fundamental business model of both Google and Facebook is to attract a large number of users and build rich data sets about their users. The ubiquity of these platforms and their presence in related markets enable them to build particularly valuable data sets. This enables them to offer highly targeted or personalised advertising opportunities to advertisers.

In the research I've been conducting since 2013, I have sought to apply Kant's ethics to digital privacy. By contrast, the ACCC took a much more expansive approach: commissioning quantitative research into news media use; inviting submissions and holding public forums; and commissioning independent reports (including from the Centre for Media Transition, where I work). Despite the contrasting approaches, our recommendations largely overlap. In its final report, the ACCC recommended (among other things): broader reform of Australian privacy law; the implementation of a right to be forgotten; and the enactment of a statutory tort for serious invasions of privacy. It also recommended that certain unfair trading practices and unfair contract terms be outlawed, in line with overseas consumer protections. This would outlaw particularly invasive privacy terms that far outweigh the benefits of services provided.

But there is at least one point of difference. Like the ACCC, I have been arguing that privacy protections ought to take a cue from consumer law protections. Unlike the ACCC, however, I want to add that internet users should be treated as more than consumers. Rather, internet users should be treated as *persons*, courtesy of privacy protections drafted in a manner analogous to consumer law protections. The distinction is significant. Throughout this book, I have been talking of persons, individuals and citizens. The concept of an internet user that I have been trying to sketch is in a Kantian sense: of a rational being with dignity and (relational) autonomy.

As legal scholar Cass Sunstein writes, 'the role of citizen is very different from the role of consumer'. The former role concerns people's engagement with democracy and public life; the latter concerns a person's role in the marketplace, with respect to the goods and services being consumed. The two roles are sometimes at odds. A person may vote for a pro-environment party, for instance, even though she litters, doesn't recycle and has an environmental footprint too big for any shoe. As Sunstein argues, citizens can be less selfish than consumers: 'In their role as citizens, people might seek to implement their highest aspirations when they do not do so in private consumption … they might attempt to satisfy altruistic or other-regarding desires, which diverge from the self-interested preferences often characteristic of the behaviour of consumers in markets.' For these reasons, writes Sunstein, 'we should evaluate communications technologies and social media by asking how they affect us as citizens, not only by asking how they affect us as consumers.'

If we are to build privacy protections modelled on consumer law, it is important that these laws protect us not just as consumers, but as citizens.

BEYOND CONSENT: EXTRA-LEGAL PROTECTIONS

Sometimes, however, law is irrelevant. As James Grimmelmann notes: 'Many privacy harms, embarrassing though they may be, are beneath the threshold at which the law ought to take notice. The fact that your mother found out your plans to attend International Skip School Day is not, and should not be, a legally cognizable harm.'

In fact, says Ruth Gavison, perhaps the law is *mostly* out of place when it comes to privacy: 'The law, as one of the most public mechanisms society has developed, is completely out of place in most of the contexts in which privacy is deemed valuable.' For many privacy breaches, the collective consent of the law simply has no role to play.

These are often the privacy breaches that occur in our personal relationships: when your mother discovers you plan to attend International Skip School Day; when your spouse stumbles upon your diary; or when your best friend learns that you're planning a holiday without her. As I argued in chapter 5, our relationships are inseparably linked to our privacy. And increasingly, our relationships are playing out on the internet, as we sign up to social media, dating platforms, hookup apps and adultery sites to meet and mate.

In this section, I explore the extra-legal means by which privacy (and relationships) can be supported and protected. The three non-legal means I address are social norms, market forces and coding. In this, I follow Lawrence Lessig, who writes that the four regulatory 'modalities' of law, norms, market and architecture work together, and sometimes in contradiction, to influence behaviour: 'The constraints are distinct, yet they are plainly interdependent. Each can support or oppose the others.'

A two-tier model of consent is not enough. In order to encourage behaviour that protects privacy appropriately, which includes taking into account privacy's effect on relationships, we need to look beyond consent and the law. In some cases, this involves calling upon the ends-in-themselves principle of the formula of humanity, which exhorts us to follow the positive, imperfect duty of treating all others (and ourselves) always as persons, as (relationally) autonomous agents pursuing their own projects. In other words, what follows is built not just on consent, but on respect. Once we acknowledge that privacy is relational, and once we recognise that privacy is constitutive of our relationships, we can see the need to reach beyond the law to protect privacy more fully.

The role of social norms

For Kant, only the law can embody the united will of the people. Social norms cannot have the same binding force; but clearly they play a significant role in moulding people's behaviour. In 2019, columnist Jessica Irvine reflected on the social norms that prevail on Twitter:

> Twitter ... exploded onto the social scene in 2006, throwing everyone in together on a wild ride. And didn't we behave like it. Like a teenage party with no parents, things quickly got a bit out of control. Pretty soon, we were word vomiting all over the place and getting a bit too rowdy.

In its early years, the internet was commonly regarded as an unprecedented enabler of *freedom*. It would allow unfettered connection, free speech and the flow of ideas. In 2004, when Facebook's arrival ushered in the era of social media, this faith became stronger. Surely now the net's great democratising potential would be fully realised. Things were rowdy, certainly, but the upside was that now finally everyone could be heard.

The downside was that now finally everyone could be heard.

Not everyone *should* be heard, and not all content should be shared. Some actors aim to harm; some speech is unequivocally dangerous. The livestreaming of the Christchurch massacre in March 2019 is a clear example. So is pornographic material featuring children. On the internet, white supremacists want a voice, as do ISIS terrorists, companies using slave labour and authoritarian nations that trample on human rights. These groups all want to exert their influence, sell their wares or promote their agenda.

Openness and free speech cannot be unlimited. This is a fundamental ethical truth: no right or freedom is absolute, nor should it be. Indeed, this is the social contract, as described in chapter 6. Freedoms must be limited, so that freedom can be protected. If someone is plotting a terrorist act, they can be arrested and jailed. Rightfully so. Their freedom can be taken away so that other citizens can be free to *live*. As political philosopher John Rawls wrote, 'The precedence of liberty means that liberty can be restricted only for the sake of liberty itself.'

The law recognises this ethical truth, even in the US, where the First Amendment comes with a range of qualifications. Threats of intimidation are unlawful, for instance. This means that the First Amendment has been interpreted to protect the right of a white supremacist to burn a cross in a field, but not in front of an African-American family's home. As the Supreme Court found in the 2003 case of *Virginia v Black*, under the Constitution states may not outlaw cross burnings, but may pass laws that 'prohibit only those forms of intimidation that are most likely to inspire fear of bodily harm'.

At first, digital platforms were wedded to the idea that information deserves to be free. Increasingly, however, digital platforms are coming to admit and accept that not all content should be published. To this end, platforms are refining the rules and standards they seek to enforce. On Twitter, these are The Twitter Rules. Their breach can lead to accounts being suspended. And on Google and YouTube users must abide by 'community guidelines'. If content reviewers are notified of a policy violation, content may be removed. As YouTube's community guidelines page says, 'If you think content is inappropriate, use the flagging feature to submit it for review by our YouTube staff. Our staff carefully reviews flagged content 24 hours a day, 7 days a week to determine whether there's a violation of our Community Guidelines.' Violations cover a range of areas, including spam, harassment and copyright issues.

Facebook, similarly, removes content that violates its 'community standards'. Unfortunately, Facebook's standards have been secret for most of the social network's history. Only in April 2018, following rolling scandals about fake news, exploitative content and the role of social media in fomenting violence, did Facebook publish these standards. This ought to be mandatory: all digital platforms hosting and publishing user content should publish their community standards and enforcement procedures.

The increasing recognition that community standards are vital has created an exploding workforce of content moderators. As Casey Newton wrote in *The Verge* in early 2019, Facebook has about 30 000 employees working on safety and security, about half as content moderators. They have a tough job: 'I hate all men' violates Facebook's standards, but 'I just broke up with my boyfriend, and I hate all men' does not. In less than 30 seconds, a moderator decides whether to purge content, or allow it. When I last checked, Facebook's community standards ran to 27 pages, and included a section devoted to privacy:

> Privacy and the protection of personal information are
> fundamentally important values for Facebook. We work hard
> to keep your account secure and safeguard your personal
> information in order to protect you from potential physical or
> financial harm. You should not post personal or confidential
> information about others without first getting their consent.
> We also provide people with ways to report imagery that they
> believe to be in breach of their privacy rights.

This is a concise and commendable statement of the value of privacy and the role of consent. It needs to be enforced.

The community standards of digital services explicitly recognise that not all content should be allowed. They are works-in-progress, and it is right that they are published and debated. These standards do not have the force of law, but they set important benchmarks.

It isn't just digital platforms seeking to impose community standards. Tim Berners-Lee has long argued that we need core principles to bind governments, companies and citizens. In 2018, Berners-Lee convinced Google and Facebook to agree to key ethical principles, including around respecting people's data and privacy.

More broadly, a code of conduct for the internet would be a significant step. The code ought to be global in its scope; and, to a significant degree, its guidelines for internet behaviour might overlap with the consumer-style protections outlined above. The question is, once we have drafted and adopted a global set of norms, how can users be encouraged to adopt them? The answer includes three key strategies: habituation; setting a good example; and education.

For philosophers and psychologists, habit plays a major role in the cultivation of virtue. This includes Kant, for whom virtue does not lie in actions performed merely by habit, as if by rote. Rather, it lies in habits and aptitudes that have been acquired by 'considered, firm, and continually purified principles'. This is how our virtue can become sufficiently robust to cope with new situations and new temptations.

Second, it is important to set a good example. As Sharon Anderson-Gold writes, we can promote respectful behaviours in others through our own respectful behaviour. One way to do this is to contribute to the moral development of others, including future generations, through the support of good manners in our social interactions. Her argument applies well to the net: if the norms we bring are respectful and polite, we encourage this in others. Otherwise, disrespect can flourish. When Jessica Irvine compared Twitter to a rowdy party, it was in the course of explaining why she had quit the platform. 'We shouldn't have to leave the party in order to feel safe and secure,' she wrote. 'It's time to raise the tone.' The same holds for privacy. By refraining from inappropriate sharing, I might encourage others to do the same. By preferring privacy-respecting platforms, I will hopefully prompt others to follow.

And third, education – including digital literacy education – has a significant role to play in informing people about desirable norms and safe behaviour. On this, there has been considerable research. In their study of sexting, communications scholars Amy Hasinoff and Tamara Shepherd argue that education ought to avoid victim blaming and abstinence-only advice. Instead, it ought to recognise that sexting involves a careful negotiation between risks (including to privacy) and benefits for identity, intimacy, sociability and, ultimately, trust. More broadly, scholars such as Catharine Lumby and Kath Albury have recommended age-appropriate education in schools about media material concerning love, sexuality, gender and relationships, and that parents be trained to talk to children about the information and values they take from the media they consume.

Admittedly, there are varying approaches to digital literacy education. What's more, its effectiveness remains contested, with scholars including Emma Rush arguing that education and 'empowerment' are less effective than legal regulation. As I have been arguing, legal regulation is crucial. Digital literacy education needs to be a supplement to legal regulation, for children as for adults. But with many online interactions, users are unclear about how their data is used. Here, education can help to validate consent. If a user is properly informed about potential data uses, then it is more likely that consent will be genuine.

Some scholars argue for *privacy* education, including researchers Martin Degeling and Thomas Herrmann. They argue that the only way for users to be autonomous in the information society, where internet profiling is often conducted without consent, is via digital privacy literacy. This will enable users to understand profiling and thus to interact with their own profiles. Further, such education is needed not just for users, but for companies and governments, so that they too are aware of the importance and limits of individual and collective consent. In this way, pessimistic resignation might give way to determined involvement.

Each of these three strategies – habituation, setting a good example and education – are especially crucial for children, who are in a state of heightened moral (and neural) plasticity. On philosopher Barbara Herman's Kantian account, the moral *sensitivity* of children must be cultivated. As part of their socialisation, she argues, children must learn 'rules of moral salience', akin to an early warning system for moral danger, which can then help provide a practical framework within which to act: 'When the rules of moral salience are well internalised, they cause the agent to be aware of and attentive to the significance of "moral danger" … The rules of moral salience constitute the structure of moral sensitivity.'

Education can make school-aged children sensitive to moral danger by explaining appropriate privacy norms, both for themselves, and for others. As we've seen, many young people share explicit images and videos. If the moral sensitivity of children is cultivated through education, there would hopefully be less non-consensual sharing.

And finally, we need to consider more than just *restrictions*. We also need to clarify the types of content and interaction that we want to encourage. Forget limits and prohibitions. How can we shape platforms in ways that foster civility, positivity and healthy communities, rather than abuse, negativity and toxicity? Here social norms play a key role. They help drive behaviour. If social norms come to reflect a greater value for privacy, then CreepShots, spyware and the non-consensual on-sharing of sexts will be more widely and reflexively recognised as the serious, harmful invasions they are, and all those who respect privacy will be more likely to receive the credit they deserve.

Market mechanisms

The market provides another way to regulate the internet.

Currently, business imperatives (harness data for profit) often compete with moral imperatives (respect privacy). However, there may be a way to align these imperatives. In a 2018 paper, privacy researcher Lital Helman proposes to link the compensation of executives in social network systems directly to the privacy protections they provide. We currently have a behavioural market failure, Helman argues, where many social media users act against their own best interests, and where social media firms have no incentive to internalise the privacy interests of users. Her proposal is to factor data management practices into executive pay by giving companies an annual privacy rating based on technological measures and user satisfaction. Pay rates would then be assessed with the help of a compensation committee. This, she contends, would inject privacy competition into the market.

As I have shown, privacy is valuable for many reasons, including the non-instrumental justification of dignity. As such, there are potential risks with putting a dollar value on its protection. However, as one of four regulatory modalities, market forces could justifiably and effectively prompt companies to respect privacy. In 2013, Google's Eric Schmidt and Jared Cohen presciently argued that technology companies would increasingly find themselves beset by public concerns over privacy, and would thus be wise to take proactive steps, including: offering a digital 'eject button' that liberates all of a user's data from a given platform; not selling personally identifying information to third parties or advertisers; or perhaps even not selling *any* data to third parties. A group of companies might band together, they suggested, and make a pledge to abide by such steps. To some extent, we are now seeing such suggestions adopted, including with the privacy principles that Google and

Facebook have signed up to, at the urging of Tim Berners-Lee.

There is much more work to be done in this space. The basic point is that, just like social norms, market forces can be shaped and shifted to protect privacy more effectively.

Coding: privacy by design

Finally, and crucially, we have the regulatory power of 'architecture'. That is, the regulatory power of *code*. If we want to regulate the web, we need to consider the way software and hardware are encoded, including the way apps, platforms, websites, operating systems and more are built. Code is law, writes Lawrence Lessig. We can 'build, or architect, or *code* cyberspace' either to protect or to doom the values we take to be fundamental.

This gets to the notion of free will, and how we use it on the net. When I talk to students, they sometimes suggest that users are free to choose how they engage online. Yes, I respond, but they can only ever engage within the parameters of the platform on which they are interacting. In other words, free will is constrained by coding. As I argued in chapter 3, technology doesn't determine our behaviour, but it does have values encoded in it. It allows us to behave in certain ways, but not in others. To use the language favoured by academics, technology has 'affordances'.

The point is well made by Jaron Lanier, an outlier among tech innovators. In his 2010 book, *You Are Not a Gadget,* Lanier rejects the unqualified optimism about tech espoused by many of his peers. This is partly, he writes, because key coding decisions lock in the development of further technology. Hence technology doesn't just liberate, it limits. As evidence, Lanier cites the MIDI music system, developed in the 1980s by synthesiser designer Dave Smith. The MIDI system represented music as a keyboard player would, with tones and semi-tones. As a result, it failed to incorporate the in-between frequencies, which can be accessed by, for instance, guitarists and singers. When MIDI then became the standard scheme to represent music in software, its limitations only grew more entrenched. The same happens in the real world. The London Tube, with its narrow tunnels, can't accommodate air conditioning. There just isn't enough room for ventilation. And for software, such limitations can be particularly problematic. 'Lock-in,' writes Lanier, 'is an absolute tyrant in the digital world.'

This means that we need to think very carefully about the code we allow. But the good news is that if the problem lies in coding, so does the potential solution. Sure, code limits our online behaviour, but *we make the code*. As Lessig writes, code isn't found, but made, 'and only ever made by us'. Hence Lessig recommends 'privacy enhancing technologies': 'These are technologies designed to give the user more technical control over data associated with him or her.' For instance, one coding solution is the ability to put locks on photos. Another is the development of ephemeral messages. (Admittedly, these are partial solutions at best.)

The shift towards coding *for* privacy – in contrast to against privacy – is captured by the phrase 'privacy by design'. As legal researcher Ira Rubinstein and computer scientist Nathaniel Good wrote in 2013, privacy by design involves considering privacy principles and mechanisms at the very beginning of the development process, rather than merely tacking them on at the end. In their paper, Rubinstein and Good analysed ten privacy incidents involving Google and Facebook, arguing that all ten might have been avoided by privacy engineering and usability principles identified by the authors. They argued that firms need clearer direction about applicable design principles and how to incorporate them. Accordingly, regulators ought to provide greater guidance on balancing privacy interests and business interests, and also ought to establish effective oversight mechanisms.

To date, digital platforms have been slow to adopt privacy by design. Google Street View is a good example. Only after public outcry was the system reconfigured to respect privacy adequately. On the net, this pattern is painfully familiar among tech giants: overstep the mark, await outcry, shuffle back a bit, repeat. To be fair, there has been a shift. Google, like other digital platforms, is doing more to protect privacy, and wants to be seen to be doing more. At the top of the chapter, I mentioned Dashboard. And in May 2019, at its annual I/O developer conference, Google announced that users could from then on go into their Google account and choose that their data be deleted automatically after three months. A week earlier, Mark Zuckerberg had opened Facebook's annual developer conference, F8, at San Jose. Behind him were four simple words: 'The future is private'.

Certainly, the regulatory mechanism of privacy by design has great potential. What's more, there's no reason it can't be combined with the regulatory mechanism of the law. For Woodrow Hartzog, a professor of law and computer science, privacy by design ought to be regulated. This ought to involve flexibility, with general prescriptions supplemented by specific regulation, much in the way I have argued above. As Hartzog said in a 2018 interview:

> Of course, certain problems deserve robust responses. Spyware is a scourge. The Internet of Things is a runaway train headed for catastrophe. More significant regulation might be needed for these technologies, but a broad spectrum of regulatory and policy options will help make sure legal responses across the board are proportional … To ignore design is to leave power unchecked.

In Europe, privacy by design is now enshrined in law in the GDPR. In the same breath as it enacts privacy by design, the GDPR also enshrines the requirement that privacy be protected by default. Article 25 of the GDPR, 'Data protection by design and by default', provides for the implementation of 'appropriate technical and organisational measures, such as pseudonymisation, which are designed to implement data-protection principles'. In Hartzog's vision and under the GDPR, two regulatory modalities – the law and coding – work together.

On a personal level too, individuals can adopt tactics that help preserve their privacy. Some of these I addressed in chapter 3. They include tactics of obfuscation such as browser extensions that confuse trackers by hiding actual web searches within fake web searches. They include the search engine DuckDuckGo, the social network Diaspora and the use of the TOR network or virtual private networks (VPNs). (Although beware: best choose a VPN based in a country with strong privacy laws; and note that some free VPNs may be unsafe.) Further strategies involve anonymity and encryption. These are no panaceas. As Bruce Schneier writes: 'My guess is that most encryption products from large US companies have NSA-friendly back doors.'

Privacy by design seeks to embed privacy on a wider level, including within the major platforms. One example is Apple Pay, which enables users to make purchases via smartphone. The system is based on Near Field Communication (NFC) technology, which doesn't transmit name, phone number or address, unlike traditional magnetic stripe credit cards. This means that Apple doesn't know what you bought, where you bought it or how much you paid.

Another technology employed by digital platforms is 'differential privacy', which shares *aggregate* data about user habits, while safeguarding individually identifiable data about users. Imagine that a company wants to track the most popular routes taken by people walking in a park. As cybersecurity academic Tianqing Zhu writes, a company can track 100 regular park traversers, including whether they stick to paths or walk on the grass. This data can be collected in such a way that we know 25 of the 100 took a shortcut over the grass, but not which 25. How? As Zhu writes, differential privacy works by adding random noise to the aggregate data, meaning that characteristics cannot be inferred about individuals. And so, for instance, we might supplement our 100 park traversers with a handful of fictitious walkers. This will not significantly alter the results, but it will prevent data being linked to identifiable individuals.

The inventor of differential privacy, Cynthia Dwork, has presented mathematical proofs showing just how much noise is needed to safeguard privacy. This has tremendous potential for doing good. Using differential privacy, broad patterns in mental health could be identified and potentially even addressed, without any individual ever being identified as a sufferer of mental illness. As Dwork writes, 'In many cases, extremely accurate information about the database can be provided while simultaneously ensuring very high levels of privacy.'

Proposals keep sprouting. In 2015, NYU data scientist Foster Provost proposed a tool enabling e-marketers to target individuals based on their location using 'geosimilarity': the similarity of anonymised smartphone users based on the patterns of the locations they've visited. And in 2019, researchers Flora Salim, Salil Kanhere and Seng Loke proposed the concept of 'algorithmic guardians', in the shape of 'bots, personal assistants or hologram technology … which could be programmed to manage our digital interactions with social platforms and apps according to our personal preferences'.

We communicate with our children via messaging apps; we arrange to meet prospective partners via dating apps; and we joke around with friends by sending digitally altered versions of ourselves in comic poses. Here's me with whiskers and cat ears! Here's our family as elves! Privacy by design can help to ensure that our relationships are treated as more than just data. It can help to ensure

that my intimate conversation with my wife will not be sold or surveilled. And it can go further still. Kant, remember, told us never to
treat persons merely as means. But he also told us always to treat persons with respect. Coding – together with social norms and market
forces – can either diminish respect or promote it. Which will it be?

THE ENTIRE FUTURE OF US

The legal right to privacy needs an update for the digital age. The
law needs more effectively to take account of the fundamental way
that my privacy can affect you – that is, the relational nature of
privacy. The law needs to incorporate a series of legislated general
principles, based in the formula of humanity, which mandate fairness and outlaw deception. And the law needs to take a globally
aligned approach that harnesses the robust protections of Europe's
GDPR. Meanwhile, social norms, market forces and coding have a
role to play too. After all, not every privacy violation deserves the
attention of the law. Some occur on the level of relationships, where
the law often has no place.

In *The Entire History of You*, the outcome isn't good. As Liam's
suspicions grow, re-dos follow. So does violence. The episode was
inspired, apparently, by writer Jesse Armstrong reflecting on the
importance of being able to forget things in relationships. When
grains are implanted, total forgetting is impossible. People can
always try to access what was said or done in their absence.

Before such technology is developed, we need to answer a few
questions. What should the law say? Should there be encoded protections? And besides, do we have a duty not to use it? The first two
questions we have answered. The third is the subject of the next and
final chapter.

8
WHICH WAY TO *COSMOIKOPOLIS*?

The future used to be bright.

A few short decades ago, the world was forcast to become a 'global village', where everyone would freely share in an abundance of information and experience. This was the future envisaged by media scholar Marshall McLuhan in 1964, five years before the internet was born: 'As electrically contracted, the globe is no more than a village. Electric speed in bringing all social and political functions together in a sudden implosion has heightened human awareness of responsibility to an intense degree.'

On this view, ordinary people would take back power, connecting to those in far-flung places, precipitating a more open and equal world.

Two years earlier, in 1962, philosopher Jürgen Habermas published *Strukturwandel der Öffentlichkeit*, which was translated into English in 1989 as *The Structural Transformation of the Public Sphere*. Habermas charted how the public sphere had been transformed since the time of the bourgeois salons of the 18th century. These bourgeois salons hosted inclusive critical discussion, free from social and economic constraints, as all participants treated one another as equals in the cooperative quest to reach an understanding on matters of general concern. With the emergence of the capital-driven mass media of the 20th century, however, ideas became commodities and people became consumers. Still, Habermas didn't give up on the public sphere. Instead, he called for its structural transformation. And soon enough scholars were lining up to nominate the internet as a shining hope to become a Habermasian public sphere, where people could be equals and discourse could be free of commercial and social constraints. Habermas, after all, wanted to 'de-centre' democracy under conditions of complexity and pluralism.

So far, I have bookended every chapter with a fictional story, chosen because it illuminates some aspect of digital privacy. I've used these films and TV shows in the same way that philosophers have always used thought experiments, to ask, 'What if ...?' For this final chapter, however, I'm going to take a more straightforward approach. I'm going to focus squarely on our global future. This will lead me to make a provocation. Sure, privacy matters. And yes, digital media – including the way it is used by us and on us – is putting significant pressure on our privacy. Even so, maybe we have been concentrating *too much* on the right to privacy. Maybe it's the *duty* of privacy that we need to develop.

Of course, the democratising promise of the internet, as signalled by McLuhan and Habermas, isn't dead. In Australia, a fledgling political party aims to give its citizens a direct voice in democracy, by enabling everyone to vote on each issue. 'Everyone on the Electoral Roll will be able to vote on any – or every – new law, or changes to existing laws in Australia, for free,' writes the party at onlinedirect-democracy.org 'Using the internet we can return to a system that reflects your true positions on important issues.'

What's more, the internet's democratising potential really does exist on a global scale. The internet transcends the national. In some ways, it transcends the international, as a network that exists in the virtual beyond. This presents grand opportunities. The potential is there for the internet to realise a global village, or to become a Habermasian public sphere.

However, it also presents grand challenges. Hackers can bypass border guards. Google and Facebook are globe-straddling multinationals. One nation's intelligence agency collects data worldwide, then exchanges its data with the intelligence agencies of other countries, which then exchange with a long list of other government acronyms. In 2018, 'techlash' was one of the Oxford Dictionaries runners-up for the word of the year. It denotes the growing backlash against Silicon Valley companies. No doubt privacy concerns were a part of the reason. What's more, the international nature of the internet presents a significant challenge for any type of regulation.

Drawing on Kant's formula of humanity, I have built my core argument upon consent: individual consent; and collective consent in the shape of the law. But what happens when the mood is bleak and the medium is so comprehensively international? How do these various possibilities and challenges play out? The logical solution lies in transnational and international law. In other words, we need global collective consent. That isn't easy, but it's hardly impossible. As privacy advocate Nigel Waters says:

> It has been and will continue to be a constant struggle for both
> domestic and international law to deal particularly with online
> privacy … but I don't think that's an argument for giving
> up or being fatalistic about the ability to have an appropriate
> framework. I think there have been some surprisingly well-
> developed attempts at cross-border regulation.

Transnational and international instruments already play a pivotal role, as we've seen. Currently, privacy is protected by the International Covenant on Civil and Political Rights (ICCPR), which came into effect in 1976 and provides, in Article 17, that: 'No one shall be subjected to arbitrary or unlawful interference with his privacy, family, home or correspondence, nor to unlawful attacks on his honour and reputation'. As at September 2019, 173 nations were party to the ICCPR, including Canada, Australia, the UK, the US and European countries such as Germany and France. Six countries, including China, have signed but not ratified the covenant; and 22 countries, including Saudi Arabia, Singapore and Myanmar, have not signed.

And since May 2018, the European Union's GDPR has set the standards for consent, the transparent processing of data and the right to erasure, among other provisions. In Article 51, the GDPR stipulates that each member state shall establish its own independent public authority to 'contribute to the consistent application of this Regulation throughout the Union'; and, under Article 60, each member state's supervisory authority is directed to cooperate with a lead supervisory authority. Already, then, privacy regulation exists in forms that are international and transnational, and that transcend individual nation states, just as the internet does. Meanwhile, each country must enact its own particular privacy provisions. In practice, jurisdictions operate within a layered blend of regulation.

In which jurisdictions can the best privacy protections be found? For Graham Greenleaf, who has published extensively on global privacy regimes, the European Union's General Data Protection Regulation sets the standard.

> I think that the GDPR – and aspects of its subsequent
> enforcement – mean that the EU countries are now further
> ahead of the rest of the world than they were even before
> it came into force in 2018. Other countries' laws, and
> enforcement, have their strengths, but none come close to the
> EU countries.

The GDPR has raised the prospect of global alignment. Its significance in this regard is hard to overstate.

Greenleaf also gives honourable mention to various non-GDPR countries:

With many caveats, I would also give honourable mentions to at least South Korea, Canada, New Zealand, Mauritius, but *not* Australia. I would also have to include some non-EU European countries – Norway, Switzerland, Jersey, Guernsey for sure, probably others as well. And if my French and Spanish were up to the task there would be some additions, perhaps including Senegal, Mexico or Argentina.

Law professor David Lindsay agrees that EU countries lead the way, but not solely because of the GDPR.

Lindsay argues that the best privacy protections are to be found in jurisdictions with a strong constitutional right to privacy. These include the constitutional protections that exist at a European level. As noted in chapter 3, privacy across Europe is protected under two significant transnational instruments: Article 8 of the European Convention on Human Rights (ECHR), which grants everyone 'the right to respect for his private and family life, his home and his correspondence'; and the Charter of the Fundamental Rights of the European Union (EU Charter), which became binding in 2009 and protects both the right to privacy and the right to data protection. Together, the ECHR and EU Charter provide a robust overarching framework, which can work together with the GDPR and national bills of rights.

In Germany, for instance, there are five layers of privacy law: local, state, national, European and international. On the first two rungs sit local and state instruments; on the third rung, fundamental rights are protected nationally under the *Grundgesetze* of Germany's Constitution; on the fourth rung, the EU Charter and the ECHR operate Europe-wide, protecting the fundamental rights that are then informed by the more specific provisions of the GDPR; and on the fifth and top international rung, the Universal Declaration of Human Rights and the International Covenant on Civil and

Political Rights are powerful statements of principle and law (albeit with shortcomings of enforceability).

The due legal protection of privacy *requires* a layered approach. Of course, this layering ought not be overly complicated. Some layers might be removed altogether. In the US, as I have mentioned, calls are growing for the passage of a coherent federal law. This might render some state laws redundant. The law must be as clear, coherent and uncomplicated as possible. The fact that I am arguing in favour of privacy regulation is not to suggest I am arguing for *more* privacy regulation. Rather, I am arguing for *better* privacy regulation. This entails repealing some existing laws, amending others, and making new ones. Ultimately, the hope is that fewer laws will do more work, and will also be more coherent, domestically and globally.

Still, layers are needed, chiefly because a layered approach allows for variation between regions and countries. In this way, the law of privacy can be tailored to the history and values of a particular populace. This may come as a surprise. I have been advocating a Kantian approach. How can we reconcile Kantian ethics with regional variations? How can universalism be tailored? Isn't this a fundamental contradiction?

Yes, I have been arguing that we must never treat any person merely as a means, and that privacy deserves universal respect. However, I have also been arguing that privacy must be balanced against other values, rights and freedoms. This is extensively recognised in the law, including in the secondary, qualifying provisions of Article 8 of the European Convention on Human Rights:

> There shall be no interference by a public authority with the
> exercise of this right except such as is in accordance with the
> law and is necessary in a democratic society in the interests
> of national security, public safety or the economic well-being
> of the country, for the prevention of disorder or crime, for

the protection of health or morals, or for the protection of the rights and freedoms of others.

I have not been arguing that privacy ought to be valued absolutely. This is evident from the privacy principles articulated in chapter 7. What's more, I have not been arguing that privacy must be respected and protected in one single fashion. Rather, our Kantian approach allows for, and even encourages, variation.

As I described in chapter 4, every known society values and respects privacy, but privacy norms vary dramatically over time and between cultures. In 2018, for instance, the CEO and chairman of search engine Baidu, Robin Li Yanhong, said China's citizens don't care about privacy as much as US citizens. 'The Chinese people are more open or less sensitive about the privacy issue,' he said. 'If they are able to trade privacy for convenience, safety and efficiency, in a lot of cases, they are willing to do that.' Whether or not this characterisation of Chinese people is fair, the underlying point is valid: privacy expectations vary.

Kant's formula of humanity gives us the dual principles of always treating others as ends in themselves, and never simply as means. These principles allow for no exception. Nonetheless, we can allow for variation. The categorical imperative must apply universally, but can adapt to local circumstances, customs and social norms. Above, I noted Barbara Herman's rules of moral salience, or RMS, which can help us identify situations when moral judgment is needed. These rules, she writes, are not fixed, but represent the prevailing moral climate: 'What is attractive about introducing RMS into a Kantian theory of moral judgment is that it would seem to let us have it both ways: while morality has an objective foundation, we have good *positive* reason to tolerate *some* culturally based moral differences.'

Privacy matters universally, but respect for privacy can take different forms. This means that some uses of technology are universally impermissible. The misogynistic use of spyware is one example. By contrast, other uses of technology might be permissible in some cultures, but not in others. This might include consensual sexting. Recall that Kant's categorical imperative specifies what is forbidden, and what is required, but also provides for a range of actions that are *permissible*. Here there is wide scope. For instance, Kant writes that we each have a duty to make others happy, which leaves tremendous room for interpretation.

It's the same with privacy. In a chapter entitled 'Privacy in the electronic global metropolis', from his book *Digital Media Ethics*, Charles Ess describes the way US-style conceptions of privacy as strongly individual contrast with certain Thai notions of privacy as primarily familial. For the ethical relativist, Ess argues, this suggests there can be no universal values or norms. For the ethical monist, a decision needs to be made as to which of these approaches is absolutely, finally and universally true. By contrast, Ess advocates ethical pluralism, which avoids cultural imperialism and promotes tolerance. The ethical pluralist position is that 'privacy – however widely understood and practised in diverse cultures and times – indeed appears to be a human universal'.

What I am advocating is a global vision of privacy, which is universal (respect privacy …) yet pluralistic (… within the context of your culture's norms). A global vision, after all, is what Kant ultimately had in mind. With the formula of humanity, Kant prescribed a normative ideal for individuals; but he also described a world in which the categorical imperative is universally observed. For Kant, this ideal state of perfect morality is a 'realm of ends', where people only ever treat one another, and themselves, as ends in themselves, and never merely as means. A realm of ends can prevail only if privacy is respected in such a way that the formula of humanity is universally adhered to.

The realm of ends is merely an ideal. However, Kant also prescribed a moral and political *goal* in the shape of cosmopolitanism, or world citizenship. The notion has its origins in Classical Greece, where the philosopher Diogenes declared his allegiance not to the *polis*, but to the *cosmopolis*, or world city. For Kant, who argued that all individuals are self-legislating members of a universal moral community, cosmopolitanism was a perfect fit. At the level of the state, Kant wrote, we find a mirror of individual morality: just as people are to be governed by the internal legislation of morality and the external legislation of just laws, so too states must be internally organised and externally organised in a manner consistent with peace. Further, wrote Kant in his essay 'Toward perpetual peace', all states must recognise the rights not only of their own citizens, but of the citizens of other countries.

Just as individuals ought never to treat others merely as a means, so too nations ought never treat one another without regarding the rights of other nations' citizens. For this to be realised, Kant argued that we need a universal association of states. In *The Metaphysics of Morals*, he wrote: 'Only in a universal *association of states* (analogous to that by which a people becomes a state) can rights come to hold *conclusively* and a true *condition of peace* come about.' Herein lies hope, especially because, in 'Toward perpetual peace', Kant is finally optimistic about both human nature and ethical progress: 'In this way, remote parts of the world can establish relations peacefully with one another, relations which ultimately become regulated by public laws and can thus finally bring the human species ever closer to a cosmopolitan constitution.'

In this future world envisioned by Kant, cosmopolitan right prevails.

Admittedly, there are wildly varying accounts of cosmopolitanism. On the one hand, John Rawls's 'law of peoples' is a minimal model, dispensing with the requirement for a strong international legal, political or democratic order. Indeed, there is debate as to whether this qualifies Rawls as a cosmopolitan. On the other hand, Jürgen Habermas and David Held demand more of cosmopolitanism, citing the emergence of international public law as a key element in a just global political order.

Like Habermas and Held, I think we ought to demand more. And more than 200 years after Kant's death, the beginnings of cosmopolitanism have arrived. The United Nations, founded in the wake of World War II, is a septuagenarian realisation of the notion that people belong to a single world order bound by moral universals. Presumably, its existence would have impressed Kant – although no doubt he would have been critical of its failures. Instruments such as the Universal Declaration of Human Rights and the International Covenant on Civil and Political Rights, complete with privacy protections, comprise cosmopolitan law. Meanwhile, a quasi-cosmopolitan approach is embodied in transnational protocols such as the GDPR. To some extent, a cosmopolitan right of privacy *has* been articulated and protected. This cosmopolitan approach perfectly suits the internet, with all its convergence, ubiquity and multi-directionality.

To supplement what already exists, there have been further proposals. Amy Webb, a 'quantitative futurist' at NYU's business school, argues that targeted international regulation is exactly what we need. In her 2019 book, *The Big Nine: How the tech titans and their thinking machines could warp humanity*, Webb argues for an international oversight body with enforcement power specifically to regulate artificial intelligence. This might look like a version of the International Atomic Energy Agency, which polices nuclear programs. Such an approach could also oversee aspects of the regulation of privacy. The alternative is an increasingly balkanised internet, where the lack of a coherent framework leads to a 'splinternet', or rival versions of the net that vary dramatically from one place to another. Instead of promoting connection, egalitarianism and shared knowledge, such a balkanised splinternet would tend to create divisions, disharmony and inequity.

Another proposal is for an international bill of rights for the internet. In 2014, Tim Berners-Lee called for an online Magna Carta to protect the rights of users worldwide, partly in the face of increasing threats from corporations and governments. Berners-Lee and the World Wide Web Foundation refined their approach in November 2018, when they published their 'Contract for the Web'. The succinct contract (at fortheweb.webfoundation.org/principles/) opens with brief description of core principles, including that, 'Everyone has a role to play to ensure the web serves humanity'. It then asks governments, companies and citizens to make contrasting commitments. Governments are asked to agree to 'respect people's fundamental right to privacy so everyone can use the internet freely, safely and without fear'. Companies are asked to agree to 'respect consumers' privacy and personal data so people are in control of their lives online'. And citizens are asked to agree to 'build strong communities that respect civil discourse and human dignity so that everyone feels safe and welcome online'.

'We're at a 50/50 moment for the web,' Berners-Lee tweeted when the contract was published. 'We've created something amazing together, but half the world is still not online, and our online rights and freedoms are at risk. The web has done so much for us, but now we need to stand up #ForTheWeb #WebSummit.'

Such principles could then be enshrined in law. Whether in the form of an online Magna Carta, or a 'Contract for the Web', clear and concise *legal* principles that apply globally would not only create enforceable general obligations, but could also detail the way in which the obligations of government, company and citizen differ.

And right now, we have an opportunity. Traditionally, digital platforms have lobbied hard against regulation, including privacy regulation. Recently, however, they've changed their tune. Even tech companies agree that now is the time to regulate. In an opinion piece in the *Washington Post* on 30 March 2019, Mark Zuckerberg argued that companies such as Facebook have 'immense responsibilities':

> I believe we need a more active role for governments and regulators. By updating the rules for the Internet, we can preserve what's best about it – the freedom for people to express themselves and for entrepreneurs to build new things – while also protecting society from broader harms. From what I've learned, I believe we need new regulation in four areas: harmful content, election integrity, privacy and data portability.

Specifically on the topic of privacy, Zuckerberg called for a global response:

> Effective privacy and data protection needs a globally harmonised framework. People around the world have called for comprehensive privacy regulation in line with the European Union's General Data Protection Regulation, and I agree. I believe it would be good for the Internet if more countries adopted regulation such as the GDPR as a common framework. New privacy regulation in the United States and around the world should build on the protections the GDPR provides. It should protect your right to choose how your information is used – while enabling companies to use information for safety purposes and to provide services. It shouldn't require data to be stored locally, which would make it more vulnerable to unwarranted access. And it should establish a way to hold companies such as Facebook accountable by imposing sanctions when we make mistakes.

We need to hold Zuckerberg to these words. Other tech leaders are saying much the same, and we need to hold them to their words too. In September 2018, Microsoft's Brad Smith called for a principle-based international agreement to govern law enforcement's access to data. A month later, Apple's Tim Cook called for GDPR-style privacy laws to be enacted federally in the US. And on 1 April 2019, Google too said it supported the 'general notion' of more privacy regulation globally, citing the GDPR as a 'workable model', even if 'different countries will want to make adjustments.' (Something the GDPR already allows.) As Kent Walker, Google's senior vice-president for global affairs, said: 'The pendulum has swung from the relatively uncritical support of technology to significant concerns about unintended side effects and abuses of technological platforms.'

And in a blog post of 19 February 2019, Cisco general counsel Mark Chandler called for US law that aligns with a global outlook. This law should aim to 'avoid further fracturing of legal obligations for data privacy through a uniform federal law that aligns with the emerging global consensus'.

Of course, there may be ulterior motives for these pronouncements. Companies may want to avoid the cost of adhering to regulatory regimes that vary dramatically. This is understandable. However, as I argued above, a layered legal approach is exactly what is required to allow for regional variations. More seriously, companies may quietly believe that the GDPR is tough on paper, but soft in practice. All bark, no bite. For this reason, enacting GDPR-style provisions is only the first step. The second step is ensuring that GDPR-style provisions are effectively enforced.

The time is right for a globally aligned approach founded on the GDPR, and which extends international human rights–style protections for online conduct. Increasingly, regulators, legislators and innovators are coming to agree that privacy requires regulation, and that such regulation must be, as far as possible, globally harmonised. In other words, that we need to take a cosmopolitan approach to digital privacy.

Naturally, there will be resistance. As Australia's competition watchdog chair Rod Sims has noted, worldwide regulatory alignment is unlikely in the short term. In Washington DC, for instance, an anti-globalist mood prevails. In September 2019, US President Donald Trump said 'the future belongs to patriots not globalists', adding that 'the future belongs to sovereign and independent nations, who protect their citizens, respect their neighbours and honour the differences that make each country special and unique'. Pointedly, he made these comments during an address to the United Nations.

The encouraging news is that the mood has shifted, however, and once moves for globally aligned privacy protections take hold, momentum can build. Perhaps quickly. Moving quickly, after all, is digital's strength. To paraphrase Facebook's now-abandoned motto, 'Move fast and break things', the opportunity exists to move fast and fix things.

And as we move fast and fix things, we must remember to keep privacy in context. That means taking a holistic approach. The proper protection of privacy involves taking into account other rights, freedoms and interests, including freedom of speech. Following the livestreaming of the massacre of 50 people in Christchurch in March 2019, there were calls to regulate online content. In early April, the Australian government moved first, hastily creating two offences to thwart 'abhorrent violent material'. My point isn't about the worth of the legislation (other than to commend its minimum viable legislation approach). Rather, it's that the complex of issues concerning our online engagements needs to be considered in totality. We ought to consider our approach to privacy in conjunction with our approach to: offensive and abhorrent content; personal and national security; defamation, libel and slander; free speech and free expression; the freedom of the press; and misinformation and fake news. And we need to remember the benefits of data, including the way diseases are being contained, child pornographers are being caught, and illegal fishing is getting harder due to public surveillance from space.

Privacy should only be addressed in the context of other rights, freedoms and interests. What's more, privacy should only be addressed in the context of underlying social conditions. All of our engagements are contingent upon our bodies and our social relations. Once we acknowledge that women are less empowered and valued than men, for instance, this will deepen our understanding that privacy is gendered, just as it discriminates in other ways. These underlying inequities need to be addressed.

The law of privacy urgently needs an overhaul. The overhaul needs to be comprehensive and coherent. It needs to be conducted nationally, yet globally oriented. But privacy regulation can only work, ultimately, as a carefully calibrated component in a broader regulatory package that also takes into account other rights, freedoms and interests, and that further takes into account underlying preconditions, including inequities of gender, sexuality, race, and so on. And luckily, the law doesn't have to protect privacy all on its own. Social norms, market forces and coding also have a significant role to play, enabling universal prescriptions to be applied with local inflexions.

True, universalism is sometimes condemned, particularly on the internet. In 2013, communications scholar Anita Say Chan described 'the myth of digital universalism'. Similarly, digital media researcher Guy T. Hoskins has critiqued the 'draft once; deploy everywhere' approach. But I am proposing a pluralistic universalism. This approach recognises that there are principles that ought to apply globally. I ought never treat another merely as a means. Privacy warrants respect. Consent matters. But regional and cultural differences can flourish, as long as an overarching and global respect for privacy prevails. Kant's formula of humanity enables us to protect privacy (and other freedoms) on the basis of the dual principles of not using others merely as means, and of respecting others as end-setters. In doing so, it can enable the citizens of individual countries simultaneously to be citizens of a globally connected internet.

But finally, I want to throw in a provocation. I want to challenge the notion that rights will save us. What we need to begin to focus on, and to foster, are privacy *duties*.

In 2002, Onora O'Neill presented a series of lectures under the title, 'A question of trust'. In the wake of the attacks of 11 September 2001, amid a growing climate of fear and suspicion, O'Neill argued that we need to revisit the role and value of human rights:

> The list of rights proclaimed in the Universal Declaration of
> 1948 is often seen as canonical. The list is untidy and unargued
> … The Declaration defines rights poorly, and it says almost
> nothing about the corresponding duties … it assumes a
> passive view of human life and citizenship. Rights answer the
> questions 'What are my entitlements?' or 'What should I get?'
> They don't answer the active citizen's question 'What should I
> do?'

This applies to all rights, including free speech. The right to free speech is, O'Neill said, 'mere rhetoric', unless others have duties to respect free speech. As she said, 'Duties are the business end of justice: they formulate the requirements to which Declarations of Rights merely gesture; they speak to all of us whose action is vital for real, respected rights.'

The problem is that individuals and governments are keen to sign up for rights, but much less eager to commit to duties:

In thinking about ethics and politics, we would I believe do
better to begin by thinking about what ought to be done and
who ought to do it, rather than about what we ought to get.
Passive citizens, who wait for others to accord and respect their
rights and mistakenly suppose that states alone can do so, are,
I think, doomed to disappointment. Active citizens who meet
their duties thereby secure one another's rights.

All the rights in the world are meaningless unless the corresponding duties are observed. Protecting privacy such that humanity is respected requires us to fulfil our *duties* to privacy. And it is in
articulating the duties of privacy, I suggest, that we will be able more
effectively to recognise and protect a privacy that is relational.

The internet is boundless and quixotic. Like nothing before, it
has the potential to be *cosmopolis*, the world city. This is not a new
idea. The globalising potential of the internet has been foreshadowed
by the likes of McLuhan and Habermas since before its inception.
However, the internet also has the potential to be something else
too: *cosmoikos*, the global home. This we can conceive as a globally
connected space where the private and domestic can flourish too. In
this way, the goal of *cosmopolis* can be joined by the goal of *cosmoikos*.
We might dub this synthesis of goals *cosmoikopolis*, a blend of *cosmos*
(world), *oikos* (private) and *polis* (public). In *cosmoikopolis*, private
and public are valued globally and in balance.

The *condition* of privacy is under serious threat. In this regard,
we appear to be headed for the dystopia of Panopticon 3.0. By contrast, the *right* to privacy persists. In fact, the legal right to privacy
is gaining strength, protected by laws against image-based abuse,
Europe's General Data Protection Regulation, global protocols, and
more. In this regard, we may be headed for the utopia of *cosmoikopolis*. Given the choice between Panopticon 3.0 or *cosmoikopolis*, I
know where I'd rather live.

As I noted above, Kant himself belonged to the school of philosophers who are optimistic about the future of humanity and morality. People are capable of moral improvement, wrote Kant, and humanity has the potential for moral progress. In the spirit of such optimism, in the face of the significant challenges posed by our online interactions, our goal ought to be *cosmoikopolis*, where citizens globally enjoy a relational privacy that is valued universally, even as it varies regionally. For that, we need to be active citizens, whose pressing task is to articulate more clearly what our duties to privacy ought to look like.

In its potential for a global connectivity, in its capacity for all humanity to engage as equals, the internet is a place well suited to approaching Kant's ideal of a cosmopolitan realm of ends. A place where we can treat one another, and ourselves, as persons.

CONCLUSION:
FREE TOGETHER

In November 2019, Google announced it was buying Fitbit for US$2.1 billion, joining the rush of companies getting into health tracking.

In a statement, Google's Rick Osterloh expressed his company's commitment to privacy and security. 'When you use our products, you're trusting Google with your information,' Osterloh said. 'We understand this is a big responsibility and we work hard to protect your information, put you in control and give you transparency about your data.' What's more, Google said Fitbit health and wellness data would not be used for Google ads, and further committed to giving Fitbit users the chance to 'review, move or delete their data'.

That wasn't enough for some. 'Given the history of digital platforms making statements as to what they intend to do with data and what they actually do down the track, it is a stretch to believe any commitment Google makes in relation to Fitbit users' data will still be in place five years from now,' said Rod Sims, chair of the Australian competition regulator, the ACCC. Some users weren't impressed either. 'I tossed my Fitbit into the trash today,' one tweeted, while another responded: 'I am usually careful about big tech companies gobbling up too much data, but especially Google. I have a knee-jerk reaction to Google having any of my data. I try to opt out of most of the stuff they do.' As a European, this user had the legal right to request such deletion under the General Data Protection Regulation.

Here is just one more privacy story, soon to be forgotten amid the avalanche. Still, it shows the limitations of user control, given Fitbit users had no say whatsoever in Google's acquisition. And it shows the power of the GDPR, which gives individuals the right to request that their data be deleted.

What would Kant make of it all? As a man of routine, Kant might have liked health trackers. Taking his daily constitutional around Königsberg, he might have enjoyed monitoring his pulse rate and steps taken, and whether he was likely to hit his personal targets. If a large company moved to acquire his health data, however, he probably would have wanted the opportunity to opt out. Otherwise, given his sensitive metrics were being traded for corporate profit, he might have felt he was being treated as less than a person. He might have felt he was being used merely as a means.

And what would Kant have made of 'Project Nightingale'? A few days after the Fitbit sale was announced, the *Wall Street Journal* reported that Google had struck a partnership with healthcare provider Ascension, giving it access to the personal medical data of up to 50 million Americans, all without patients and doctors knowing. And what about the sale of Grindr to a Chinese company? In 2016, the gay hook-up app Grindr was sold to Chinese firm Kunlun for US$100 million, prompting concerns that the Chinese government could access the highly sensitive data of millions of users. (Kunlun later agreed to sell Grindr by June 2020 after the Committee on Foreign Investment in the United States raised national security concerns.) And what about 'deepfake porn'? As tech writer Samantha Cole reported in 2018, pornographic videos have emerged featuring Hollywood stars including Gal Gadot and Daisy Ridley. In these fakes, the actors' faces have been superimposed onto porn actors' bodies. Making these deepfakes isn't too hard, apparently, requiring only 100 or so still images. Or even fewer. Without knowing it, any one of us might be currently appearing in an explicit video.

My guess is that Kant would have been deeply troubled by all these developments, which disregard individual consent and are clear breaches of the formula of humanity. And my guess is that the more he learnt about the internet and privacy, the more he would have agreed that strong laws are needed to protect citizens in their online interactions. And further, I'm guessing he would have supported supplementary extra-legal measures, including the implementation of market mechanisms, social norms and coding intended to promote the due respect of privacy.

• • •

This book has addressed three main questions. First, what is going on with privacy and the internet? Second, what is privacy and why should we care? And third, how can we best protect it? In light of our analysis, we can now ask some better questions:

- **Shadow profiles.** Who has them? Which social networks have profiles of people who don't use that social network? What do these shadow profiles contain?
- **Facial recognition.** Who is using it? How? For what, exactly?
- **Eavesdropping.** Who is listening in? How? Why?
- **Data brokers.** Where do they get their data? With whom do they share it?
- **Data sharing.** Which companies share data? Facebook, Instagram and WhatsApp (all owned by Facebook)? Google and Ascension? Who else?
- **Encryption.** If my messaging service is encrypted, so that only my wife and I can see one another's messages, can the messaging service unencrypt what we're saying?

- **Deleting data and profiles.** If I delete my account, is it completely erased? What if I delete my Facebook, but keep my Instagram? Deleted means deleted, right?
- **Inferred data.** What if data is collected ethically and legally, but this allows sensitive data (about political opinions, religious views and sexuality, for instance) to be inferred? Who is inferring what?
- **Loyalty schemes and credit cards.** What do they collect? With whom do they share it? Insurance companies? Finance companies? Who else?
- **Government agencies.** What data are government agencies collecting about citizens, residents and others, including from other governments? Who is able to access this data?
- **Children.** What data is being collected about our kids? By whom?
- **Other vulnerable groups.** Again, what data is being collected?
- **Democracy hacking.** What manipulative techniques are being used to sway voters, and to keep them away from the ballot box?
- **Human hacking.** What other manipulative techniques are being employed?

We need clearer answers, so that we can then decide which practices we are prepared to accept, and which practices should be outlawed or restricted.

This book has provided some answers. The evidence suggests that shadow profiles exist, are ethically problematic, and ought to be addressed with laws. We need laws to ban them altogether, or, at the least, set strict limits and mandate substantial transparency. Data brokers are problematic too. As with shadow profiles, there is a fundamental failure of morally satisfactory consent. Again, a requirement for greater transparency is a bare minimum. The same goes for government data collection, including practices of domestic surveillance. Secret laws and policies are less likely to be just laws and policies. Here again, greater transparency is needed. This has been one of my fundamental recommendations: the law ought to enshrine a series of general prescriptions founded on the formula of humanity, including a commitment to transparency. Greater transparency would also help with the algorithms that determine the content we see on social media and elsewhere. Just what signals – and what personal data – are being used to determine this content? Some regulatory oversight of algorithms would help. Currently, much of the problem arises because data about us is flowing in secret, without any mechanisms for oversight.

Apart from a transparency principle, these general prescriptions also ought to contain a consent principle. Consent is imperfect, but remains fundamental for an ethical approach to privacy. This doesn't mean bombarding people with a notice-and-consent dialogue box before every click. Quite the reverse. It means setting up streamlined processes to recognise what people do and do not agree to. The principle is simple. If I say, 'Don't track my location', then don't track my location. If I say, 'Don't track my web activity', then don't track my web activity. If I say, 'Do not record or use any audio captured by my phone', then don't record or use any audio. (With the exceptions detailed in chapter 6, such as when the law sets limits, or where there is an ethical imperative.) Individuals need to be given the chance to make their preferences clear. And whenever these preferences are contravened, the consequences need to have impact. The collective consent of the law would thus work hand-in-hand with individual consent.

Of course, there may be better proposals than those I've been making. Recently, law scholars Jack Balkin and Jonathan Zittrain have advanced the notion of 'information fiduciaries'. The idea is that Google, Facebook and other digital platforms ought to carry special duties of care, confidentiality and loyalty in respect to their users, just as doctors, lawyers and accountants have special duties of care, confidentiality and loyalty. One attraction of this approach, as Balkin wrote in 2016, is that the conversation switches to a discussion about 'the kinds of *relationships* – relationships of trust and confidence – that governments may regulate in the interests of privacy'. Meanwhile, California's innovative new privacy law came into effect on 1 January 2020. An alternative to the GDPR, the *California Consumer Privacy Act* gives consumers the right to opt out of the sale of personal information, to request the deletion of personal information, and to access their personal information in a 'readily useable format' that enables them to take it to third parties.

Ultimately, my allegiance is less to the proposals I have been making, and more to the ethical principle that underpins them: that we treat all others never simply as means, and always as imperfectly self-determining agents.

There's a lot at stake. I have detailed how invasions of privacy threaten dignity, autonomy, relationships, society and democracy. Beyond all this, there is a further concern. And that is that our new data-driven, privacy-challenging world has the potential to worsen social inequity, creating a widening gulf between haves and have-nots. The fear is that the hidden assumptions that underlie big data and algorithms are reinforcing existing systems of privilege and prejudice. As our identities are compressed from persons into marketing niches such as 'Urban Scramble' or 'Mobile Mixers' – data-broker categories consisting mainly of minority communities with lower incomes – isn't it all too likely that existing inequities will be reinforced? As law scholar Orla Lynskey writes, the law has started to recognise the way algorithmic data profiling can classify people by categories such as race, ethnicity, gender or sexual orientation, even when such classifications are legally prohibited as discriminatory. Welfare activist Virginia Eubanks adds that coercive big data is creating a 'digital poorhouse', and that the cost of big data use in social policy is falling more heavily on the poor and vulnerable. The nightmare scenario invokes the film *Gattaca*, where an elite class of 'valids' are given opportunities far beyond those offered the 'in-valids'. In *Gattaca*, superiority is determined by DNA. Where we're headed, superiority might be determined by privacy. Only for the select few, and not for others, would privacy and the freedom it brings ever be an option.

An added complication is that privacy isn't always good. Sometimes privacy can be misused to cloak criminality, or unethical behavior. What we want to do is to find a way to protect *warranted* privacy, justified in the light of other rights, interests and freedoms. Privacy laws need to be framed in such a way as to minimise misuse. And further, they need to take into account the key point that privacy is not just about the individual. It's a collective concept. In a digital age more than ever, privacy is networked and relational.

Since 2017, Facebook has been using artificial intelligence to identify users who might be about to attempt suicide. The platform then notifies police and helps locate at-risk users. In 2019, the *Guardian* reported that Facebook had initiated more than 3500 such 'wellness checks' globally. This reveals the relational nature of privacy: the privacy surrounding a suicide attempt extends beyond the individual to encompass friends and family. It also reveals the delicate balancing act required. As a society, we want to minimise suicides, and suicide attempts. At the same time, we want to value privacy. It will be an ongoing task to spell out exactly how we ought to perform our privacy balancing act, and to distinguish exactly the sort of privacy we want.

Earlier, I cited Anita Allen, who has written of how we need a liberating, rather than a restrictive, form of privacy. Women should be encouraged to discover individual forms of personal privacy, Allen wrote, including easy access to contraception and abortion which would afford the decisional privacy to choose whether or not to bear a child. Privacy has the potential to be both liberating and stifling, and the challenge is to conceptualise more clearly a positive privacy. That is, we want a privacy that affords liberty instead of confinement, and creates opportunities rather than making people more vulnerable to domestic violence and oppressive control. What we want is a privacy in the service of equity.

Here we can articulate a second set of questions. Whereas the first set of questions is intended to enable us to see the problem still more clearly, the second set is intended to help us to devise better protections.

- How can we best ensure that we are protecting privacy in a manner that is **positive and promotes equity,** rather than in a way that fosters confinement and oppression?
- How can the law, and extra-legal measures, best articulate **an appropriate balancing act** with other rights, interests and freedoms?
- How do we best protect **relational privacy?** That is, how can we best protect privacy in a way that simultaneously benefits the individual and the group/family/society?
- What exactly does **the duty of privacy** involve?
- And finally, what should *cosmoikopolis* – a world where relational privacy is protected globally and in balance – look like in practice, in a way that takes account of **both universal and local privacy** norms?

Again, this book has provided some answers, but more detailed responses are required.

The great ethicists of history, including Kant, may well have been confounded by the internet. On the internet, flux is constant. From one day to the next, it is reinvented. As Shannon Vallor wrote in 2016: 'The founders of the most enduring classical traditions of ethics – Plato, Aristotle, Aquinas, Confucius, the Buddha – had the luxury of assuming that the practical conditions under which they and their cohorts lived would be, if not wholly static, at least relatively stable.'

What I hope to have shown, however, is that we don't need to devise a new ethics for the digital age. Rather, the ethics we have are more than adequate. In fact, new media needs old ethics. Or at least, the internet can be illuminated by venerable ethical principles. And while I have taken a Kantian approach, non-Kantian ethical approaches might well yield similar results. 'It has been widely believed that there are such deep disagreements between Kantians, Contractualists, and Consequentialists,' wrote philosopher Derek Parfit in 2011. 'That, I have argued, is not true. These people are climbing the same mountain on different sides.'

If our particular mountain is the ethics and regulation of digital privacy, then my suggestion is that the best way to climb is with the simple recognition that what matters isn't the network, but the people who use it. 'The network by itself is meaningless,' wrote Jaron Lanier in 2018. 'Only the people were ever meaningful.' Kant would second that.

Privacy matters for every one of us, not just as individuals, but as social beings. Privacy enables us to be free, but also to be connected. Our goal ought to be the realisation of a privacy and a freedom that transcend the excessively individualistic, and also the excessively collective. In a world at risk of becoming something worse than Panopticon 3.0 – a world of unchecked spyware, shadow profiles and facial recognition – privacy can enable us all to be free together. Increasingly, privacy will be the yardstick by which to measure a society's commitment to freedom. For only when privacy is duly protected can we hope to be free as individuals, and as societies.

ACKNOWLEDGMENTS

While considering a privacy matter in 1956, a federal judge in the US described a 'haystack in a hurricane'. Today, we might better describe privacy as a sandcastle in a cyclone. The topic has a tendency to disintegrate in front of our eyes. The following beneficent beings helped me to see it more clearly.

This book started life in early 2013, when I embarked on a PhD at Macquarie University in Sydney with Catriona Mackenzie, Sherman Young and Paul Formosa as supervisors. Catriona, you read drafts on public holidays; Sherman, you read drafts at 36 000 feet; Paul, you read drafts while infants slept. Thank you. I'm also grateful to a stack of librarians, and to Timothy Pilgrim, Nigel Waters and Sam Yorke, who generously answered my early questions about privacy and consent. And big thanks to the PhD's three examiners: Beate Rössler, Shannon Vallor and Tim Dwyer. Your charitable and insightful feedback provided motivation, and rich suggestions for further lines of inquiry.

Then, in 2017, Phillipa McGuinness at NewSouth Books received an unsolicited and eccentric proposal about Kant and digital privacy. Instead of blocking me, she championed the project unfailingly, to the extent of finding a northern hemisphere co-publisher in McGill-Queen's University Press. Thanks Pip, and Emma Hutchinson, and everyone at NewSouth and McGill-

Queen's, as well as freelance copyeditor Tricia Dearborn for your keen eye and astute adjustments.

As the book took shape, various colleagues from my current life as an academic and my former life as a journalist provided feedback and input. To all of you, I apologise. In many cases, the drafts you read were less comprehensible than a standard set of online privacy terms and conditions. So apologies – and thanks – to Karen O'Connell, James Meese, Alecia Simmonds, Laura Smith-Khan, Graham Greenleaf and David Lindsay, and to Cath Keenan, Julia Baird and Joel Gibson.

Many of those I have cited are colleagues at the University of Technology Sydney, where I work at the Centre for Media Transition. There are more to thank. At the CMT, Derek Wilding and Peter Fray paid me a great compliment by granting me the autonomy to realise this work. For a project about freedom, you let me be free. And at UTS, Lesley Hitchens, Brian Opeskin and Attila Brungs are fostering a spirit of collaboration and inquiry in the service of social justice, for which I am deeply grateful. Meanwhile, the support from NYU Sydney, and especially director Mal Semple, has been unwavering.

At heart, this book is about the importance of relationships. It's about the way privacy connects us, even as it also enables us to keep a distance. And so it's appropriate that the project was only ever possible due to a network of relationships with a long list of people, including those I've named. I consider you all to be more than colleagues; I consider you all as good friends.

On that note, thanks also to my mum, dad and Uli, poppa Pat, Lynne and Bill, for much love and support. As the saying goes, it takes a village to raise a book. Or something like that. Dave and Ingrid, Ange and Jamie, Nick and Anna, Boris and Marion, Michael and Bridget, Eric and Sacha, Tim and Pete – each of you helped more than you realise. And above all, biggest thanks go to my wife

Jo and my daughters Edie and Lola. Jo, you encouraged me always to do this for the right reasons: to create something good. And Edie and Lola, every day you make me want to make the world a better place for you, and for all.

Covered in hay and blasted by sand, I thank you all, with love and respect.

NOTES

To improve readability, I have not included citations in the text. Instead, details provided in the text indicate the relevant reference in the bibliography.

Chapter 1: I can see the present you, the past you and the future you

1   Just what sort of public spaces exist on the net? Indeed, can a genuine public space exist online? To answer, media scholars have taken various approaches. For instance, in 2001 Lincoln Dahlberg invoked the six normative conditions prescribed by Jürgen Habermas's theory of democratic communication to find that the internet does facilitate an expansion of the public sphere, but that the quality of online discourse falls short of Habermas's model. That was before social media boomed, so what about now? I won't linger on this important issue regarding the qualitative nature of online public spaces. Rather, I'll take it as axiomatic that some kinds of public spaces and interactions can be found on the net.

Chapter 2: It's hard to opt out of a service you've never used

1   There are, naturally, tough in-between cases. How do we classify a non-government organisation (NGO) such as Greenpeace or the Electronic Frontier Foundation? What about WikiLeaks? And what about when private enterprise and government are mixed, as with some prisons and police departments? In chapter 7, I argue that in some instances governments are justified to encroach upon privacy but companies are not. Does this mean that privately run police departments, say, should be required to abide by the information-handling standard set for governments, or rather by the stricter standard set for companies?

2   These quotes come from a 2015 BBC story by Regan Morris. Since then, TeenSafe has reinvented itself. As the teensafe.com website says (as at December 2019), it is now a 'subscription service for parents of young drivers that disables your young driver's phone, except for the ability to send and receive phone calls, while they are driving. TeenSafe ensures your young driver keeps their eyes on the road (and off their phone).'

3   This section is heavily indebted to Bruce Schneier's 2015 account of digital surveillance, *Data and Goliath: The hidden battles to collect your data and control your world*.

Chapter 4: Privacy is *not* all about control

1   There are further complications for applying the Fourth Amendment online, including the third-party doctrine. Laid down in 1976 in *United States v Miller*, the third party doctrine provides that any data voluntarily provided to a third party, such as a telecommunications company, does not attract Fourth Amendment protections. In 1979, the court ruled in *Smith v Maryland* that the doctrine extends to call records held by phone companies. Recently, however, the third-party doctrine has been challenged: in 2018, the doctrine was limited dramatically in *Carpenter v United States*. In a 5-4 ruling, the Supreme Court held that the US government generally needs a warrant to access cell site location data, generated automatically when a mobile phone connects to a cell tower.

2   In January 2019, Max Schrems was vindicated when Google was fined €50 million by France's data protection authority. It was the first major fine imposed for a GDPR breach.

3   Several scholars, such as Herman Tavani, have sought to develop a hybrid control/access model. I would suggest that the model I have been describing could also be considered a hybrid model: it too allows for both access and control. It is, however, better characterised as an access model.

4   My primary focus, as I have noted, is the privacy of the individual. However, to accommodate the relational nature of privacy, a fuller and more accurate definition might run: 'The right to privacy is my or our right that others be deprived of unauthorised access to me or us and to information about me or us. In some cases, though not all, this right will involve my or our ability to control such access. The condition of privacy, meanwhile, is the state of others being denied such access.'

Chapter 5: My privacy is for your benefit

1   This is distinct from the reductionist argument outlined in the previous chapter, which proposed that everything privacy seeks to protect can be protected by another right, such as security.

2   The value of privacy may not be exclusive to humans. In 1967, Alan Westin wrote, 'virtually all animals seek periods of individual seclusion or small group intimacy'; this is 'territoriality, in which an organism lays private claim to an area of land, water, or air and defends it against intrusion by members of its own species'.

3   Others prefer the term 'intrinsic' to 'non-instrumental'. The terms are sometimes used interchangeably. However, I prefer 'non-instrumental' to denote something valuable for its own sake and 'intrinsic' to denote something whose value is self-generated.

BIBLIOGRAPHY

Acquisti, A. & Fong, C.M. 2015, 'An experiment in hiring discrimination via online social networks', viewed 11 December 2019, <ssrn.com/abstract=2031979>.

Acquisti, A., Gross, R. & Stutzman, F. 2014, 'Face recognition and privacy in the age of augmented reality', *Journal of Privacy and Confidentiality*, vol. 6, no. 2, pp. 1–20.

Acxiom 2016, 'Acxiom Privacy Principles', viewed 16 September 2016, <www.acxiom. com/about-acxiom/privacy/privacy-principles/>.

Albrechtslund, A. 2008, 'Online social networking as participatory surveillance', *First Monday*, vol. 13, no. 3, viewed 11 December 2019, <journals.uic.edu/ojs/index.php/fm/article/view/2142/1949>.

Allen, A.L. 1988, *Uneasy Access: Privacy for women in a free society*, Rowman & Littlefield, Lanham, Maryland.

—— 2013, 'An ethical duty to protect one's own informational privacy?', *Alabama Law Review*, vol. 65, pp. 845–66, viewed 11 December 2019, <scholarship.law.upenn.edu/faculty_scholarship/451/>.

—— 2016, 'Protecting one's own privacy in a big data economy', *Harvard Law Review Forum*, vol. 130, pp. 71–78, University of Pennsylvania Law School, Public Law Research Paper No. 17-1, viewed 11 December 2019, <ssrn.com/abstract=2894545>.

Almuhimedi, H., Schaub, F., Sadeh, N., Adjerid, I., Acquisti, A., Gluck, J., Cranor, L.F. & Agarwal, Y. 2015, 'Your location has been shared 5,398 times! A field study on mobile app privacy nudging', *Proceedings of the 33rd Annual ACM (Association for Computing Machinery) Conference on Human Factors in Computing Systems*, pp. 787–96, viewed 11 December 2019, <dl.acm.org/citation.cfm?id=2702210>.

Altman, I. 1975, *The Environment and Social Behavior: Privacy, personal space, territory, and crowding*, Brooks/Cole Publishing Co., Monterey, California.

Anderson-Gold, S. 2010, 'Privacy, respect and the virtues of reticence in Kant', *Kantian Review*, vol. 15, no. 2, pp. 28–42.

Anitha, S. & Gill, A. 2009, 'Coercion, consent and the forced marriage debate in the UK', *Feminist Legal Studies*, vol. 17, no. 2, pp. 165–84.

Antón, A.I., He, Q. & Baumer, D.L. 2004, 'Inside JetBlue's privacy policy violations', *IEEE Security and Privacy*, vol. 2, no. 6, pp. 12–18.

Arendt, H. 1974, 'Hannah Arendt: From an interview', *New York Review of Books*, viewed 11 December 2019, <www.nybooks.com/articles/1978/10/26/hannah-arendt-from-an-interview/>.

—— 1977, 'Public rights and private interests', in M. Mooney & F. Stuber (eds), *Small*

Comforts for Hard Times: Humanists on public policy, Columbia University Press, New York, pp. 103–108.

Asimov, I. 1982, *Foundation's Edge*, Granada, London.

Audi, R. (ed.), 1999, *The Cambridge Dictionary of Philosophy*, 2nd edn, Cambridge University Press, Cambridge, UK.

Australian Competition & Consumer Commission 2018, *Digital Platforms Inquiry – Preliminary Report*, viewed 6 January 2020, <www.accc.gov.au/focus-areas/inquiries-ongoing/digital-platforms-inquiry/preliminary-report>.

——— 2019, *Digital Platforms Inquiry – Final Report*, viewed 6 January 2020, <www.accc.gov.au/focus-areas/inquiries-ongoing/digital-platforms-inquiry/final-report-executive-summary>.

Australian Law Reform Commission 2003, *Essentially Yours: The protection of human genetic information in Australia*, ALRC Report 96, <www.alrc.gov.au/publication/essentially-yours-the-protection-of-human-genetic-information-in-australia-alrc-report-96/>.

——— 2007, *Review of Australian Privacy Law*, DP 72, viewed 6 January 2020, <www.alrc.gov.au/publication/review-of-australian-privacy-law-dp-72/>.

——— 2014, *Serious Invasions of Privacy in the Digital Era*, DP 80, viewed 6 January 2020, <www.alrc.gov.au/wp-content/uploads/2019/08/whole_dp80.pdf>.

Bagrow, J.P., Liu, X. & Mitchell, L. 2019, 'Information flow reveals prediction limits in online social activity', *Nature Human Behaviour*, vol. 3, no. 2, pp. 122–28, viewed 11 December 2019, <arxiv.org/abs/1708.04575>.

Baig, E.C. 2018, 'Facebook gives more details on how it tracks non-users', *USA Today*, 16 April 2018, viewed 15 February 2019, <www.usatoday.com/story/tech/columnist/baig/2018/04/16/facebook-gives-more-details-how-tracks-non-users/522455002/>.

Baker, R. 2015, 'Facebook makes data deal with Quantium, Acxiom and Experian to fuse offline and online data', *AdNews*, 21 July 2015, viewed 12 August 2016, <www.adnews.com.au/news/facebook-makes-data-deal-with-quantium-acxiom-and-experian-to-fuse-offline-and-online-data>.

Balkin, J.M. 2016, 'Information fiduciaries and the First Amendment', *University of California Davis Law Review*, vol. 49, no. 4, pp. 1183–234, viewed 20 December 2019, <lawreview.law.ucdavis.edu/issues/49/4/Lecture/49-4_Balkin.pdf>.

Bambauer, D.E. 2013, 'Privacy versus security', *Journal of Criminal Law and Criminology*, vol. 103, pp. 667–84, viewed 11 December 2019, <ssrn.com/abstract=2208824>.

Bane, A.F. & Milheim, W.D. 1995, 'Internet insights: how academics are using the internet', *Computers in Libraries*, vol. 15, no. 2, pp. 32–36.

Bannerman, S. 2018, 'Relational privacy and the networked governance of the self', *Information, Communication & Society*, vol. 22, no. 14, pp. 2187–202.

Barrett, B. 2018, 'A location-sharing disaster shows how exposed you really are', *Wired*, 19 May 2018, viewed 15 November 2019, <www.wired.com/story/locationsmart-securus-location-data-privacy/>.

Bartlett, R.C. & Collins, S.D. 2011, *Aristotle's Nicomachean Ethics: A new translation*, University of Chicago Press, Chicago.

BBC 2015, 'How I was "cyber-flashed"', *BBC News*, vol. 13, August 2015, viewed 12 December 2019, <www.bbc.com/news/technology-33905578?d96a349c52fc4f68eea46a47ccb3d360>.

Beauchamp, T.L. 2010, 'Autonomy and consent', in F. Miller & A. Wertheimer (eds), *The Ethics of Consent: Theory and practice*, Oxford Scholarship Online, pp. 55–78.

Becher, S. 2019, 'Research shows most online consumer contracts are incomprehensible, but still legally binding', *The Conversation*, vol. 4, February 2019, viewed 15 November 2019, <theconversation.com/research-shows-most-online-consumer-contracts-are-incomprehensible-but-still-legally-binding-110793>.

Behar, R. 2004, 'Never heard of Acxiom? Chances are it's heard of you', *FORTUNE – European Edition*, vol. 149, no. 3, pp. 58–64, viewed 15 November 2019, <archive.fortune.com/magazines/fortune/fortune_archive/2004/02/23/362182/index.htm>.

Benn, S.I. 1971, 'Privacy, freedom, and respect for persons', in J.R. Pennock & J.W. Chapman (eds), *Nomos XIII: Privacy*, Atherton Press, New York, pp. 1–26.

Bennett, C.J. 1992, *Regulating Privacy: Data protection and public policy in Europe and the United States*, Cornell University Press, Ithaca, New York.

Bentham, J. 1826, 'Outline of the plan of construction, alluded to in the "Proposal for a new and less expensive mode of employing and reforming convicts"', *Remarks on the Form and Construction of Prisons: With appropriate designs*, Committee of the Society for the Improvement of Prison Discipline etc., London, viewed 19 November 2019, <archive.org/details/remarksonforman00englgoog>.

———— 1996, *The Collected Works of Jeremy Bentham: An introduction to the principles of morals and legislation*, J.H. Burns & H.L.A. Hart (eds), Clarendon Press, Oxford, UK.

Berger, A. 2009, 'Brandeis and the history of transparency', *Sunlight Research*, vol. 26, May 2009, viewed 15 November 2019, <sunlightfoundation.com/blog/2009/05/26/brandeis-and-the-history-of-transparency/>.

Bergman, M.K. 2001, 'White Paper: The Deep Web: Surfacing hidden value', *Journal of Electronic Publishing*, vol. 7, no. 1.

Berners-Lee, T. 1999, *Weaving the Web: The original design and ultimate destiny of the World Wide Web by its inventor*, HarperInformation, San Francisco.

———— 2017, 'Three challenges for the web, according to its inventor', *Web Foundation*, 12 March 2017, viewed 15 November 2019, <webfoundation.org/2017/03/web-turns-28-letter/>.

Berners-Lee, T., Hendler, J. & Lassila, O. 2001, 'The semantic web', *Scientific American*, vol. 284, no. 5, pp. 28–37, viewed 11 December 2019, <www.scientificamerican.com/article/the-semantic-web/>.

Biddle, S. 2012, 'Facebook ruined your birthday', *Gizmodo*, 16 June 2012, viewed 15 November 2019, <www.gizmodo.com.au/2012/06/facebook-ruined-your-birthday/>.

Bloustein, E.J. 1964, 'Privacy as an aspect of human dignity: An answer to Dean Prosser', *New York University Law Review*, vol. 39, pp. 962–1007.

Blue, V. 2013, 'Firm: Facebook's shadow profiles are "frightening" dossiers on everyone', *ZDNet*, 24 June 2013, viewed 15 November 2019, <www.zdnet.com/article/firm-facebooks-shadow-profiles-are-frightening-dossiers-on-everyone/>.

Bogost, I. 2018, 'Apple's Airpods are an omen', *Atlantic*, 12 June 2018, viewed 9 December 2019, <www.theatlantic.com/technology/archive/2018/06/apples-airpods-are-an-omen/554537/>.

Bok, S. 1982, *Secrets: On the ethics of concealment and revelation*, Pantheon, New York.

Botsman, R. 2017, 'Big data meets Big Brother as China moves to rate its citizens', *Wired*, 21 October 2017, viewed 15 November 2019, <www.wired.co.uk/article/chinese-government-social-credit-score-privacy-invasion>.

Boyd, D. 2014, 'It's complicated: the social lives of networked teens', viewed 15 November 2019, <www.danah.org/books/ItsComplicated.pdf>.

Brafman, O. & Brafman, R. 2009, *Sway: The irresistible pull of irrational behaviour*, Virgin Books, London.

Brandeis, L.D. 2009, *Other People's Money and How the Bankers Use It*, Cosimo, Inc., New York.

Brin, D. 1998, *The Transparent Society: Will technology force us to choose between privacy and freedom?*, Perseus Books, Reading, Massachusetts.

Brown, L. 1993, *The New Shorter Oxford English Dictionary on Historical Principles*, Clarendon, Oxford, UK.

Brown, W. 2004, '"The subject of privacy": a comment on Moira Gatens', in B. Rössler (ed.), *Privacies: Philosophical evaluations*, Stanford University Press, Stanford, California, pp. 133–41.

Bruns, A. 2007, 'Produsage: towards a broader framework for user-led content creation', *Proceedings of the 6th ACM SIGCHI Conference on Creativity & Cognition*, pp. 99–106, <eprints.qut.edu.au/6623/>.

Burk, D.L. 2008, 'Privacy and property in the global datasphere', in S. Hongladaram & C. Ess (eds), *Information Technology Ethics: Cultural perspectives*, IGI Global, Hershey, Pennsylvania, pp. 94–107.

Butler, D.A. & Rodrick, S. 2015, *Australian Media Law*, 5th edn, Thomson Reuters (Professional), Sydney.

Cacioppo, J.T. & Patrick, W. 2008, *Loneliness: Human nature and the need for social connection*, WW Norton & Company, New York.

Calpito, D. 2015, 'Google received 350,000 right to be forgotten requests for 1.2 million links in Europe', *Tech Times*, 26 November 2015, viewed 1 December 2016, <www.techtimes.com/articles/110823/20151126/google-received-350-000-right-to-be-forgotten-requests-for-1-2-million-links-in-europe.htm>.

Canning, S. 2016, 'Facebook and Quantium sign deal to measure advertising impact on store sales', *Mumbrella*, 8 June 2016, viewed 15 August 2016, <mumbrella.com.au/facebook-quantium-sign-deal-372301>.

Castells, M. 1996, *The Rise of the Network Society: The information age: Economy, society, and culture*, vol. 1, John Wiley & Sons, Oxford, UK.

Centre for Media Transition 2018, 'Trends in Digital Defamation: Defendants, plaintiffs, platforms', viewed 18 November 2019, <www.uts.edu.au/sites/default/files/article/downloads/Trends%20in%20Digital%20Defamation_0.pdf>.

Chadwick, R. & Berg, K. 2001, 'Solidarity and equity: new ethical frameworks for genetic databases', *Nature Reviews Genetics*, vol. 2, no. 4, pp. 318–21, viewed 11 December 2019, <www.nature.com/articles/35066094>.

Chan, A. 2013, *Networking Peripheries: Technological futures and the myth of digital universalism*, MIT Press, Cambridge, Massachusetts.

Chandler, M. 2019, 'Executive Platform: Cisco calls for US Federal Privacy Legislation — Leveling the privacy playing field', 7 February 2019, viewed 18 November 2019, <blogs.cisco.com/news/cisco-calls-for-us-federal-privacy-legislation-leveling-the-privacy-playing-field>.

Chideya, F. 2015, 'Your data is showing: breaches wreak havoc while the government plays catch-up', *Intercept*, 28 May 2015, viewed 18 November 2019, <theintercept.com/2015/05/27/data-breaches-wreak-havoc/>.

Christians, C.G., Fackler, M., Richardson, K., Kreshel, P. & Woods, R.H. 2012, *Media Ethics: Cases and moral reasoning*, 9th edn, Pearson Education, Glenview, Illinois.

Citizenfour 2014, Radius-TWC, US/Germany.

CNBC 2018, 'Zuckerberg: We collect data from people who haven't signed up for Facebook for security purposes', 11 April 2018, viewed 18 November 2019, <www.cnbc.com/video/2018/04/11/zuckerberg-we-collect-data-from-people-who-havent-signed-up-for-facebook-for-security-purposes.html>.

Cocking, D. & Kennett, J. 1998, 'Friendship and the self', *Ethics*, vol. 108, no. 3, pp. 502–27.

Cole, S. 2019, 'We are truly fucked: Everyone is making AI-generated fake porn now', *Vice*, viewed 21 November 2019, <www.vice.com/en_au/article/bjye8a/reddit-fake-porn-app-daisy-ridley>.

Coleman, G. 2014, *Hacker, Hoaxer, Whistleblower, Spy: The many faces of Anonymous*, Verso Books, London.

Cooke, R. 2013, 'How NSA surveillance destroys privacy and undermines our sovereignty', *Monthly*, July 2013, viewed 18 November 2019, <www.themonthly.com.au/issue/2013/july/1372600800/richard-cooke/how-nsa-surveillance-destroys-privacy-and-undermines-our-so>.

Copeland, R. 2019, 'Google's "Project Nightingale" gathers personal health data on millions of Americans', *Wall Street Journal*, viewed 18 November 2019, <www.wsj.com/articles/google-s-secret-project-nightingale-gathers-personal-health-data-on-millions-of-americans-11573496790>.

Corrigan, R. 2015, 'Mass surveillance not effective for finding terrorists', *New Scientist*, 15 January 2015, viewed 18 November 2019, <www.newscientist.com/article/dn26801-mass-surveillance-not-effective-for-finding-terrorists/>.

CreepShots, 'About: Photographer rights', viewed 16 March 2017, <creepshots.com/about/photographer-rights/>.

Cullins, A. 2019, 'Facebook must face biometric privacy class action after losing appeal', *Hollywood Reporter*, 9 August 2019, viewed 18 November 2019, <www.hollywoodreporter.com/thr-esq/facebook-face-biometric-privacy-class-action-losing-appeal-1230618>.

Curran, G. & Gibson, M. 2013, 'WikiLeaks, anarchism and technologies of dissent', *Antipode*, vol. 45, no. 2, pp. 294–314.

Dahlberg, L. 2001, 'Computer-mediated communication and the public sphere: a critical analysis', *Journal of Computer-Mediated Communication*, vol. 7, no. 1.

Daniel, C. & Palmer, M. 2007, 'Google's goal: to organise your daily life', *Financial Times*, 23 May 2007, viewed 18 November 2019, <next.ft.com/content/c3e49548-088e-11dc-b11e-000b5df10621>.

de Mars, S. & O'Callaghan, P. 2016, 'Privacy and search engines: forgetting or contextualizing?', *Journal of Law and Society*, vol. 43, no. 2, pp. 257–84.

Dearden, L. 2016, 'Burkini ban: why is France arresting Muslim women for wearing full-body swimwear and why are people so angry?', *independent.co.uk*, 25 August 2016, viewed 18 November 2019, <www.independent.co.uk/news/world/europe/burkini-ban-why-is-france-arresting-muslim-women-for-wearing-full-body-swimwear-and-why-are-people-a7207971.html>.

Debatin, B., Lovejoy, J.P., Horn, A.K. & Hughes, B.N. 2009, 'Facebook and online privacy: attitudes, behaviors, and unintended consequences', *Journal of Computer-Mediated*

Communication, vol. 15, no. 1, pp. 83–108, viewed 18 November 2019, <academic.oup.
com/jcmc/article/15/1/83/4064812>.

DeCew, J. 2015, 'Privacy', in E.N. Zalta (ed.), *The Stanford Encyclopedia of Philosophy*
(Spring 2015 edition), viewed 18 November 2019, <plato.stanford.edu/archives/
spr2015/entries/privacy/>.

Degeling, M. & Herrmann, T. 2016, 'Your interests according to Google: a profile-centered
analysis for obfuscation of online tracking profiles', *Computers and Society*, viewed
11 December 2019, <arxiv.org/ftp/arxiv/papers/1601/1601.06371.pdf>.

Denis, L. 1997, 'Kant's ethics and duties to oneself', *Pacific Philosophical Quarterly*, vol. 78,
pp. 321–48.

—— 2012, *Moral Self-Regard: Duties to oneself in Kant's moral theory*, Routledge, New
York.

Department of Homeland Security 2017, 'Privacy Policy Guidance Memorandum',
viewed 18 November 2019, <www.dhs.gov/sites/default/files/publications/Privacy%20
Policy%20Guidance%20Memo%202017-01%20-%20FINAL.pdf>.

Dinello, D. 2005, *Technophobia! Science fiction visions of posthuman technology*, University of
Texas Press, Austin, Texas.

Dorling, P. 2013, 'X-Keyscore spy program tracks "nearly all" web use', *smh.com.au*,
2 August 2013, viewed 12 December 2019, <www.smh.com.au/technology/xkeyscore-
spy-program-tracks-nearly-all-web-use-20130802-hv17w.html>.

—— 2014, 'Edward Snowden reveals tapping of major Australia–New Zealand
undersea telecommunications cable', *smh.com.au*, 15 September 2014, viewed
18 November 2019, <www.smh.com.au/technology/edward-snowden-reveals-tapping-
of-major-australianew-zealand-undersea-telecommunications-cable-20140915-10h96v.
html>.

Dreyfuss, E. 2019, 'German regulators just outlawed Facebook's whole ad business',
Wired, 7 February 2019, viewed 15 February 2019, <www.wired.com/story/germany-
facebook-antitrust-ruling/>.

Duckett, C. 2016, '61 agencies after warrantless access to Australian telecommunications
metadata', *ZDNet*, viewed 18 November 2019, <www.zdnet.com/article/61-agencies-
after-warrantless-access-to-australian-telecommunications-metadata/>.

Duhigg, C. 2012, 'How companies learn your secrets', *New York Times*, vol. 16, pp.
1–16, viewed 18 November 2019, <128.59.177.251/twiki/pub/CompPrivConst/
HowCompaniesLearnOurConsumingSecrets/How_Companies_Learn_Your_
Secrets_-_NYTimes.com.pdf>.

Duke, J. 2019, '"Pendulum has swung" against digital giants: Google executive', *smh.com.
au*, 1 April 2019, viewed 18 November 2019, <www.smh.com.au/business/companies/
pendulum-has-swung-against-digital-giants-google-executive-20190401-p519ll.html>.

Dunbar, R.I. 2016, 'Do online social media cut through the constraints that limit the size of
offline social networks?', *Royal Society Open Science*, vol. 3, no. 1.

Dutton, W.H. 1996, *Information and Communication Technologies: Visions and realities*,
Oxford University Press, Oxford, UK.

Dwork, C. 2006, 'Differential privacy', in M. Bugliesi, B. Preneel, V. Sassone & I. Wegener
(eds), *Automata, Languages and Programming. ICALP 2006. Lecture Notes in Computer
Science,* vol. 4052, Springer, Berlin, pp. 1–12, viewed 18 November 2019, <link.
springer.com/chapter/10.1007/11787006_1#citeas>.

Dwyer, T. 2015, *Convergent Media and Privacy*, Palgrave Macmillan, London.

———— 2015, 'Evolving concepts of personal privacy: Locative media in online mobile spaces', in R. Wilken & G. Goggin (eds), *Locative Media*, Routledge, New York, pp. 121–35.

Edwards, C.R. 2016, 'Snap Inc. does what Google couldn't – exemplifies privacy by design', *Digerati*, 28 September 2016, viewed 29 September 2016, <digeratimag. com/2016/09/28/snap-inc-google-couldnt-exemplifies-privacy-design/>.

Edwards, J. 2012, 'How Facebook is hunting down and deleting fake accounts', *Business Insider Australia*, 30 December 2012, viewed 18 November 2019, <www. businessinsider.com.au/facebook-fake-likes-and-accounts-2012-12>.

Elgesem, D. 1996, 'Privacy, respect for persons, and risk', in C. Ess (ed.), *Philosophical Perspectives on Computer-Mediated Communication*, State University of New York Press, Albany, New York, pp. 45–66.

Elmer, G. 2013, 'IPO 2.0: The panopticon goes public', *MediaTropes*, vol. 4, no. 1, pp. 1–16, viewed 18 November 2019, <www.mediatropes.com/index.php/Mediatropes/article/view/20371>.

———— 2015, 'Going public on social media', *Social Media + Society*, vol. 1, no. 1.

Ericson, R.V. & Haggerty, K.D. 1997, *Policing the Risk Society*, University of Toronto Press, Toronto, Canada.

Ess, C. 2011, 'Self, community, and ethics in digital mediatized worlds', in C. Ess & M. Thorseth (eds), *Trust and Virtual Worlds: Contemporary perspectives*, Peter Lang, Bern, Switzerland, pp. 3–30.

———— 2014, *Digital Media Ethics*, 2nd edn, Polity, Cambridge, UK.

———— 2019, 'Intercultural privacy: a Nordic perspective', in H. Behrendt, W. Loh, T. Matzner & C. Misselhorn (eds), *Privatsphäre 4.0: Eine Neuverortung des Privaten im Zeitalter der Digitalisierung*, Springer, Berlin, pp. 73–88.

Ess, C. & Fossheim, H. 2013, 'Personal data: changing selves, changing privacies', in M. Hildebrandt, K. O'Hara & M. Waidner (eds), *The Digital Enlightenment Yearbook 2013: The value of personal data*, IOS Press, Amsterdam, pp. 40–55.

Etzioni, A. 2015, 'A cyber age privacy doctrine: more coherent, less subjective, and operational', *Brooklyn Law Review*, vol. 80, no. 4, pp. 1263–308.

Eubanks, V. 2018, *Automating Inequality: How high-tech tools profile, police, and punish the poor*, St. Martin's Press, New York.

Evers, C. & Goggin, G. 2012, 'Mobiles, men and migration: mobile communication and everyday multiculturalism in Australia', in L. Fortunati, R. Pertierra & J. Vincent (eds), *Migrations, Diaspora and Information Technology in Global Societies*, Routledge, New York, pp. 78–90.

Fairfield, J.A. & Engel, C. 2015, 'Privacy as a public good', *Duke Law Journal*, vol. 65 (3), pp. 385–421.

Federal Trade Commission 2014, 'Data Brokers: A call for transparency and accountability', viewed 18 November 2019, <www.ftc.gov/system/files/documents/reports/data-brokers-call-transparency-accountability-report-federal-trade-commission-may-2014/140527databrokerreport.pdf>.

———— 2019, 'Dissenting Statement of Commissioner Rebecca Kelly Slaughter regarding the matter of FTC vs. Facebook, 24 July 2019', viewed 21 November 2019, <www. ftc.gov/public-statements/2019/07/dissenting-statement-commissioner-rebecca-kelly-slaughter-regarding-matter>.

———— 2019, 'Statement of Chairman Joe Simons and Commissioners Noah Joshua

Phillips and Christine S. Wilson regarding the Matter of Facebook, Inc., 24 July 2019', viewed 21 November 2019, <www.ftc.gov/public-statements/2019/07/statement-chairman-joe-simons-commissioners-noah-joshua-phillips-christine>.

Ferguson, A.G. 2017, 'Policing predictive policing', *Washington University Law Review*, vol. 94, no. 5, pp. 1109–89, viewed 18 November 2019, <openscholarship.wustl.edu/cgi/viewcontent.cgi?article=6306&context=law_lawreview>.

Finley, K. 2018, 'Gmail is getting a long-overdue upgrade', *Wired*, 25 April 2018, viewed 18 November 2019, <www.wired.com/story/gmail-is-getting-a-long-overdue-upgrade/>.

Fleischer, P. 2015, 'Fireside chat with Peter Fleischer, Google's global privacy counsel, 24 October 2015', Amsterdam Privacy Conference.

Flew, T. 2019, 'Digital communication, the crisis of trust, and the post-global', *Communication Research and Practice*, 11 January 2019, pp. 1–19.

Foot, P. 1972, 'Morality as a system of hypothetical imperatives', *Philosophical Review*, vol. 81, no. 3, pp. 305–16.

Formosa, P. 2008, '"All politics must bend its knee before right": Kant on the relation of morals to politics', *Social Theory and Practice*, vol. 34, no. 2, pp. 157–81.

——— 2013, 'Evils, wrongs and dignity: how to test a theory of evil', *Journal of Value Inquiry*, vol. 47, no. 3, pp. 235–53.

——— 2013, 'Kant's conception of personal autonomy', *Journal of Social Philosophy*, vol. 44, no. 3, pp. 193–212.

——— 2014, 'The ends of politics: Kant on sovereignty, civil disobedience, and cosmopolitanism', in P. Formosa, A. Goldman & T. Patrone (eds), *Politics and Teleology in Kant*, University of Wales Press, Cardiff, pp. 37–58.

——— 2017, *Kantian Ethics, Dignity and Perfection*, Cambridge University Press, Cambridge, UK.

Foucault, M. 1977, *Discipline and Punish: The birth of the prison*, Vintage, New York.

Fowler, G. 2018, 'No, Mark Zuckerberg, we're not really in control of our data', *Washington Post*, 12 April 2018, viewed 18 November 2019, <www.washingtonpost.com/news/the-switch/wp/2018/04/12/no-mark-zuckerberg-were-not-really-in-control-of-our-data/?noredirect=on>.

Franks, M.A. 2015, 'Drafting an effective "revenge porn" law: a guide for legislators', viewed 18 November 2019, <papers.ssrn.com/sol3/papers.cfm?abstract_id=2468823>.

Fried, C. 1968, 'Privacy', *Yale Law Journal*, vol. 77, no. 3, pp. pp. 475–93.

Frier, S. 2019, 'Facebook paid contractors to transcribe users' audio chats', *Bloomberg*, 14 August 2019, viewed 18 November 2019, <www.bloomberg.com/news/articles/2019-08-13/facebook-paid-hundreds-of-contractors-to-transcribe-users-audio>.

Fukuyama, F. 1995, *Trust: The social virtues and the creation of prosperity*, Penguin, London.

Funk, M. 2016, 'Cambridge Analytica and the secret agenda of a Facebook quiz', *New York Times*, 20 November 2016, viewed 18 November 2019, <www.nytimes.com/2016/11/20/opinion/cambridge-analytica-facebook-quiz.html>.

Gair, K. 2015, 'Privacy concerns mount as drones take to the skies', *smh.com.au*, 12 December 2015, viewed 18 November 2019, <www.smh.com.au/digital-life/consumer-security/privacy-concerns-mount-as-drones-take-to-the-skies-20151208-glijvk.html>.

Gallagher, R. & Greenwald, G. 2014, 'How the NSA plans to infect "millions" of computers with malware', *Intercept*, 13 March 2014, viewed 18 November 2019,

<theintercept.com/2014/03/12/nsa-plans-infect-millions-computers-malware/>.

Gander, K. 2014, 'Miss Teen USA webcam hacker Jared James Abrahams sentenced to 18 months in prison', *independent.co.uk*, 18 March 2014, viewed 22 February 2017, <www.independent.co.uk/news/world/americas/miss-teen-usa-webcam-hacker-jared-james-abrahams-sentenced-to-18-months-in-prison-9200575.html>.

Garcia, D. 2017, 'Leaking privacy and shadow profiles in online social networks', *Science Advances*, vol. 3, no. 8, 4 August 2017, viewed 15 February 2019, <advances.sciencemag.org/content/3/8/e1701172>.

Garcia, D., Goel, M., Agrawal, A.K. & Kumaraguru, P. 2018, 'Collective aspects of privacy in the Twitter social network', *EPJ Data Science*, vol. 7, viewed 6 January 2020, <epjdatascience.springeropen.com/articles/10.1140/epjds/s13688-018-0130-3>.

Gatford, S. 2015, 'Revenge porn makes new law', *LexisNexis*, 29 September 2015, viewed 13 September 2016, <lexisnexis.com.au/media-centre/blog-articles/2015-Sep-29-Revenge-porn-makes-new-law.html>.

Gavison, R. 1980, 'Privacy and the limits of law', *Yale Law Journal*, vol. 89, no. 3, pp. 421–71.

Gerety, T. 1977, 'Redefining privacy', *Harvard Civil Rights-Civil Liberties Law Review*, vol. 12, no. 2, pp. 233–96.

Gerstein, R.S. 1978, 'Intimacy and privacy', *Ethics*, vol. 89, no. 1, pp. 76–81.

Gibbs, W.W. 2018, 'Eyes on the high seas', *Anthropocene Magazine*, September 2018, viewed 20 December 2019, <www.anthropocenemagazine.org/2018/09/eyes-on-the-high-seas/>.

Godwin, M. 2003, *Cyber Rights: Defending free speech in the digital age*, MIT Press, Cambridge, Massachusetts.

Goode, L. 2015, 'Anonymous and the political ethos of hacktivism', *Popular Communication*, vol. 13, no. 1, pp. 74–86.

Google UK 2014, 'Google terms of service', 30 April 2014, viewed 16 August 2016, <www.google.co.uk/intl/en/policies/terms/regional.html>.

Goos, K., Friedewald, M., Webster, W. & Leleux, C. 2015, 'The co-evolution of surveillance technologies and surveillance practices', in D. Wright & R. Kreissl (eds), *Surveillance in Europe*, Routledge, New York, pp. 51–100.

Gordon, E. & de Souza e Silva, A. 2011, *Net Locality: Why location matters in a networked world*, John Wiley & Sons, Oxford, UK.

Gorrey, M. 2018, '"Predatory": man jailed for upskirting women at Central Station', *smh.com.au*, 30 May 2018, viewed 18 November 2019, <www.smh.com.au/national/nsw/predatory-man-jailed-for-upskirting-women-at-central-station-20180530-p4zies.html>.

Grassegger, H. & Krogerus, M. 2017, 'The data that turned the world upside down: how Cambridge Analytica used your Facebook data to help the Donald Trump campaign in the 2016 election', *Vice Motherboard*, 29 January 2017, viewed 18 November 2019, <www.vice.com/en_us/article/mg9vvn/how-our-likes-helped-trump-win>.

Greenberg, A. 2016, 'Great. Now even your headphones can spy on you', *Wired*, 22 November 2016, viewed 23 November 2016, <www.wired.com/2016/11/great-now-even-headphones-can-spy/?mbid=nl_112216_p3&CNDID=44897850>.

Greenleaf, G. 2012, 'The influence of European data privacy standards outside Europe: implications for globalization of Convention 108', *International Data Privacy Law*, vol. 2, no. 2, pp. 68–92.

———— 2015, 'Global tables of data privacy laws and bills (4th ed., January 2015)', *Privacy Laws & Business International Report,* vol. 133, pp. 18–28, viewed 18 November 2019, <ssrn.com/abstract=2603502>.

———— 2017, 'Countries with data privacy laws – by year 1973–2016 (Tables) (2 April, 2017)', *Privacy Laws & Business International Report*, vol. 146, p. 18, viewed 18 November 2019, <ssrn.com/abstract=2996139>.

———— 2018, '"GDPR Creep" for Australian businesses but gap in laws widens (6 June 2018)', *Privacy Laws & Business International Report 1*, vol. 154, pp. 4–5, viewed 15 February 2019, <ssrn.com/abstract=3226835 >.

Greenwald, G. 2013, 'Edward Snowden: NSA whistleblower answers reader questions', *Guardian*, 18 June 2016, viewed 22 August 2016, <www.theguardian.com/world/2013/jun/17/edward-snowden-nsa-files-whistleblower>.

———— 2014, *No Place To Hide: Edward Snowden, the NSA, and the US surveillance state*, Metropolitan Books, New York.

Greenwald, G. & MacAskill, E. 2013, 'NSA Prism program taps in to user data of Apple, Google and others', *Guardian*, 8 June 2013, viewed 6 February 2017, <www.theguardian.com/uk-news/2014/jul/14/gchq-tools-manipulate-online-information-leak?CMP=twt_gu>.

Greenwald, G., MacAskill, E. & Poitras, L. 2013, 'Edward Snowden: the whistleblower behind the NSA surveillance revelations', *Guardian*, 11 June 2013, viewed 18 November 2019, <www.theguardian.com/world/2013/jun/09/edward-snowden-nsa-whistleblower-surveillance>.

Grimmelmann, J. 2009, 'Privacy as product safety', *Widener Law Journal*, vol. 19, pp. 793–827, viewed 19 November 2019, <james.grimmelmann.net/files/articles/privacy-as-product-safety.pdf>.

Gross, R. & Acquisti, A. 2005, 'Information revelation and privacy in online social networks', *Proceedings of the 2005 ACM Workshop on Privacy in the Electronic Society*, pp. 71–80.

Guthrie, S. 2016, 'These celebrities fell victim to a spam email', *New Daily*, 16 March 2016, viewed 9 August 2016, <thenewdaily.com.au/entertainment/celebrity/2016/03/16/celebrity-nude-photos-hacking/>.

Habermas, J. 1989, *The Structural Transformation of the Public Sphere*, trans. T. Burger & F. Lawrence, vol. 85, MIT Press, Cambridge, Massachusetts.

Hafner, K. & Lyon, M. 1996, *Where Wizards Stay Up Late: The origins of the Internet*, Simon & Schuster, New York.

Haggart, B. & Tusikov, N. 2019, 'What the UK's Online Harms white paper teaches us about internet regulation', *The Conversation*, viewed 18 November 2019, <theconversation.com/what-the-u-k-s-online-harms-white-paper-teaches-us-about-internet-regulation-115337>.

Halavais, A. 2017, *Search Engine Society*, Polity Press, Cambridge, UK.

Harari, Y.N. 2018, *21 Lessons for the 21st Century*, Random House, New York.

———— 2019, 'Will Artificial Intelligence enhance or hack humanity? Fei-Fei Li & Yuval Noah Harari in conversation with Nicholas Thomson', *Wired*, 20 April 2019, viewed 20 November 2019, <www.wired.com/story/will-artificial-intelligence-enhance-hack-humanity/>.

Hartcher, P. 2019, 'There's a good chance Beijing already has your face on file', *smh.com.au*, 22 October 2019, viewed 18 November 2019, <www.smh.com.au/world/asia/there-s-a-good-chance-beijing-already-has-your-face-on-file-20191021-p532lu.html>.

Hasinoff, A.A. & Shepherd, T. 2014, 'Sexting in context: privacy norms and expectations', *International Journal of Communication*, vol. 8, pp. 2932–55, viewed 18 November 2019, <ijoc.org/index.php/ijoc/article/viewFile/2264/1262>.

Haskins, C. 2019, 'Revealed: this is Palantir's top-secret user manual for cops', *Vice Motherboard*, viewed 18 November 2019, <www.vice.com/en_us/article/9kx4z8/revealed-this-is-palantirs-top-secret-user-manual-for-cops>.

Hatmaker, T. 2018, 'Zuckerberg denies knowledge of Facebook shadow profiles', *TechCrunch*, viewed 18 November 2019, <techcrunch.com/2018/04/11/facebook-shadow-profiles-hearing-lujan-zuckerberg/>.

Held, V. 2005, 'Feminist transformations of moral theory', in A.D. Moore (ed.), *Information Ethics: Privacy, property and power*, University of Washington Press, Seattle, pp. 85–109.

Helman, L. 2018, 'Pay for (Privacy) Performance', viewed 18 November 2019, <ssrn.com/abstract=3160992>.

Henley, J. 2005, '55 years on, the controversial kiss that could be worth £10,000', *Guardian*, 13 April 2005, viewed 30 March 2017, <www.theguardian.com/world/2005/apr/13/france.arts>.

Henry, N., Powell, A. & Flynn, A. 2017, *Not Just 'Revenge Pornography': Australians' experience of image-based abuse*, viewed 8 May 2017, <www.rmit.edu.au/content/dam/rmit/documents/college-of-design-and-social-context/schools/global-urban-and-social-studies/revenge_porn_report_2017.pdf>.

Herman, B. 1993, *The Practice of Moral Judgment*, Harvard University Press, Cambridge, Massachusetts.

Hern, A. 2016, 'Uber employees "spied on ex-partners, politicians and Beyoncé"', *Guardian*, 13 December 2016, viewed 18 November 2019, <www.theguardian.com/technology/2016/dec/13/uber-employees-spying-ex-partners-politicians-beyonce>.

—— 2017, 'Vibrator maker ordered to pay out C$4m for tracking users' sexual activity', *Guardian*, 14 March 2017, viewed 23 March 2017, <www.theguardian.com/technology/2017/mar/14/we-vibe-vibrator-tracking-users-sexual-habits>.

—— 2019, 'Google fined record £44m by French data protection watchdog', *Guardian*, 22 January 2019, viewed 18 November 2019, <www.theguardian.com/technology/2019/jan/21/google-fined-record-44m-by-french-data-protection-watchdog>.

Hern, A. & Cadwalladr, C. 2018, 'Revealed: Aleksandr Kogan collected Facebook users' direct messages', *Guardian*, 13 April 2018, viewed 18 November 2019, <www.theguardian.com/uk-news/2018/apr/13/revealed-aleksandr-kogan-collected-facebook-users-direct-messages>.

Hill, K. 2011, 'Fitbit moves quickly after users' sex stats exposed', *Forbes*, 5 July 2011, viewed 18 November 2019, <www.forbes.com/sites/kashmirhill/2011/07/05/fitbit-moves-quickly-after-users-sex-stats-exposed/#7d9b11c79e73>.

—— 2017, 'How Facebook figures out everyone you've ever met', *Gizmodo*, 11 November 2017, viewed 11 December 2019, <www.gizmodo.com.au/2017/11/how-facebook-figures-out-everyone-youve-ever-met/>.

—— 2020, 'The secretive company that might end privacy as we know it', *New York Times*, 18 January 2020, <www.newyorktimes.com/2020/01/18/technology/clearview-privacy-facial-recognition.html>.

Hoffman, C. 2010, 'The battle for Facebook', *Rolling Stone*, 15 September 2010, viewed 13 February 2017, <www.rollingstone.com/culture/news/the-battle-for-facebook-20100915>.

Holten, E., Jackson, N., Bodker, C., Carson, M., Rinvolucri, B., Liggett, A. & Monzani, C. 2015, 'Someone stole naked pictures of me. This is what I did about it – video', *Guardian*, 21 January 2015, viewed 18 November 2019, <www.theguardian.com/ commentisfree/video/2015/jan/21/naked-pictures-this-is-what-i-did-revenge-porn-emma-holten-video>.

Hoofnagle, C.J. 2018, 'Designing for consent', *Journal of European Consumer and Market Law*, vol. 7, no. 4, pp. 162–71, viewed 3 December 2019, <www.kluwerlawonline.com/ document.php?id=EuCML2018033>.

Hoskins, G.T. 2018, 'Draft once; deploy everywhere? Contextualizing digital law and Brazil's Marco Civil da Internet', *Television & New Media*, vol. 19, no. 5, pp. 431–47.

House of Commons (UK) 2019, 'Digital, Culture, Media and Sport Committee: Disinformation and "Fake News": Final report', viewed 18 November 2019, <publications.parliament.uk/pa/cm201719/cmselect/cmcumeds/1791/1791.pdf>.

Hu, M. 2018, 'Cybersurveillance intrusions and an evolving Katz privacy test', *American Criminal Law Review*, vol. 55, pp. 127–53.

Hull, G., Lipford, H.R. & Latulipe, C. 2011, 'Contextual gaps: privacy issues on Facebook', *Ethics and Information Technology*, vol. 13, no. 4, pp. 289–302.

Hunter, F., '"It is a stretch": ACCC's Sims questions Google assurances over Fitbit data', *smh.com.au*, 19 November 2019, viewed 20 December 2019, <www.smh.com.au/ politics/federal/it-is-a-stretch-accc-s-sims-questions-google-assurances-over-fitbit-data-20191119-p53by8.html>.

Inness, J.C. 1992, *Privacy, Intimacy, and Isolation*, Oxford University Press, Oxford.

Irvine, J. 2019, 'Twitter was like a wild teenage party I had to leave', *smh.com.au*, 11 April 2019, viewed 19 November 2019, <www.smh.com.au/politics/federal/twitter-was-like-a-wild-teenage-party-i-had-to-leave-20190410-p51cwa.html>.

Isaak, J. & Hanna, M.J. 2018, 'User data privacy: Facebook, Cambridge Analytica, and privacy protection', *Computer*, vol. 51, no. 8, pp. 56–59, viewed 19 November 2019, <ieeexplore.ieee.org/stamp/stamp.jsp?arnumber=8436400>.

Jane, E.A. 2016, *Misogyny Online: A short (and brutish) history*, SAGE Swifts, London.

———— 2016, 'Online misogyny and feminist digilantism', *Continuum*, vol. 30, no. 3, pp. 284–97.

Jee, C. 2019, 'China's social credit system stopped millions of people from buying travel tickets', *MIT Technology Review*, 4 March 2019, viewed 19 November 2019, <www. technologyreview.com/f/613070/chinas-social-credit-system-stopped-millions-of-people-buying-travel-tickets/>.

Jenkins, H. 2006, *Convergence Culture: Where old and new media collide*, NYU Press, New York.

Jenkins Jr, H.W. 2010, 'Google and the search for the future', *Wall Street Journal*, 14 August 2010, viewed 26 July 2016 <www.wsj.com/articles/SB1000142405274870490 1104575423294099527212>.

Johnson, B. 2010, 'Privacy no longer a social norm, says Facebook founder', *Guardian*, 11 January 2010, viewed 19 November 2019, <www.theguardian.com/technology/2010/ jan/11/facebook-privacy>.

Johnson, R. 2004, 'Kant's moral philosophy', in E.N. Zalta (ed.), *The Stanford Encyclopedia of Philosophy*, (Spring 2015 edition), viewed 19 November 2019, <plato.stanford.edu/ archives/spr2004/entries/kant-moral/>.

Joye, C. 2014, 'Interview transcript: former head of the NSA and commander of the

US cyber command, General Keith Alexander', *Australian Financial Review*, 8 May 2014, viewed 19 November 2019, <www.afr.com/technology/web/security/interview-transcriptformer-head-of-the-nsa-and-commander-of-the-us-cyber-command-general-keith-alexander-20140507-itzhw#ixzz4HZhlKMUf>.

Kadidal, S. 2015, 'Surveillance after the *USA FREEDOM Act*: how much has changed?', *Huffington Post*, 17 December 2015, viewed 9 February 2017, <www.huffingtonpost.com/the-center-for-constitutional-rights/surveillance-after-the-us_b_8827952.html>.

Kant, I. 1785, *Grundlegung zur Metaphysik der Sitten*, Johann Friedrich Harknoch, Riga, viewed 19 November 2019, <gutenberg.spiegel.de/buch/grundlegung-zur-methaphysik-der-sitten-3510/1>.

—— 1996, *The Metaphysics of Morals*, trans. M. Gregor (from German original, 1797), Cambridge University Press, Cambridge, UK.

—— 1996, 'On a supposed right to lie from philanthropy', in M. Gregor (ed.), *Practical Philosophy*, trans. M. Gregor (from German original, 1797), Cambridge University Press, Cambridge, UK.

—— 1996, 'On the common saying: that may be correct in theory, but it is of no use in practice', in M. Gregor (ed.), *Practical Philosophy*, trans. M. Gregor (from German original, 1793), Cambridge University Press, Cambridge, UK.

—— 1996, 'Toward perpetual peace', in M. Gregor (ed.), *Practical Philosophy*, trans. M. Gregor (from German original, 1795), Cambridge University Press, Cambridge, UK.

—— 2009, *Groundwork of the Metaphysic of Morals*, trans. H.J. Paton (from German original, 1785), Harper Perennial Modern Thought, New York.

Kennedy, H., Elgesem, D. & Miguel, C. 2017, 'On fairness: User perspectives on social media data mining', *Convergence*, vol. 23, no. 3, pp. 270–88.

Kerstein, S. 2009, 'Treating others merely as means', *Utilitas*, vol. 21, no. 2, pp. 163–80.

Kidd, K. 2018, 'Federal judge declines to dismiss Facebook photo tagging class-action', *Northern California Record*, 12 March 2018, viewed 19 November 2019, <norcalrecord.com/stories/511359801-federal-judge-declines-to-dismiss-facebook-photo-tagging-class-action>.

Kiss, J. 2014, 'An online Magna Carta: Berners-Lee calls for bill of rights for web', *Guardian*, 12 March 2014, viewed 17 February 2017, <www.theguardian.com/technology/2014/mar/12/online-magna-carta-berners-lee-web>.

Kleingeld, P. 2014, 'The development of Kant's cosmopolitanism', in P. Formosa, A. Goldman & T. Patrone (eds), *Politics and Teleology in Kant*, University of Wales Press, Cardiff.

—— 2014, 'Kant's second thoughts on colonialism', in K. Flikschuh & L. Ypi (eds), *Kant and Colonialism: Historical and critical perspectives*, Oxford University Press, Oxford, pp. 43–67.

Kleingeld, P. & Brown, E. 2014, 'Cosmopolitanism', in E.N. Zalta (ed.), *The Stanford Encyclopedia of Philosophy* (Winter 2019 edition), viewed 19 November 2019, <plato.stanford.edu/entries/cosmopolitanism/>.

Korsgaard, C.M. 1996, *Creating the Kingdom of Ends*, Cambridge University Press, Cambridge, UK.

—— 2013, 'Kantian ethics, animals, and the law', *Oxford Journal of Legal Studies*, vol. 33, no. 4, pp. 629–48.

Kosinski, M., Stillwell, D. & Graepel, T. 2013, 'Private traits and attributes are predictable from digital records of human behavior', *Proceedings of the National Academy of Sciences*, vol. 110, no. 15, pp. 5802–805.

Kramer, A.D., Guillory, J.E. & Hancock, J.T. 2014, 'Experimental evidence of massive-scale emotional contagion through social networks', *Proceedings of the National Academy of Sciences*, vol. 111, no. 24, pp. 8788–90, viewed 19 November 2019, <www.pnas.org/content/111/24/8788>.

Kranenborg, H. 2015, 'Google and the right to be forgotten', *European Data Protection Law Review*, vol. 1, pp. 70–79.

Kranzberg, M. 1986, 'Technology and history: "Kranzberg's Laws"', *Technology and Culture*, vol. 27, no. 3, pp. 544–60.

Kuchler, H. 2018, 'Max Schrems: the man who took on Facebook – and won', *Irish Times*, 5 April 2018, viewed 19 November 2019, <www.irishtimes.com/business/technology/max-schrems-the-man-who-took-on-facebook-and-won-1.3451485>.

Kupfer, J. 1987, 'Privacy, autonomy, and self-concept', *American Philosophical Quarterly*, vol. 24, no. 1, pp. 81–89.

Kurzweil, R. 2005, *The Singularity is Near: When humans transcend biology*, Penguin, New York.

Lanier, J. 2010, *You Are Not a Gadget: A manifesto*, Vintage, New York.

——— 2018, *Dawn of the New Everything: A journey through virtual reality*, Vintage, New York.

——— 2018, *Ten Arguments for Deleting your Social Media Accounts Right Now*, Random House, New York.

Lanzing, M. 2016, 'The transparent self', *Ethics and Information Technology*, vol. 18, no. 1, pp. 9–16, viewed 19 November 2019, <link.springer.com/article/10.1007/s10676-016-9396-y>.

Lapowsky, I. 2018, 'How the LAPD uses data to predict crime', *Wired*, 22 May 2018, viewed 19 November 2019, <www.wired.com/story/los-angeles-police-department-predictive-policing/>.

Lardinois, F. 2015, 'Google launches native ads in Gmail to all advertisers', *Tech Crunch*, 1 September 2016, viewed 11 August 2016, <techcrunch.com/2015/09/01/google-launches-new-native-ad-format-in-gmail/>.

Lavoie, A. 2009, 'The online zoom lens: why internet street-level mapping technologies demand reconsideration of the modern-day tort notion of public privacy', *Georgia Law Review*, vol. 43, pp. 575–616.

Leahy, P. & Sensenbrenner, J. 2013, 'The case for NSA reform', *Politico*, 29 October 2013, viewed 19 November 2019, <www.politico.com/story/2013/10/leahy-sensenbrenner-nsa-reform-098953>.

Lee, M., Crofts, T., McGovern, A. & Milivojevic, S. 2015, *Sexting and Young People: Report to the Criminology Research Advisory Council*, viewed 19 November 2019, <www.criminologyresearchcouncil.gov.au/reports/1516/53-1112-FinalReport.pdf>.

Leiner, B.M., Cerf, V.G., Clark, D.D., Kahn, R.E., Kleinrock, L., Lynch, D.C., Postel, J., Roberts, L.G. & Wolff, S. 2009, 'A brief history of the Internet', *ACM SIGCOMM Computer Communication Review*, vol. 39, no. 5, pp. 22–31, viewed 19 November 2019, <www.isoc.org/internet/history/brief.shtml>.

Lenhart, A. 2009, 'Teens and sexting: how and why minor teens are sending sexually suggestive nude or nearly nude images via text messaging. A Pew Internet & American

Life Project Report', viewed 10 August 2016, <ncdsv.org/images/PewInternet_
TeensAndSexting_12-2009.pdf>.

Lessig, L. 2006, *Code: Version 2.0*, Basic Books, viewed 19 November 2019, <codev2.cc/>.

Levy, S. 1984, *Hackers: Heroes of the computer revolution*, Doubleday, New York.

—— 2016, 'Why are we fighting the crypto wars again?', *Wired*, 11 March 2016, viewed
19 November 2019, <www.wired.com/2016/03/why-are-we-fighting-the-crypto-wars-
again/>.

Lewis, K., Kaufman, J. & Christakis, N. 2008, 'The taste for privacy: an analysis of college
student privacy settings in an online social network', *Journal of Computer-Mediated
Communication*, vol. 14, no. 1, pp. 79–100.

Lindsay, D. 2005, 'An exploration of the conceptual basis of privacy and the implications
for the future of Australian privacy law', *Melbourne University Law Review*, vol. 29,
viewed 19 November 2019, <www5.austlii.edu.au/au/journals/MelbULawRw/2005/4.
html>.

—— 2012, 'Digital eternity or digital oblivion: some difficulties in conceptualising and
implementing the right to be forgotten', in D. Dorr & R.L. Weaver (eds), *The Right to
Privacy in the Light of Media Convergence: Perspectives from three continents*, Walter de
Gruyter, Berlin, pp. 322–43.

—— 2014, 'The "right to be forgotten" in European data protection law', in
N. Witzleb, D. Lindsay, M. Paterson & S. Rodrick (eds), *Emerging Challenges in
Privacy Law: Comparative perspectives*, Cambridge University Press, Cambridge, UK,
pp. 290–337.

Locke, J. 2005, *Second Treatise of Government*, Hackett Publishing Co., Cambridge, UK,
viewed 17 December 2019, <www.gutenberg.org/files/7370/7370-h/7370-h.htm>.

Lumby, C. & Albury, K. 2010, 'Too much? Too young? The sexualisation of children
debate in Australia', *Media International Australia*, vol. 135, no. 1, pp. 141–52.

Lupton, D. 2014, 'Self-tracking modes: reflexive self-monitoring and data practices',
presented at *The Social Life of Big Data* 2015 symposium, Perth, WA, 2 June, 2015,
viewed 20 December 2019, <ro.ecu.edu.au/slbd/1>.

Lymn, S. 2012, 'Living in Orwell's world: how to disappear completely online', *The
Conversation*, 3 April 2012, viewed 22 August 2016, <theconversation.com/living-in-
orwells-world-how-to-disappear-completely-online-5990>.

Lynskey, O. 2018, 'The power of providence: the role of platforms in leveraging the
legibility of users to accentuate inequality', in M. Moore & D. Tambini (eds), *Digital
Dominance: The power of Google, Amazon, Facebook, and Apple*, Oxford University
Press, New York.

Mackenzie, C. 2014, 'Three dimensions of autonomy: a relational analysis', in A. Veltman
& M. Piper (eds), *Autonomy, Oppression and Gender*, Oxford University Press, New
York, pp. 15–41.

Mackenzie, C. & Stoljar, N. 2000, *Relational Autonomy: Feminist perspectives on autonomy,
agency, and the social self*, Oxford University Press, New York.

Madrigal, A.C. 2012, 'Reading the privacy policies you encounter in a year would take
76 work days', *Atlantic*, 1 March 2012, viewed 19 November, <www.theatlantic.com/
technology/archive/2012/03/reading-the-privacy-policies-you-encounter-in-a-year-
would-take-76-work-days/253851/>.

Malheiros, M., Jennett, C., Patel, S., Brostoff, S. & Sasse, M.A. 2012, 'Too close for comfort:
a study of the effectiveness and acceptability of rich-media personalized advertising',

Proceedings of the SIGCHI Conference on Human Factors in Computing Systems,
pp. 579–88.

Manjoo, F. 2019, 'It's time to panic about privacy', *New York Times*, 10 April 2019, viewed
20 December 2019, <www.nytimes.com/interactive/2019/04/10/opinion/internet-data-
privacy.html>.

Mansour, R.F. 2016, 'Understanding how big data leads to social networking vulnerability',
Computers in Human Behavior, vol. 57, pp. 348–51.

Marks, M. 2019, 'Facebook is predicting if you'll kill yourself. That's wrong',
Guardian, 30 January 2019, viewed 19 November 2019, <www.theguardian.com/
commentisfree/2019/jan/30/facebook-is-predicting-if-youll-kill-yourself-thats-wrong>.

Marshall, A. 2018, 'Uber makes peace with cities by spilling its secrets', *Wired*, 16 April
2018, viewed 19 November 2019, <www.wired.com/story/uber-nacto-data-sharing/>.

Marshall, J. 2016, 'Facebook wants to help sell every ad on the web', *Wall Street Journal*,
27 May 2016, viewed 19 November 2019, <www.wsj.com/articles/facebook-wants-to-
help-sell-every-ad-on-the-web-1464321603>.

Marwick, A.E. & boyd, d. 2014, 'Networked privacy: how teenagers negotiate context in
social media', *New Media & Society*, vol. 16, no. 7, pp. 1051–67.

Matheson, R. 2014, 'A market for emotions: with emotion-tracking software, Affectiva
attracts big-name clients, aims for "mood-aware" Internet', *MIT News*, 31 July 2014,
viewed 19 November 2019, <news.mit.edu/2014/with-emotion-tracking-software-
affectiva-attracts-clients-mood-aware-internet-0731>.

Mathiesen, T. 1997, 'The viewer society: Michel Foucault's "Panopticon" revisited',
Theoretical Criminology, vol. 1, no. 2, pp. 215–34.

Matsakis, L. 2018, 'Mozilla diagnoses the health of the global internet', *Wired*, 10 April
2018, viewed 19 November 2019, <www.wired.com/story/mozilla-internet-health-
report/>.

Maxwell, J. 2019, 'Face to face with the future', *Inside Story*, 18 October 2019, viewed
19 November 2019, <insidestory.org.au/face-to-face-with-the-future/>.

Mayer, J.R. & Mitchell, J.C. 2012, 'Third-party web tracking: policy and technology',
2012 *IEEE Symposium on Security and Privacy*, pp. 413–27, viewed 19 December 2019,
<ieeexplore.ieee.org/document/6234427/?arnumber=6234427>.

Mayer-Schönberger, V. 2010, 'Beyond privacy, beyond rights – toward a "systems" theory
of information governance', *California Law Review*, vol. 98 (6), pp. 1853–85.

——— 2015, 'Keynote Address: Privacy by regulation', 26 October 2015, Amsterdam
Privacy Conference 2015.

Mayer-Schönberger, V. & Cukier, K. 2013, *Big Data: A revolution that will transform how
we live, work, and think*, Houghton Mifflin Harcourt, London.

Mazzetti, M., Goldman, A., Bergman, R. & Perlroth, N. 2019, 'A new age of warfare:
how internet mercenaries do battle for authoritarian governments', *New York Times*,
21 March 2019, viewed 19 November 2019, <www.nytimes.com/2019/03/21/us/politics/
government-hackers-nso-darkmatter.html?>.

McCabe, D. 2017, 'Facebook targets children with Messenger Kids app', *Axios*, 5 December
2017, viewed 19 November 2019, <www.axios.com/facebook-targets-children-with-
messenger-kids-app-1513388352-3d15df91-8c4f-4610-99e5-8442b41d8633.html>.

McGoogan, C. 2016, 'Twitter to verify more users: how to get a blue tick', *Telegraph*,
20 July 2016, viewed 12 August 2016, <www.telegraph.co.uk/technology/2016/07/20/
twitter-to-verify-more-users-how-to-get-a-blue-tick/>.

McKenzie, D.F. 1984, 'The sociology of a text: orality, literacy and print in early New Zealand', *Library*, vol. 6, no. 4, pp. 333–65.

McLuhan, M. 1964, *Understanding Media: The extensions of man*, Taylor & Francis, London.

Meese, J. 2015, 'Google Glass and Australian privacy law: regulating the future of locative media', in R. Wilken & G. Goggin (eds), *Locative Media*, Routledge, New York, pp. 136–47.

———— 2018, *Authors, Users, and Pirates: Copyright law and subjectivity*, MIT Press, Cambridge, Massachusetts.

Meese, J. & Wilken, R. 2014, 'Google Street View in Australia: privacy implications and regulatory solutions', *Media and Arts Law Review*, vol. 19, no. 4, pp. 305–24.

Meikle, G. & Young, S. 2012, *Media Convergence: Networked digital media in everyday life*, Palgrave Macmillan, London.

Metz, R. 2019, 'Yes, tech companies may listen when you talk to your virtual assistant. Here's why that's not likely to stop', *CNN*, 19 August 2019, viewed 19 November 2019, <edition.cnn.com/2019/08/19/tech/siri-alexa-people-listening/index.html>.

Michael, K. & Michael, M. 2013, 'The future prospects of embedded microchips in humans as unique identifiers: the risks versus the rewards', *Media Culture & Society*, vol. 35, no. 1, pp. 78–86, viewed 19 November 2019, <ro.uow.edu.au/cgi/viewcontent.cgi?article=2150&context=eispapers>.

Mill, J.S. 2011, *On Liberty*, Walter Scott Publishing Co., London, viewed 19 November 2019, <www.gutenberg.org/files/34901/34901-h/34901-h.htm>.

Miller, N. 2015, '"Naked Rambler" Stephen Gough makes UK legal history by facing court in the nude', *smh.com.au*, 10 June 2015, viewed 17 November 2016, <www.smh.com.au/world/naked-rambler-stephen-gough-makes-uk-legal-history-by-facing-court-in-the-nude-20150609-ghk9wy>.

———— 2016, 'Behave, the Ministry of Nudge is watching you', *smh.com.au*, 15 September 2016, viewed 15 September 2016, <www.smh.com.au/world/government-nudge-unit-to-attempt-to-change-peoples-behaviours-20160914-grg5sb.html>.

Mislove, A., Viswanath, B., Gummadi, K.P. & Druschel, P. 2010, 'You are who you know: Inferring user profiles in online social networks', *Proceedings of the Third ACM International Conference on Web Search and Data Mining*, pp. 251–60.

Mitchelson, A. 2017, 'Peeping Tom drones prompt calls for a close look at privacy laws', *New Daily*, 27 April 2017, viewed 19 November 2019, <thenewdaily.com.au/news/national/2017/04/27/drones-privacy-law/>.

Mizrahi, S.K. 2018, 'Ontario's new invasion of privacy torts: do they offer monetary redress for violations suffered via the internet of things?', *Western Journal of Legal Studies*, vol. 8, p. 1.

Mo, J.Y. 2017, 'Misuse of private information as a tort: The implications of *Google v Judith Vidal-Hall*', *Computer Law & Security Review*, vol. 33, no. 1, pp. 87–97.

Molitorisz, S. 2018, 'It's time for third-party data brokers to emerge from the shadows', *The Conversation*, 4 April 2018, viewed 15 February 2019, <theconversation.com/its-time-for-third-party-data-brokers-to-emerge-from-the-shadows-94298>.

Moor, J.H. 1990, 'The ethics of privacy protection', *Library Trends*, vol. 39, no. 1–2, pp. 69–82.

———— 1997, 'Towards a theory of privacy in the information age', *Computers and Society*, vol. 27, no. 3, pp. 27–32.

Moore, A.D. 2003, 'Privacy: its meaning and value', *American Philosophical Quarterly*, vol. 40, no. 3, pp. 215–27, viewed 19 November 2019, <ssrn.com/abstract=1980880>.

—— 2013, 'Privacy', in H. LaFollette (ed.), *The International Encyclopedia of Ethics*, Wiley Online Library, viewed 19 November 2019, <ssrn.com/abstract=2017214>.

—— 2013, 'Privacy, speech, and the law', *Journal of Information Ethics*, vol. 22, no. 1, pp. 21–43, viewed 19 November 2019, <ssrn.com/abstract=1984807>.

Moore, M. & Tambini, D. 2018, *Digital Dominance: The Power of Google, Amazon, Facebook, and Apple*, Oxford University Press, New York.

Moores, S. 2004, 'The doubling of place', in N. Couldry & A. McCarthy (eds), *MediaSpace: Place, scale, and culture in a media age*, Routledge, London, pp. 21–36.

Morozov, E. 2011, 'Don't be evil', *New Republic*, 13 July 2011, viewed 19 November 2019, <hci.stanford.edu/courses/cs047n/readings/morozov-google-evil.pdf>.

Morris, R. 2015, 'Child watch: the apps that let parents "spy" on their kids', *BBC News*, 29 January 2015, viewed 10 December 2019, <www.bbc.com/news/technology-30930512>.

Morse, J. 2018, 'Mark Zuckerberg awkwardly dodges question about shadow profiles from European Parliament', *Mashable*, 23 May 2018, viewed 19 November 2019, <mashable.com/2018/05/22/zuckerberg-european-parliament-shadow-profiles/#0NMHeXIB1gqT>.

Murphy, R.F. 1964, 'Social distance and the veil', *American Anthropologist*, vol. 66, no. 6, pp. 1257–74.

National Telecommunications and Information Administration 2016, 'Lack of trust in internet privacy and security may deter economic and other online activities', 13 May 2016, viewed 19 November 2019, <www.ntia.doc.gov/blog/2016/lack-trust-internet-privacy-and-security-may-deter-economic-and-other-online-activities>.

Nedelsky, J. 1989, 'Reconceiving autonomy: sources, thoughts and possibilities', *Yale Journal of Law & Feminism*, vol. 1, no. 1, viewed 19 December 2019, <digitalcommons.law.yale.edu/yjlf/vol1/iss1/5>.

—— 1993, 'Reconceiving rights as relationship', *Review of Constitutional Studies*, vol. 1, no. 1, viewed 19 November 2019, <ssrn.com/abstract=2045687>.

New South Wales Standing Committee on Law and Justice 2016, 'Remedies for the serious invasion of privacy in New South Wales', 3 March 2016, viewed 19 November 2019, <www.parliament.nsw.gov.au>.

Newton, C. 2019, 'The trauma floor: the secret lives of Facebook moderators in America', *Verge*, 25 February 2019, viewed 19 November 2019, <www.theverge.com/2019/2/25/18229714/cognizant-facebook-content-moderator-interviews-trauma-working-conditions-arizona>.

Nightingale, V. 2007, 'New media worlds? Challenges for convergence', in V. Nightingale & T. Dwyer (eds), *New Media Worlds: Challenges for convergence*, Oxford University Press, Oxford, pp. 19–36.

Nimmer, M.B. 1954, 'The right of publicity', *Law and Contemporary Problems*, vol. 19, no. 2, pp. 203–23.

Nissenbaum, H. 2010, *Privacy in Context: Technology, policy, and the integrity of social life*, Stanford University Press, Stanford, California.

—— 2011, 'A contextual approach to privacy online', *Daedalus*, vol. 140, no. 4, pp. 32–48, viewed 19 November 2019, <ssrn.com/abstract=2567042>.

Nissenbaum, H. & Brunton, F. 2015, *Obfuscation: A user's guide for privacy and protest*, MIT Press, Cambridge, Massachusetts.

Noack, R. 2016, 'This city embedded traffic lights in the sidewalks so that smartphone
    users don't have to look up', *Washington Post*, 25 April 2016, viewed 31 May 2016,
    <www.washingtonpost.com/news/worldviews/wp/2016/04/25/this-city-embedded-
    traffic-lights-in-the-sidewalks-so-that-smartphone-users-dont-have-to-look-up/>.

Nott, G. 2019, 'Microsoft moves fast to write the regulation on facial recognition',
    Computerworld, 29 March 2019, viewed 19 November 2019,.

Nwaneri, C. 2017, 'Ready lawyer one: legal issues in the innovation of virtual reality',
    Harvard Journal of Law & Technology, vol. 30, no. 2, pp. 601–27, viewed 19 November
    2019, <jolt.law.harvard.edu/assets/articlePDFs/v30/30HarvJLTech601.pdf>.

Obar, J.A. & Oeldorf-Hirsch, A. 2018, 'The biggest lie on the internet: ignoring the privacy
    policies and terms of service policies of social networking services', *Information,
    Communication & Society*, 3 July 2018.

Ofcom 2016, *Adults' Media Use and Attitudes Report 2016*, April 2016, viewed 19 November
    2019, <www.ofcom.org.uk/__data/assets/pdf_file/0026/80828/2016-adults-media-use-
    and-attitudes.pdf>.

Olding, R. & Munro, P. 2016, 'The day Laura Pilati saw her photo on a schoolgirl porn
    site', *smh.com.au*, 19 August 2016, viewed 22 August 2016, <www.smh.com.au/
    national/the-day-i-saw-myself-on-a-schoolgirl-porn-site-20160818-gqw371.html>.

O'Neill, O. 1989, *Constructions of Reason: Explorations of Kant's practical philosophy*,
    Cambridge University Press, Cambridge, UK.

—— 1996, *Towards Justice and Virtue: A constructive account of practical reasoning*,
    Cambridge University Press, Cambridge, UK.

—— 2002, *Autonomy and Trust in Bioethics*, Cambridge University Press, Cambridge,
    UK.

—— 2002, 'A question of trust: the BBC Reith Lectures 2002', viewed 19 November
    2019, <www.immagic.com/eLibrary/ARCHIVES/GENERAL/BBC_UK/B020000O.
    pdf>.

—— 2003, 'Some limits of informed consent', *Journal of Medical Ethics*, vol. 29, no. 1,
    pp. 4–7.

Parent, W.A. 1983, 'Privacy, morality, and the law', *Philosophy & Public Affairs*, vol. 12,
    no. 4, pp. 269–88.

Parfit, D. 2011, *On What Matters*, vol. 1, Oxford University Press, Oxford.

Parham, J. 2019, 'When influencers switch platforms – and bare it all', *Wired*, 19 August
    2019, viewed 20 November 2019, <www.wired.com/story/culture-fan-tastic-planet-
    influencer-porn/>.

Pateman, C. 1980, 'Women and consent', *Political Theory*, vol. 8, no. 2, pp. 149–68.

Paul, K. 2019, '"Tossed my Fitbit in the trash": users fear for privacy after Google
    buys company', *Guardian*, 7 November 2019, viewed 20 November 2019, <www.
    theguardian.com/technology/2019/nov/05/fitbit-google-acquisition-health-data>.

Perera, C., Ranjan, R., Wang, L., Khan, S.U. & Zomaya, A.Y. 2015, 'Big data privacy in the
    internet of things era', *IT Professional*, vol. 17, no. 3, pp. 32–39.

Perez, E., Prokupecz, S. & Cohen, T. 2014, 'More than 90 people nabbed in global hacker
    crackdown', *CNN*, 20 May 2014, viewed 9 August 2016, <edition.cnn.com/2014/05/19/
    justice/us-global-hacker-crackdown/index.html?iref=allsearch>.

Perlroth, N. 2016, 'Apple rushes out iPhone software fix to avoid conversation
    eavesdropping', *smh.com.au*, 26 August 2016, viewed 26 August 2016, <www.smh.

com.au/technology/consumer-security/apple-rushes-out-iphone-software-fix-to-avoid-conversation-eavesdropping-20160825-gr1krv.html>.

—— 2017, 'Spyware's odd targets: backers of Mexico's soda tax', *New York Times*, 11 February 2017, viewed 14 February 2017, <www.nytimes.com/2017/02/11/technology/hack-mexico-soda-tax-advocates.html?_r=0>.

Pesce, J.P., Casas, D.L., Rauber, G. & Almeida, V. 2012, 'Privacy attacks in social media using photo tagging networks: A case study with Facebook', *Proceedings of the 1st Workshop on Privacy and Security in Online Social Media*, pp. 1–8.

Peters, J. 2016, *The Idealist: Aaron Swartz and the rise of free culture on the internet*, Simon & Schuster, New York.

Peterson, A. 2016, 'Why a staggering number of Americans have stopped using the Internet the way they used to', *Washington Post*, 13 May 2016, viewed 17 December 2019, <www.washingtonpost.com/news/the-switch/wp/2016/05/13/new-government-data-shows-a-staggering-number-of-americans-have-stopped-basic-online-activities/>.

Pettit, P. 1995, 'The cunning of trust', *Philosophy & Public Affairs*, vol. 24, no. 3, pp. 202–25.

Pilgrim, T. 2015, interviewed by S. Molitorisz, 8 October 2015.

Pinker, S. 2008, 'The stupidity of dignity', *New Republic*, 28 May 2008, viewed 20 November 2019, <newrepublic.com/article/64674/the-stupidity-dignity>.

Piwek, L. & Joinson, A. 2016, '"What do they *snapchat* about?" Patterns of use in time-limited instant messaging service', *Computers in Human Behavior*, vol. 54, pp. 358–67, viewed 20 November 2019.

Plato 2014, *Laws*, trans. B. Jowett, University of Adelaide, viewed 20 November 2019, <ebooks.adelaide.edu.au/p/plato/p71l/complete.html>.

Poirier, A. 2017, 'One of history's most romantic photographs was staged', BBC News, 14 February 2017, viewed 19 December 2019, <www.bbc.com/culture/story/20170213-the-iconic-photo-that-symbolises-love>.

Posner, R.A. 1977, 'The right of privacy', *Georgia Law Review*, vol. 12, no. 3, pp. 393–422, viewed 17 December 2019, <chicagounbound.uchicago.edu/cgi/viewcontent.cgi?article=2803&context=journal_articles>.

Price, R. 2014, 'These videos demonstrate exactly what is wrong with Google Glass', *Daily Dot*, 28 March 2014, viewed 11 December 2019, <www.dailydot.com/via/google-glass-surveillance-camera-man/>.

Prosser, W.L. 1960, 'Privacy', *California Law Review*, vol. 48, pp. 383–423.

Provost, F., Martens, D. & Murray, A. 2015, 'Finding similar mobile consumers with a privacy-friendly geosocial design', *Information Systems Research*, 19 June 2015.

Quantified Self 2016, viewed 12 August 2016, <quantifiedself.com>.

Quodling, A. 2018, 'Shadow profiles – Facebook knows about you, even if you're not on Facebook', *The Conversation*, 13 April 2018, viewed 20 November 2019, <theconversation.com/shadow-profiles-facebook-knows-about-you-even-if-youre-not-on-facebook-94804>.

Rachels, J. 1975, 'Why privacy is important', *Philosophy & Public Affairs*, vol. 4, no. 4, pp. 323–33.

Rauhofer, J. 2008, 'Privacy is dead, get over it! Information privacy and the dream of a risk-free society', *Information & Communications Technology Law*, vol. 17, no. 3, pp. 185–97.

Rauscher, F. 2016, 'Kant's social and political philosophy', in E.N. Zalta (ed.), *The Stanford Encyclopedia of Philosophy* (Fall 2016 edition), viewed 20 November 2019, <plato.

stanford.edu/archives/fall2016/entries/kant-social-political/>.

Rawls, J. 1971, *A Theory of Justice*, Harvard University Press, Cambridge, Massachusetts.

Regalado, A. 2019, 'More than 26 million people have taken an at-home ancestry test', *MIT Technology Review*, 11 February 2019, viewed 20 November 2019, <www. technologyreview.com/s/612880/more-than-26-million-people-have-taken-an-at-home-ancestry-test/>.

Regan, P.M. 1995, *Legislating Privacy: Technology, social values, and public policy*, University of North Carolina Press, Chapel Hill, North Carolina.

———— 2002, 'Privacy as a common good in the digital world', *Information, Communication & Society*, vol. 5, no. 3, pp. 382–405.

———— 2015, 'Response to *Privacy as a Public Good*', *Duke Law Journal Online*, vol. 65, pp. 51–65, viewed 20 November 2019, <scholarship.law.duke.edu/cgi/viewcontent. cgi?article=1013&context=dlj_online>.

Reiman, J. 1976, 'Privacy, intimacy, and personhood', *Philosophy & Public Affairs*, vol. 6, pp. 26–44.

———— 2004, 'Driving to the panopticon: A philosophical exploration of the risks to privacy posed by the information technology of the future', in B. Rössler (ed.), *Privacies: Philosophical evaluations*, Stanford University Press, Stanford, US, pp. 194–214.

Richards, N.M. & Solove, D.J. 2010, 'Prosser's privacy law: A mixed legacy', *California Law Review*, vol. 98 (6), pp. 1887–924, viewed 20 November 2019, <scholarship.law. berkeley.edu/cgi/viewcontent.cgi?article=1059&context=californialawreview>.

Roberts, D. & Ackerman, S. 2015, 'NSA mass phone surveillance revealed by Edward Snowden illegal', *Guardian*, 8 May 2015, viewed 6 February 2017, <www.theguardian. com/us-news/2015/may/07/nsa-phone-records-program-illegal-court>.

Roderick, L. 2014, 'Discipline and power in the digital age: The case of the US consumer data broker industry', *Critical Sociology*, vol. 40, no. 5, pp. 729–46.

Ronson, J. 2015, *So You've Been Publicly Shamed*, Picador, London.

Rooney, T. 2015, 'Spying on your kid's phone with Teensafe will only undermine trust', *The Conversation*, 29 April 2015, viewed 19 November 2019.

Rosen, J. 2003, 'PressThink: An introduction', *PressThink*, 1 September 2003, viewed 20 November, 2019, <archive.pressthink.org/2003/09/01/introduction_ghost.html>.

Rosenblatt, J. 2018, 'Facebook photo-scanning suit is a multibillion-dollar threat', *Bloomberg*, 17 April 2018, viewed 20 November 2019, <www.bloomberg.com/news/ articles/2018-04-16/facebook-must-face-group-suit-claiming-it-stole-biometric-data>.

Rosenzweig, R. 2004, 'How will the net's history be written? Historians and the internet', in H. Nissenbaum & M.E. Price (eds), *Academy and the Internet*, Peter Lang, New York.

Rössler, B. 2004, *Privacies: Philosophical evaluations*, Stanford University Press, Stanford, US.

———— 2005, *The Value of Privacy*, trans. R.D.V. Glasgow, Polity, Malden, Massachusetts.

Rotenberg, M. & Jacobs, D. 2013, 'Updating the law of information privacy: The new framework of the European Union', *Harvard Journal of Law and Public Policy*, vol. 36, pp. 605–52.

Rubenfeld, J. 1989, 'The right of privacy', *Harvard Law Review*, vol. 102, no. 4, pp. 737–807, viewed 20 November 2019, <digitalcommons.law.yale.edu/fss_papers/1569/>.

Rubinstein, I.S. & Good, N. 2013, 'Privacy by design: A counterfactual analysis of Google and Facebook privacy incidents', *Berkeley Technology Law Journal*, vol. 28, pp. 1333–1414, viewed 20 November, <scholarship.law.berkeley.edu/cgi/viewcontent. cgi?article=2007&context=btlj>.

Rudesill, D.S., Caverlee, J. & Sui, D. 2015, 'The deep web and the darknet: a look inside the internet's massive black box', *Woodrow Wilson International Center for Scholars*, vol. 3, pp. 1–20, viewed 20 November 2019, <www.wilsoncenter.org/sites/default/files/ stip_dark_web.pdf>.

Rudmin, F. 2006, 'Why does the NSA engage in mass surveillance of Americans when it's statistically impossible for such spying to detect terrorists?', *CounterPunch*, 24 May 2006, viewed 20 November 2019, <www.counterpunch.org/2006/05/24/why-does-the-nsa-engage-in-mass-surveillance-of-americans-when-it-s-statistically-impossible-for-such-spying-to-detect-terrorists/>.

Rush, E. 2012, 'Children, media and ethics', in W. Warburton & D. Braunstein (eds), *Growing up Fast and Furious: Reviewing the impacts of violent and sexualised media on children*, Federation Press, Sydney, pp. 159–74.

Rushkoff, D. & Goodman, B. 2004, 'The persuaders', *Frontline*, viewed 20 November 2019, <www.pbs.org/wgbh/pages/frontline/shows/persuaders/etc/script.html>.

Salim, F.D., Kanhere, S.S. & Loke, S.W. 2019, 'Your period tracking app could tell Facebook when you're pregnant – an "algorithmic guardian" could stop it', *The Conversation*, 27 February 2019, viewed 20 November 2019, <theconversation.com/ your-period-tracking-app-could-tell-facebook-when-youre-pregnant-an-algorithmic-guardian-could-stop-it-111815>.

Samuels, D. 2019, 'Is big tech merging with Big Brother? Kinda looks like it', *Wired*, 23 January 2019, viewed 20 November 2019, <www.wired.com/story/is-big-tech-merging-with-big-brother-kinda-looks-like-it/>.

Sandel, M.J. 2012, *What Money Can't Buy: The moral limits of markets*, Penguin, London.

Sarigol, E., Garcia, D. & Schweitzer, F. 2014, 'Online privacy as a collective phenomenon', *Proceedings of the Second ACM Conference on Online Social Networks*, viewed 20 November 2019, <arxiv.org/pdf/1409.6197.pdf>.

Sartre, J.-P. 2005, *Huis Clos*, Routledge, Oxford, UK.

Scannell, P. 1996, *Radio, Television and Modern Life: A phenomenological approach*, Blackwell, Oxford, UK.

Schechner, S. 2019, 'Eleven popular apps that shared data with Facebook', *Wall Street Journal*, 24 February 2019, viewed 20 November 2019, <www.wsj.com/articles/eleven-popular-apps-that-shared-data-with-facebook-11551055132>.

Schmidt, E. & Cohen, J. 2013, *The New Digital Age: Reshaping the future of people, nations and business*, Hachette, London.

Schneier, B. 2015, *Data and Goliath: The hidden battles to collect your data and control your world*, W.W. Norton & Company, New York.

Schoeman, F. 1984, 'Privacy: philosophical dimensions', *American Philosophical Quarterly*, vol. 21, no. 3, pp. 199–213.

Scott, E. 2015, 'Senate passes controversial metadata laws', *Sydney Morning Herald*, 27 March 2015, viewed 27 July 2016, <www.smh.com.au/federal-politics/political-news/senate-passes-controversial-metadata-laws-20150326-1m8q3v>.

Scott, G.G. 2014, 'More than friends: popularity on Facebook and its role in impression formation', *Journal of Computer-Mediated Communication*, vol. 19, no. 3, pp. 358–72.

Segall, L. 2015, 'Pastor outed on Ashley Madison commits suicide', *CNN.com*, 8 September

2015, viewed 3 February 2017, <money.cnn.com/2015/09/08/technology/ashley-madison-suicide/index.html>.

Sengupta, S. 2013, 'What you didn't post, Facebook may still know', *New York Times*, 26 March 2013, viewed 9 August 2016, <www.cnbc.com/id/100590334>.

Sentas, V. & Pandolfini, C. 2017, *Policing Young People in NSW: A study of the Suspect Targeting Management Plan. A report of the Youth Justice Coalition NSW*, viewed 20 November 2019, <www.piac.asn.au/wp-content/uploads/2017/10/17.10.25-YJC-STMP-Report.pdf>.

Sherman, N. 1997, *Making a Necessity of Virtue: Aristotle and Kant on virtue*, Cambridge University Press, Cambridge, UK.

Shvartzshnaider, Y., Tong, S., Wies, T., Kift, P., Nissenbaum, H., Subramanian, L. & Mittal, P. 2016, 'Learning privacy expectations by crowdsourcing contextual informational norms', viewed 20 November 2019, <www.cs.nyu.edu/wies/publ/hcomp16.pdf>.

Sigman, A. 2009, 'Well connected? The biological implications of "social networking"', *Biologist*, vol. 56, no. 1, pp. 14–20, viewed 20 November 2019, <www.aricsigman.com/IMAGES/Sigman_lo.pdf>.

Simonite, T. 2018, 'Few rules govern police use of facial-recognition technology', *Wired*, 22 May 2018, viewed 20 November 2019, <www.wired.com/story/few-rules-govern-police-use-of-facial-recognition-technology/>.

Simpson, P.L.P. 1997, *The Politics of Aristotle*, trans. P.L.P. Simpson, University of North Carolina Press, Chapel Hill, North Carolina.

Singer, N. 2012, 'Acxiom, the quiet giant of consumer database marketing', *New York Times*, 16 June 2012, viewed 20 November 2019, <www.nytimes.com/2012/06/17/technology/acxiom-the-quiet-giant-of-consumer-database-marketing.html?_r=0>.

———— 2018, 'What you don't know about how Facebook uses your data', *New York Times*, 11 April 2018, viewed 20 November 2019, <www.nytimes.com/2018/04/11/technology/facebook-privacy-hearings.html>.

Singer, P. 1994, *Ethics*, Oxford University Press, Oxford.

Skegg, P. 2011, 'Presuming competence to consent: Could anything be sillier?', *University of Queensland Law Journal*, vol. 3, no. 2, pp. 165–87, viewed 20 November 2019, <www.austlii.edu.au/au/journals/UQLawJl/2011/11.pdf>.

Sleeper, M., Cranshaw, J., Kelley, P.G., Ur, B., Acquisti, A., Cranor, L.F. & Sadeh, N. 2013, 'I read my Twitter the next morning and was astonished: a conversational perspective on Twitter regrets', *Proceedings of the SIGCHI Conference on Human Factors in Computing Systems*, pp. 3277–86, viewed 20 November 2019, <www.academia.edu/29052733/i_read_my_Twitter_the_next_morning_and_was_astonished>.

Slefo, G.P. 2016, 'Pinterest partners with Oracle to measure offline sales', *Advertising Age*, 7 June 2016, viewed 20 November 2019, <adage.com/article/digital/pinterest-partners-oracle-offer-audience-based-buys/304343/>.

Smith, A. 2014, 'What people like and dislike about Facebook', *Pew Research Center*, 3 February 2014, viewed 20 November 2019, <www.pewresearch.org/fact-tank/2014/02/03/6-new-facts-about-facebook/>.

———— 2018, 'Declining majority of online adults say the internet has been good for society', *Pew Research Center*, 30 April 2018, viewed 20 November 2019, <www.pewinternet.org/2018/04/30/declining-majority-of-online-adults-say-the-internet-has-

been-good-for-society/>.

Smith, B. 2019, 'Microsoft President Brad Smith in conversation', 28 March 2019, viewed 19 December 2019, <www.ussc.edu.au/events/microsoft-president-brad-smith-in-conversation>.

Smith, M. 1994, *The Moral Problem*, Wiley-Blackwell, Oxford, UK.

Smith, M.R. & Marx, L. 1994, *Does Technology Drive History? The dilemma of technological determinism*, MIT Press, Cambridge, Massachusetts.

Solove, D. 2007, '"I've got nothing to hide" and other misunderstandings of privacy', *San Diego Law Review*, vol. 44, 745, pp. 745–72, viewed 20 November 2019, <ssrn.com/abstract=998565>.

———— 2008, *Understanding Privacy*, Harvard University Press, Cambridge, Massachusetts.

———— 2013, 'Privacy self-management and the consent dilemma', *Harvard Law Review*, vol. 126, pp. 1880–903, viewed 20 November 2019, <ssrn.com/abstract=2171018>.

———— 2018, 'Should privacy law regulate technological design? An interview with Woodrow Hartzog', *linkedin.com*, 11 April 2018, viewed 20 November 2019, <www.linkedin.com/pulse/should-privacy-law-regulate-technological-design-interview-solove/>.

Spinello, R.A. 2011, 'Privacy and social networking technology', *International Review of Information Ethics*, vol. 16, no. 12, pp. 41–46, viewed 20 November 2019, <www.i-r-i-e.net/inhalt/016/spinello.pdf>.

Srnicek, N. 2017, *Platform Capitalism*, Polity Press, Cambridge, UK.

Stallman, R.M. 2002, 'Chapter 4: Why software should not have owners', *Free Software, Free Society: Selected essays of Richard M. Stallman*, Free Software Foundation, Boston, US, pp. 47–51.

Stoycheff, E. 2016, 'Under surveillance: examining Facebook's spiral of silence effects in the wake of NSA internet monitoring', *Journalism & Mass Communication Quarterly*, vol. 93, no. 2, pp. 296–311.

Strachan, L.A. 2011, 'Re-mapping privacy law: how the Google Maps scandal requires tort law reform', *Richmond Journal of Law and Technology*, vol. 17, no. 4, pp. 1–30, viewed 20 November 2019, <scholarship.richmond.edu/jolt/vol17/iss4/4>.

Strassberg, D.S., McKinnon, R.K., Sustaíta, M.A. & Rullo, J. 2013, 'Sexting by high school students: An exploratory and descriptive study', *Archives of Sexual Behavior*, vol. 42, no. 1, pp. 15–21, viewed 20 November 2019, <link.springer.com/article/10.1007/s10508-016-0926-9>.

Streeter, T. 1999, '"That deep romantic chasm": libertarianism, neoliberalism, and the computer culture', in A. Calabrese & J.-C. Burgelman (eds), *Communication, Citizenship, and Social Policy: Rethinking the limits of the welfare state*, Rowman & Littlefield, Lanham, Maryland, US, pp. 49–64.

Stuart, K. 2014, 'Brianna Wu and the human cost of Gamergate: "Every woman I know in the industry is scared"', *Guardian*, 18 October 2014, viewed 20 November, <www.theguardian.com/technology/2014/oct/17/brianna-wu-gamergate-human-cost>.

Summers, C.A., Smith, R.W. & Reczek, R.W. 2016, 'An audience of one: behaviorally targeted ads as implied social labels', *Journal of Consumer Research*, vol. 43, no. 1, pp. 156–78.

Sunstein, C.R. 2017, *#Republic: Divided democracy in the age of social media*, Princeton University Press, Princeton, New Jersey.

Svoboda, T. 2015, *Duties Regarding Nature: A Kantian environmental ethic*, Routledge

Studies in Ethics and Moral Theory, London.

Sweeney, L. 2000, 'Simple demographics often identify people uniquely', *Carnegie Mellon University, Data Privacy Working Paper 3*, viewed 20 November 2019, <dataprivacylab. org/projects/identifiability/paper1.pdf>.

Taddei, S. & Contena, B. 2013, 'Privacy, trust and control: which relationships with online self-disclosure?', *Computers in Human Behavior*, vol. 29, no. 3, pp. 821–26.

Taddicken, M. 2014, 'The "privacy paradox" in the social web: The impact of privacy concerns, individual characteristics, and the perceived social relevance on different forms of self-disclosure', *Journal of Computer-Mediated Communication*, vol. 19, no. 2, pp. 248–73.

Tashea, J. 2017, 'Courts are using AI to sentence criminals. That must stop now', *Wired*, 17 April 2017, viewed 20 November 2019, <www.wired.com/2017/04/courts-using-ai-sentence-criminals-must-stop-now/>.

Tavani, H.T. 2007, 'Philosophical theories of privacy: implications for an adequate online privacy policy', *Metaphilosophy*, vol. 38, no. 1, pp. 1–22.

Taylor, L. 2017, 'What is data justice? The case for connecting digital rights and freedoms globally', *Big Data & Society*, vol. 4, no. 2, pp 1–14.

Tene, O. & Polonetsky, J. 2015, 'A theory of creepy: technology, privacy, and shifting social norms', *Yale Journal of Law and Technology*, vol. 16, no. 1, pp. 58–102, viewed 20 November 2019, <digitalcommons.law.yale.edu/yjolt/vol16/iss1/2>.

Thomas, J. 2015, 'Hurtcore porn and the dark web: why we need an ethics of technology', *BigThink*, 19 September 2015, viewed 20 November 2019, <bigthink.com/connected/hurtcore-porn-and-the-dark-web-why-we-need-an-ethics-of-technology>.

Thomson, J.J. 1975, 'The right to privacy', *Philosophy & Public Affairs*, vol. 4, no. 4, pp. 295–314.

Timberg, C. & Greene, J. 2019, 'WhatsApp accuses Israeli firm of helping governments hack phones of journalists, human rights workers', *Washington Post*, 30 October 2019, viewed 20 November 2019, <www.washingtonpost.com/technology/2019/10/29/whatsapp-accuses-israeli-firm-helping-governments-hack-phones-journalists-human-rights-workers/>.

Titcomb, J. 2016, 'Why has Mark Zuckerberg taped over the webcam and microphone on his MacBook?', *Telegraph*, 23 June 2016, viewed 20 November 2019, <www.telegraph. co.uk/technology/2016/06/22/why-has-mark-zuckerberg-taped-over-the-webcam-and-microphone-on/>.

Tomlinson, J. 2007, *The Culture of Speed: The coming of immediacy*, Sage, London.

Tran, M. 2015, 'Combatting gender privilege and recognizing a woman's right to privacy in public spaces: arguments to criminalize catcalling and creepshots', *Hastings Women's Law Journal*, vol. 26, no. 2, pp. 185–206, viewed 20 November 2019, <repository. uchastings.edu/hwlj/vol26/iss2/1>.

Trottier, D. 2016, 'Digital vigilantism as weaponisation of visibility', *Philosophy & Technology*, pp. 1–18.

Tsosie, K. & Anderson, M. 2018, 'Two Native American geneticists interpret Elizabeth Warren's DNA test', *The Conversation*, 23 October 2018, viewed 20 November 2019, <theconversation.com/two-native-american-geneticists-interpret-elizabeth-warrens-dna-test-105274>.

Tsukayama, H. 2012, 'FTC announces $22.5 million settlement with Google', *Washington Post*, 9 August 2012, viewed 20 November 2019, <www.washingtonpost.com/blogs/

post-tech/post/google-settles-ftc-privacy-case-for-225-million-agencys-largest-penalty/2012/08/09/e048f6a2-e236-11e1-a25e-15067bb31849_blog.html?utm_term=.4ff18b7b1a97>.

Turkle, S. 2011, *Alone Together: Why we expect more from technology and less from each other*, Basic Books, New York.

Turner, A. 2016, 'Google Translate becomes more polyglot', *smh.com.au*, 1 June 2016, viewed 20 November 2019, <www.smh.com.au/technology/mobiles/languages-google-translate-becomes-more-polyglot-20160524-gp28l9.html>.

Turow, J., Hennessy, M. & Draper, N.A. 2015, 'The tradeoff fallacy: How marketers are misrepresenting American consumers and opening them up to exploitation', *Report from the Annenberg School for Communication*, viewed 20 November 2019, <www.asc.upenn.edu/sites/default/files/TradeoffFallacy_1.pdf>.

Twitter 2017, 'Twitter privacy policy: Information collection and use – third-parties and affiliates', *twitter.com*, viewed 5 April 2017, <twitter.com/privacy?lang=en>.

United Nations Broadband Commission for Digital Development 2016, 'The state of broadband: broadband catalyzing sustainable development', viewed 2 March 2017, <broadbandcommission.org/Documents/reports/bb-annualreport2016.pdf>.

Vallor, S. 2012, 'Social networking and ethics', in E.N. Zalta (ed.), *The Stanford Encyclopedia of Philosophy* (Winter 2016 edition), viewed 20 November 2019, <plato.stanford.edu/archives/win2016/entries/ethics-social-networking/>.

——— 2016, *Technology and the Virtues: A philosophical guide to a future worth wanting*, Oxford University Press, New York.

Van der Nagel, E. & Frith, J. 2015, 'Anonymity, pseudonymity, and the agency of online identity: examining the social practices of r/Gonewild', *First Monday*, vol. 20, no. 3, viewed 20 November 2019, <www.firstmonday.org/article/view/5615/4346>.

van Dijk, J. 2006, *The Network Society*, Sage Publications, London.

Veltman, A. & Piper, M. 2014, 'Introduction', in A. Veltman & M. Piper (eds), *Autonomy, Oppression and Gender*, Oxford University Press, New York, pp. 1–11.

Virilio, P. 2002, 'The visual crash', in T.Y. Levin, U. Frohne & P. Weibel (eds), *CTRL [Space]*, 2nd edn, MIT Press, Cambridge, Massachusetts, pp. 108–13.

Vis-Dunbar, M., Williams, J. & Weber-Jahnke, J.H. 2011, 'Indigenous and community-based notions of privacy: a technical report of the Informational Privacy Interdisciplinary Group', viewed 17 December 2019, <www.researchgate.net/profile/Jens_Weber6/publication/310482039_Indigenous_and_Community-based_Notions_of_Privacy/links/582f93e408ae138f1c03595c/Indigenous-and-Community-based-Notions-of-Privacy.pdf>.

Waddell, K. 2019, 'Advertisers want to mine your brain', *Axios*, 4 June 2019, viewed 20 November 2019, <www.axios.com/big-tech-advertising-neuroscience-brain-scans-b676b41f-861f-4538-95b0-7fc19534a870.html>.

——— 2019, 'Brains are the last frontier of privacy', *Axios*, 22 September 2019, viewed 20 November 2019, <www.axios.com/brain-privacy-neuralink-brain-computer-interface-6ba7269e-1553-4395-a6db-3560fead7e24.html>.

Wagner, K. 2018, 'Facebook will allow users to opt out of letting Facebook collect their browsing history', *Recode*, 1 May 2018, viewed 20 November 2019, <www.vox.com/2018/5/1/17307224/facebook-data-collection-opt-out-browsing-history-targeted-ads>.

Wang, Y., Leon, P.G., Acquisti, A., Cranor, L.F., Forget, A. & Sadeh, N. 2014, 'A field trial of privacy nudges for Facebook', *Proceedings of the SIGCHI Conference on Human Factors in Computing Systems*, pp. 2367–76, viewed 29 January 2020, <dl.acm.org/doi/pdf/10.1145/2556288.2557413>.

Warren, S.D. & Brandeis, L.D. 1890, 'The right to privacy', *Harvard Law Review*, vol. 4, no. 5, pp. 193–220.

Waters, N. 2015, interviewed by S. Molitorisz, 10 December 2015.

Webb, A. 2019, *The Big Nine: How the tech titans and their thinking machines could warp humanity*, Hachette, London.

Welch, M. 2013, *Corrections: A critical approach*, Routledge, London.

Westin, A.F. 1967, *Privacy and Freedom*, Atheneum, New York.

White, A. 2018, 'Facebook must stop tracking Belgian web users, court rules', *Bloomberg*, viewed 20 November 2019, <www.bloomberg.com/news/articles/2018-02-16/facebook-must-stop-tracking-belgian-web-users-court-rules>.

Whitman, J.Q. 2004, 'The two western cultures of privacy: dignity versus liberty', *Yale Law Journal*, vol. 113, no. 6, pp. 1151–221, viewed 20 November 2019, <digitalcommons.law.yale.edu/cgi/viewcontent.cgi?article=1647&context=fss_papers>.

Williams, J., Vis-Dunbar, M. & Weber-Jahnke, J.H. 2011, 'First Nations privacy and modern health care delivery', *Indigenous Law Journal*, vol. 10, pp. 101–32, viewed 20 November 2019, <jps.library.utoronto.ca/index.php/ilj/article/view/27636>.

Wood, A. 1999, *Kant's Ethical Thought*, Cambridge University Press, Cambridge.

—— 2014, 'Kant's principles of publicity', in P. Formosa, A. Goldman & T. Patrone (eds), *Politics and Teleology in Kant*, University of Wales Press, Cardiff.

Woodlock, D. 2016, 'The abuse of technology in domestic violence and stalking', *Violence Against Women*, vol. 23, no.5, 12 May 2016, pp. 1–35.

Wright, D. & Raab, C. 2014, 'Privacy principles, risks and harms', *International Review of Law, Computers & Technology*, vol. 28, no. 3, pp. 277–98.

Yuhas, A. 2016, 'Hacker who stole nude photos of celebrities gets 18 months in prison', *Guardian*, 28 October 2016, viewed 20 November 2019, <www.theguardian.com/technology/2016/oct/27/nude-celebrity-photos-hacker-prison-sentence-ryan-collins>.

Zang, J., Dummit, K., Graves, J., Lisker, P. & Sweeney, L. 2015, 'Who knows what about me? A survey of behind the scenes personal data sharing to third parties by mobile apps', *Technology Science*, 30 October 2015, pp. 1–53, viewed 20 November 2019, <techscience.org/a/2015103001>.

Zetter, K. 2015, 'Hackers finally post stolen Ashley Madison data', *Wired*, 18 August 2015, viewed 20 November 2019, <www.wired.com/2015/08/happened-hackers-posted-stolen-ashley-madison-data/>.

Zhu, T. 2019, 'What is differential privacy and how can it protect your data?', *The Conversation*, 19 March 2018, viewed 20 November 2019, <theconversation.com/explainer-what-is-differential-privacy-and-how-can-it-protect-your-data-90686>.

Zimmer, M. & Hoffman, A. 2012, 'Privacy, context, and oversharing: reputational challenges in a web 2.0 world', in H. Masum, M. Tovey & C. Newmark (eds), *The Reputation Society: How online opinions are reshaping the offline world*, MIT Press, London, pp. 175–84.

Zittrain, J. 2008, *The Future of the Internet – and how to stop it*, Yale University Press, New Haven, Conneticut.

Zuboff, S. 2015, 'Big Other: surveillance capitalism and the prospects of an information civilization', *Journal of Information Technology*, vol. 30, no. 1, pp. 75–89.

Zuckerberg, M. 2019, 'The internet needs new rules. Let's start in these four areas', *Washington Post*, 31 March 2019, viewed 21 November 2019, <www.washingtonpost. com/opinions/mark-zuckerberg-the-internet-needs-new-rules-lets-start-in-these-four-areas/2019/03/29/9e6f0504-521a-11e9-a3f7-78b7525a8d5f_story.html>.

—— 2019, 'A privacy-focused vision for social networking', *Facebook*, 6 March 2019, viewed 20 November 2019, <www.facebook.com/notes/mark-zuckerberg/a-privacy-focused-vision-for-social-networking/10156700570096634/>.

INDEX